LIBERALISM AND HUMAN SUFFERING

Liberalism and Human Suffering

Materialist Reflections on Politics, Ethics, and Aesthetics

Asma Abbas

palgrave
macmillan

First published in 2010 by PALGRAVE MACMILLAN® in the United States—a division of St. Martin's Press LLC, 175 Fifth Avenue, New York, NY 10010.

Where this book is distributed in the UK, Europe, and the rest of the world, this is by Palgrave Macmillan, a division of Macmillan Publishers Limited, registered in England, company number 785998, of Houndmills, Basingstoke, Hampshire RG21 6XS.

Palgrave Macmillan is the global academic imprint of the above companies and has companies and representatives throughout the world.

Palgrave® and Macmillan® are registered trademarks in the United States, the United Kingdom, Europe and other countries.

ISBN: 978-0-230-10445-7

Library of Congress Cataloging-in-Publication Data

Abbas, Asma.
    Liberalism and human suffering : materialist reflections on politics, ethics, and aesthetics / Asma Abbas.
        p. cm.
    ISBN 978-0-230-10445-7 (alk. paper)
    1. Liberalism--Moral and ethical aspects. 2. Suffering—Political aspects. 3. Historical materialism. I. Title.

JC574.A274 2010
320.51—dc22   2010004031

A catalogue record of the book is available from the British Library.

Design by Scribe Inc.

First edition: October 2010

10 9 8 7 6 5 4 3 2 1

Printed in the United States of America.

They seemed to know how to blend together all that life contains, the real truth, the undeniable last word, the innermost core of all that is unbearably painful within a heart and all that is joyful, all that is loved and all that is worthy of love but remains unloved, lied to and lied about, the unimaginable depths of the soul where no other can withstand the longing and which few have the conviction to plumb, the sorrows and the indisputable rage.

—Nadeem Aslam, *Maps for Lost Lovers*

For Ammi, Abbu, and Apa

CONTENTS

Acknowledgments ix

Permissions xii

Introduction: Suffering's Dead? 1

Part I: Suffering Liberalism 17

1   Incorporating the Victim 19

2   Theater of the Ascetic 45

3   The Liberal Sensorium 73

Part II: Recuperating Materialism 95

4   The Labor of Suffering 97

5   A Fetishism of Injuries 121

6   The Tragic Art of Historical Materialists 143

Notes 189

Bibliography 221

Index 237

Acknowledgments

To claim any ability to completely acknowledge the presences, visitations, and availabilities that have necessitated and enabled this book would be hypocritical and make for a bad epic poem. The shape and existence of this work owes everything to the spaces and times within which it was thought, enacted, courted, loathed, and lived with. From home in Karachi, to the New School for Social Research, to the Pennsylvania State University, to Bard College at Simon's Rock, the procession of this artifice (from the dissertation proposal to these proofs) includes my family, teachers, friends, comrades, and students. I hope that my gratitude reaches those who are aware and those who are unaware of this—unless I have done things completely wrong, this "front matter" cannot be the only way for them to get it.

Nancy Love has taught me to embrace blessings and curses, one as the other—a necessity haunting this work—and to quest for memory, hope, and meaning beyond our own privations. She, along with John Christman, Daniel Conway, Holloway Sparks, Samuel Chambers, James Miller, and Richard Lee fanned an unapologetic courtship of the political as a question of being itself and made turning back impossible. The personal and intellectual generosity of many more teachers continues to charm my life. Beyond the confines of my home institutions, many vocational political theorists took time and care for panels, conversations, comments, counsel, and encouragement that profoundly impacted me as I clutched my project on suffering. For their care and counsel in bringing closure to this work, Sam Chambers, Gregg Horowitz, David Adams, and Leela Gandhi deserve profound thanks.

The suspected and unsuspected complicities gathered along the way became the most explicit occasion for this work and for me as the teller of this story. I could not have hoped for a more vibrant and endearing community of chosen fellow travelers, and want to thank my friends who have made needful returns, joys, habitations, and negations possible. Among many invaluable companions to whom I am indebted, these folks catalyzed specific ideas, details, and torments within this project: Michael Scoville, Chad Lavin, Barbara Alfano, Sushmita Chatterjee, Philip Mabry, George Davis, Paul Youngquist, Chris Russill, Larin McLaughlin, John Seery, Amitava Kumar, and Sarah Armstrong.

The Department of Political Science, the College of Liberal Arts, the Institute of Arts and Humanities, and Bruce Miller generously supported my work at Penn State. Bard College at Simon's Rock picked up where they left off, and has genuinely stood by me. I am grateful to the fellowship of those at Bard College at Simon's Rock who exist as if our relationships of love and learning, reverence and respect, can change something in this world. My colleagues and guides in Academic Affairs and the Social Sciences Division have amply enabled this book's completion.

Being a teacher has unwittingly scrabbled at the recesses and reaches of this project. I owe to my students the affirmation, above all, of the question of suffering as one of joy and the creation of new forms of life. Thanks to those who have made it with me all this way, who grasp redeeming and damning infinitudes (and the fact that I am ready to write this book anew), who have kept my heart, and who still manage to believe and be surprised. My dearests, you know who you are.

Farideh Koohi-Kamali, Robyn Curtis, and others at Palgrave Macmillan stood behind this project gra-ciously, trustingly, and firmly. Thanks to Sarah Breeding for making beautiful pages out of this story. The privilege is entirely mine.

I am deeply indebted to every member of my family in Pakistan, here, and abroad who continues to bless me, and for whom my chosen paths have inspired some faith and closeness rather than rejection or indifference. This work is in particular awe of the lives, struggles, strengths, and overcomings of the women in my family—the mothers, aunts, sisters, and nieces close to my heart who bring much loveliness and wonder in my life, their resilience a source both of fluster and strength.

Syed Ali Hasan's and Zaki Abbas's words and wishes suffuse this work. My tribe extends to the companions of *Manshoor* and Pakistan Mazdoor Mahaz. Ahmed, unflinching brother and keeper, is present here, too.

Dreamlike, fragrant presences of my parents permeate these pages. Bilquis Tufail led the charge with unconditional affirmation, advocacy, and patience as parent and teacher. There would be no labor, no suffering, no compassion, no defiance, no grace, and no faith without Tufail Abbas's resolute commitment to the just and the true, and without Naeema Abbas's redemptive devotion to the good and the beautiful—these words mean anything to me because of who they are. It is to their lives, loves, and hopes that this book is dedicated.

No one can breathe life and promise into absences, presences, and possibilities more potently, joyfully, heartbreakingly, and life-affirmingly than Mukhtar Alvi. She made dreaming and aspiring imperative. And she capacitated seemingly impossible steps into, and crucial claims on, the world. Her prayers and confidence are sewn into every word of mine.

Then there is Stephen Hager, my abiding witness. The poetry and music of his being, and the trust that his senses compel, humble me. That his fingers have run through these pages assures and emboldens my words. Thanks, lastly, to a feline Herman Melville for feeling and responding to what no human can.

PERMISSIONS

INTRODUCTION

SUFFERING'S DEAD?

Those crimes which place demands on our soul, which touch our spirit and less so our senses, or in other words, those crimes which move us most deeply—they don't cause blood to flow. Slaughter takes place within the realm of conventions and morality, within a society which trembles when bestial acts are committed.

—Ingeborg Bachmann, *The Book of Franza*

Man has often had enough; there are actual epidemics of having had enough; but even this nausea, this weariness, this disgust with himself—all this bursts from him with such violence that it at once becomes a new fetter. The no he says to life brings to light, as if by magic, an abundance of tender yeses; even when he wounds himself, this master of destruction, of self-destruction—the very wound itself afterward compels him to live.

—Friedrich Nietzsche, *On the Genealogy of Morals*

"It was murder," declares the narrator at the end of Ingeborg Bachmann's *Malina*. A woman disappears, leaving us to wonder whether death is the end or the perfection of suffering. This murder of the woman at the hands of her lover, her father, patriarchy, and a society at war documents some of the ways of dying in which a society and its subjects partake. The personal and the political are more than mere allegories for each other, occurring in dynamic reciprocity: wars happen on the insides and outsides of people. The unselfing suggested in this murder is not eventful—perhaps not even perceptible on the surface of language, expression, or plot—but ordinary, inarticulate, material, subterranean, everyday, perhaps inevitable, perhaps irreversible, yet not altogether undesirable if it undoes a subject that society and politics will not let live. Trying to find meaning for its words by

navigating a world written in the languages of domination, militari-
zation, and genocide—and a society unable to process both its guilt
and the memory of its own disarticulations and neuroses—the novel
is drenched in the hope and the despair, the struggles to write beautiful books, the memories and the nightmares, the loves and their necessary illusions—*and* the ways of dying that interrupt the writing of
these utopias and love stories—that define the living. The pronounce-
ment of murder comes at the end of a long novel, when suffering
has been exhausted, conscripted, and pathologized—when beauty has
given way to disbelief and the illegible. In remembering these ways of
dying lies the only chance of survival, reminds Bachmann, in a world
that has perfected its arts of death but forgotten how to suffer.

This book is haunted by this murder—murder that is not merely
the end of life but the giving up of living suffering to dead suffering.
In Bachmann's novel, "Ich"—a self-proclaimed unknown woman—
personifies the entwinement of the suffering of speech and the speech
of suffering. This weave baffles those schemes of managing human
suffering whose arbitrary claims about what suffering is and how it
matters in society form the basis of our lives and the relations that
allow us to live. These schemes determine, rank, and organize the
meaning, status, and worth of our hurt—and, then, grant us the consolations when they "empower" us to represent and express it. The
novel is a chronicle as much of a death foretold—to wit, the "murder"
announced at the end—as of death as it is suffered, as it comes to be,
dynamic, demanding, exacting, reliant on life and the living. All the
woman perhaps seeks is love, one imagines, looking to the men who
signify fatal injunctions she receives as stone inscriptions in a dream,
"Live and be amazed," "To write is to be amazed," and "Kill the
Beloved." In love, she is thwarted by those she desires, unable to
inhabit spaces that supposedly promise safety, and even less willing
to abandon them, at a loss of affirmations of happiness that affirm
only others—for what lies would *that* take in a world that burns both
inside and outside of her? Her "unknownness" is not accidental—it is
just a sign that pages upon pages of being with her and her pain will
still ironically require the declaration of murder to let the rest of us off
the hook. For the more adventurous of us, yes, there is the mystery:
who and what has died? Is the dying over and done with now? But as
if the declaration of murder was not closure enough, in yet another
gesture of assurance, Bachmann herself dies in exactly the way she
writes Ich's death. Both entwined narratives must be brought to a
close, or at least be done with, so a story can be told, once and for all.
What is the loss signified in this need? What exhaustion of suffering

does this clarity of death attest to? What passing of the capacity to suffer are these gratuitous closures mocking?

"Ich" may be Vienna itself—who knows?—in search of love and longevity, waiting for life to resurge, left capable of very little, not unlike what happens to human beings when wars that annihilate them may be easier to bear than wars waged through them—these wars that are supposed to bring them consolation, secure them, and allow them to continue living through and across death. When this happens, even the universe forgets to keep count of how it was supposed to recalibrate itself for the death of one being; at the same time as modern constitutions, laws, and "human" rights—all assurances, as such, of something—ultimately are permissions to us to let humanity be, not demand too much from it. In opposition to these artifacts of modern politics and the subterfuges they provide for a material engagement with suffering, the novel is composed of half-written letters, incomplete conversations, reverberating phone hang-ups, the rush and blush of desire and rejection, dizzying monologues, italicized prayers, stubborn to-do lists, fragments of poetry, and snapshots of our everyday trials. Also present are figments and ghosts of those with whom both Ich and Bachmann have learnt to live, speak, make sense of words, and give their senses to the world in acts of sacrifice. Such is the artistry of this novel that attempts to redeem and reclaim the human, without ever allowing the aesthetic confusion and assemblage to become merely an artistic device in the hands of a master artificer. The vulnerability is not fragile or self-important, and it is amazing how the story of this woman gets told without the paradoxical misstep of objectifying the character, for even in so much "objective" distance—there are no claims to familiarity, not even names—and in this ultimate act of dispossession, the willing reader will find herself most present, most intimate.

Bachmann's *Malina*, in its artifice and its tempting of fate, in its trauma and its committed representations, is a homage to life as lived by those who love and who suffer life, its glories, and its indignities.[1] Here, the space of the personal and the private would only criminally be separated from all the brutalities and violations that happen in a world where the culprit and the savior are the same. This is the familiar world where we are counted on to "feel" the pain of ailing capital and to save it as it rehearses its tricky death routine only to come back alive and stronger. Shockingly, we are much less capable of seeing ourselves in those who die everyday as they give up parts of their bodies and beings—their vital living labor—to the deadness that *is* capital. Any wonder, then, that in the recent economic crisis, capital took the character of an injured victim at the hands of "big government," "bad people," "greed," among other villains, and any resistance to immediately rescuing Wall Street was framed by many as a moral wrong comparable to the cruelty and godlessness of letting a bleeding man die. There are numerous deceits in this story but only one irony: as if capital was not already "dead" labor!

MATERIALIST OVERTURES

Might the story of our suffering be similar? That is, it is on the suffering of the needful subjects of liberalism, imperialism, and colonialism that edifices of society as we know it are built—edifices that claim their vital health as they reek of dead suffering and extract the labor of our senses. And that, in then seeking to save these constructions, we commit the gravest inhumanity when we cease to have any senses left for the living suffering. In every pathos that we offer up to liberal society can be found a clue to our lost senses—senses that have lost their way, forgetting where to look, what to look for, how to smell, how the dead call on us, how being tickles, how freedom tastes, what love sounds like, what intimacy suffering allows and asks for, and where a memory enters us. The limits of the political, then, are not reliant on epistemic assessment but are experienced relationally and aesthetically as a question of the nature of our very being—the degree to which our senses contest the imposed modes of the presence and absence of suffering is the degree to which we are political.

This claim of mine is rooted in the particular contrivances of time and space with which liberalism and capitalism substantiate their various subjections, something I deal with in detail throughout the book. Perhaps a brief example of the historically specific nature of this picture of the political will suffice here. During and after World War I, a peculiar profession gained some popularity: at the same time as circles of paranormal investigation and séances took off, creative ways of making the dead appear became fruitful occupations. A photographer by the name of William Hope was "considered by believers and supporters to be a true master of the art of producing spirits on ordinary photographic plates."[2] He brought a few photographers together to do this in earnest, creating and trading in "spirit photographs" that depicted the dead cohabiting with the living, capturing on photographic plates what could perhaps be kept from being forgotten. These photos and their very possibility are us, in a way, picturing the range of life and living that we deal with everyday, in no way quite comprehended by the instrumental and utilitarian relation to

suffering and death that suffuse a society that produces death prolifi-
cally (and also opens up the question of the terms on which our labors
will relate to this production).

This is a first clue to my book's partiality to the aesthetic—as sig-
nifying artistic creation but also perception and sensing on which the
artistry is premised—as the locus of a materialist response to various political philosophies that find their power (even in their declared
departures from religion) in an unclaimed or declaimed crafting of the
character of suffering that then becomes the nonnegotiable truth and
currency. There has to be a way out of religion's primordial claim on
the domain of suffering and secular modernity's mimicry of that move
by objectifying and playing god with it, trading in its lives and deaths.
This would involve a recovery of aesthetics as encompassing the
activities of the suffering, hoping, transforming, and creating body.
The aesthetic, as a pivot for my recuperated materialism, is a holistic
domain of cognition, sensation, and perception—beyond Alexander
Baumgarten's insistence that however bountiful the senses when they
dabble in the world, their retrieval remains inferior and supplementary
to reason—and of the insertion, fragmentary or wholesome, of our
bodies and minds (and permutations thereof) in the world. It follows
that suffering can encompass being and becoming to embrace our
experience of the extant world and possible other worlds that can be
constructed (or not) out of this one.

Starting with Bachmann, and returning at difficult moments to
those thinkers (like Karl Marx and Friedrich Nietzsche) who carry the
burden of their aesthetic labors, and more directly to other writers
like Iris Murdoch, Virginia Woolf, and Tony Kushner, I confess my
commitment to the irreducible commingling of the poetical and the
political substance of any text or action. My own work here might
betray why political theory, as I understand and value it, articulates its
transformative provocations best when the poetic, musical, performative, and figural elements of its artifice and representation confront
the Apollonian dominance of the stone sculptures with which the hallways of those who control the material and its meaning are strewn. In
recognizing that forms of representation and expression are primarily
and ultimately forms of sensing and suffering—and therein is the politics of *my* work—the reader may grasp my most earnest plea: I want
the question of suffering to not diminish us as human beings by giving
us readymade frameworks of action and sensual limits to our humanity but to ask more of us, even to ask for an intimacy and a devotion,
convoking a democratic moment that makes us responsible for the
material *and* the meaning, making the political "sensible," reliant on

our senses and not only on our acts of yielding, on cue, the representations that inhabit and validate it.

Malina is a provocation to senses beyond those that nourish empathy and sympathy in a narrow way. These emotions furnish the commonly accepted core redemptive move when we come to think of
right and noble ways of relating to suffering. This reliance is, ironically,
consistent with a distance from suffering that is entailed in making
the suffering into an object with cause, origin, and explanation, that
can also be made to go away. It extends into any of the representational politics that fuel the wishful transubstantiations of humans into
victims and victims into agents and that assume that the victimhood
and the agency are temporally and experientially discrete conditions.
The distancing and turning away, the philanthropic and humanitarian
recitation of stories of salvation and redemption, is fundamentally different from the sensual demands that *Malina* makes. Notably, what
is demanded is a compassion rooted not in identifying with or negating, but in an aesthetic draw and revulsion where one's own being is
at stake in a very different way than the precariousness premised on
boundedness, separation, and the climactic voluntarist communion
of our beings, bodies, and realities within bourgeois liberal morality.

There is no call for romanticizing Ich's pain (for that would make
it, again, an object to be desired, consumed, destroyed, or undone).
The repulsion that I mention above is also not for the suffering—
for that inversion does not simply undo the status of suffering as an
object. Both the romance and the repulsion emerge out of a sacralization of suffering that objectifies without interrogating, examining,
vetting its significations, and engaging its materiality as it seeks to
enter us. There is another relation to be had beyond the sacralization,
wherein the draw and the revulsion would be qualitatively different
experiences. When the objectification, sacralization, and the distancing implicit in those is not an option, how might our revulsions and
attachments be shaped in order to honor the helplessness, the decay,
the dissolution, and the conquest—the survival, the presence, the
exit, and the absence—of a woman who struggles to speak and whose
every silence and stutter pierces in a way no scream can? This is a question that connects the aesthetic to the ethical in my work and haunts
it, wishfully but not presumptively. Someone like Iris Murdoch, to
whom I return later in the book, would deem this the ethical substance of life itself: the ability to know defeat, to live past failure, to
kill the hero while we are at it, and to live and love through ordinary
honorable defeats—so our world can become too small for the surplus
and organized suffering we are subject to, and much more capacious

for the suffering and experience we ought to be subjects of and claim as our own.

So when asked whether death is the ultimate suffering or the end of it, some suspicion is requisite. Why are those the only options? And what if the certainties and the closures death provides shape how we relate to suffering in this world? The romance of finitude, inherited from idealisms of various sorts, has to be interrupted in order that we may direct our senses to what, despite claims to the contrary, is not quite dead and done, as is the suffering that, by being in excess of an idealist narrative's conferred mold, is not acknowledged as objectified and consumable. The point is not to emphasize an abstract becoming so that one can look away from what *is* but to see, in the act of imposed finitudes and closures, a kind of brutally arbitrary setting aside that would not be possible if, in the realm of the becoming and the existence of suffering, our senses were *alive* to what is—not overloaded and deadened like Borges's Funes, and not frenetically always already "productive" like codified nationalist origin stories or Apollonian memorials, identities, and other ascetic ideals.

I am trying to draw attention to a materialist stance that beholds us to the work of the living that has to always contend with the dead and the not present, and the modes of presence and materiality that the dead and the living share and call each other to—exposing, along the way, the potential fascism of all idealism. Whether in the realm of memory or of representation or of reparation, the premise cannot, and must not, exclusively be the objectification of suffering that pretends this epistemic move to either reflect ontic realities or be passive in its effect on our capacities of bearing these burdens. Perhaps it is possible to see the realm of the political to not contain only the suffering that has been defined, objectified, and domesticated—but to see political struggles transpire at the level of determining what suffering is and how our bodies become matter. The discretion to mourn and grieve is no small claim on the political—the bourgeois moral compulsion to hammer our sorrow and suffering into congealed pathos is of a piece with the misplaced mournings within capital's dead life and the disregard of the suffering to which claims of finitude and a contrived self-containment blind us.

Suffering ought to be liberated from the question of death if a democratic politics is to remain loyal to whom it is at least nominally serving. This book attempts this by proposing a materialist politics of suffering that is content with not seeking to outshine life in clarity, solutions, and lack of caveats. Rejecting the options of a huge memory like Funes's without changing the way we relate to memory, and of the dissolution of boundaries and the fusion of dichotomies—for they make a mockery of tragic necessity and betray an inability to suffer— my treatment of liberalism itself tries to enact a refusal to toss out at will what does not fit. The fixation on limit cases, on cruelty, and on the terminal nature of physical death reveals an important factor in liberalism's inability to suffer, signaling the ways in which death always stifles the suffering that lives and walks amid the dead and that would be much more complex to deal with. Such is the desperate partiality to ends that leaves no room for the complexity that is life and that should be politics. Liberalism wants ends of stories, it wants verdicts, so that it can move on to its next patient or victim. We are left with executions of laws to the detriment of how they come to be and how our lives come to be in tandem with this development. Idealist closure makes us oblivious to the ways our theories and their politics declare dead upon arrival what is actually alive.

A CRITIQUE AND A RECUPERATION: SUFFERING, REPRESENTATION, POLITICS

OCEANIA *(To the Angel of America)*: He wants to live.

PRIOR: Yes.
I am thirty years old, for God sake. I haven't done anything yet, I . . .
I want to be healthy again. And this plague, it should stop. In me and everywhere. Make it go away.

AUSTRALIA: Oh, We have tried.
We suffer with You but
We do not know. We
Do not know how.

EUROPA: This is the Tome of Immobility, of respite, of cessation. Drink of its bitter water once, Prophet, and never thirst again.

PRIOR: I . . . can't.
I still want . . . my blessing. Even sick. I want to be alive.

ANGEL: You only think you do.
Life is a habit with you.
You have not seen what is to come:
We have:
What will the grim Unfolding of these Latter Days bring?
That you or any Being should wish to endure them?
Death more plenteous than all Heaven has tears to mourn it,

The slow dissolving of the Great Design,
The spiraling apart of the Work of Eternity,
The World and its beautiful particle logic
All collapsed. All dead, forever,
In starless, moonlorn onyx night.
We are failing, failing,
The Earth and the Angels.
(The sound of a great generator, failing, the lights dim.)

ANGELS: Look up, look up,
It is Not-to-Be Time.
Oh who asks of the Order's Blessing
With Apocalypse Descending?
Who demands: More Life?
When Death Like a Protector
Blinds our eyes, shielding from tender nerve
More horror than can be borne.
Let any being on whom Fortune smiles
Creep away to Death
Before that last dreadful daybreak
When all your ravaging returns to you
With the rising, scorching, unrelenting Sun:
When morning blisters crimson
And bears all life away,
A tidal wave of Protean Fire
That curls around the planet
And bares the Earth clean as bone.
(Pause.)

PRIOR: But still. Still.
Bless me anyway.
I want more life. I can't help myself. I do.
I've lived through such terrible times, and there are people who live
through much much worse, but . . . You see them living anyway.
When they're more spirit than body, more sores than skin, when
they're burned and in agony, when flies lay eggs in the corner of
the eyes of their children, they live. Death usually has to take life
away. I don't know if that's just the animal. I don't know if it's not
braver to die. But I recognize the habit. The addiction to being
alive. We live past hope. If I can find hope anywhere, that's it,
that's the best I can do. It's so much not enough, so inadequate,
but . . . Bless me anyway, I want more life.

—Tony Kushner, *Angels in America:*
A Gay Fantasia on National Themes

In being about suffering, my book is about the labors of those who suffer, in body and in spirit, in neuroses and in wars, in speech and in silence, in humiliations and in patronage, in efforted graces and respectabilities, in announced consoling self-overcomings, at work and at home, ordinarily and heroically, in laughters and forgivenesses. These are labors, of suffering and making suffering matter, that end up confounding any theoretical enterprise that makes the claim of having understood the problem of suffering and doing its best to solve it. On the one hand, I resist both the imposed silences and the spoken silences about suffering so familiar to liberal politics, and, on the other hand, I want to retain the possibility of attending to and treating speeches and silences differently from what we have learnt, honoring those whose speeches and silences we are too ill-trained to see and hear, let alone comprehend. I hope and trust that there are other ways of making suffering present.

Liberalism is a family of modern epistemologies and political pro-grams unified by the commitment of each of its variants to the cause of managing and abating human suffering. This commitment is both informed by and frames liberalism's emphasis on preserving an indi-vidual's liberties. Liberalism demarcates the space for different kinds of contentions in society, devotes itself to the suffering that dwells in certain spaces and not others, and deems representation as a means toward redress of suffering. Within juridical discourse, for injury (and thus suffering understood only as injury) to be addressed and cor-rected, it must be represented—in speech, in legislature, in court, on the highway, after rape, and so on. The many-layered relation between suffering and making it present that inheres in the sensorium of mod-ern liberal capitalist politics begs examining.

Examining the demands of presence that liberal modernity makes on suffering brings up the question of how the "problem" of suffering is framed. In the aftermath of religious wars, modern political thought betroths itself to the question of suffering and ways of avoiding it, and formulations of justice in various ideologies correspond to how they understand suffering—all involving a certain insistence on the coordinates of presence. Every performance of justice requires a per-formance of suffering. Such enactments, whether sufferers represent themselves or are represented by others, are the struggles to make suf-fering matter that are at once political, ethical, and aesthetic. In being the realm where we make our sufferings matter, the political is consti-tuted by struggles over what matter *is*, no less than what suffering *is*. Politics is thus not limited to the battles of appropriations that begin once the form and content of presence and absence, and the sensing and suffering of these, have been determined—it includes every act that negotiates the materiality, the life, *and* the death of these forms.

Collaborations between liberal politics, ethics, and aesthetics edify presence exemplified by voice—speaking for oneself or others, ultimately of one's suffering, instrumental to a prescribed end—as an indisputable element of a liberal democracy and an index of one's inclusion in it.[3] These collaborations keep this ideology of representation and inclusion intact as a lifeworld—through the privileges granted to voice and the work of the resulting representations out there and among us—shaping, undercutting, and maiming the suffering meant to be made present. An approach to suffering that factors in the labor of making it present for liberal structures would require reconfiguring the role of these collaborations in yielding the political as a domain where suffering is more than an object of political action or a resource harnessed as injury, identity, or other currency in liberal politics.[4]

Conversations about suffering abound in what we may call the "official" public sphere. Suffering is made present in a standard way: it is domesticated into pain and harm, which become the central, overarching, occluding motifs in our experience of our own and others' suffering and in our relation and response to it. The usual locus of ethical-political discourses that take suffering seriously is why and how someone would be driven to cause harm, what history unleashes suffering, and how we must respond to scenarios of human suffering that defy human imagination. In all these, the positions of the perpetrator and the observer-respondent are often the coordinates within which the victim is evidenced. In their focus on how to acknowledge, affirm, and remove suffering, such conversations about victims and their injuries (codified harms) have suffering and sufferers as the object of diagnosis, prognosis, and remedy. Debates feature questions of whether, for whom, and for what to speak; who speaks for others; who speaks for themselves; how to make space for people to speak for themselves; whom to bid speak; whether or not we can know someone's pain; and how to make them or their speech go away. These puzzles revolve around, ironically, the agents qua respondents to someone's suffering—the saviors, liberators, lip-readers, empowerers—whose regard for others is fed by a fervor steeped in the unacknowledged privilege of framing these conversations and puzzles and is subsequently quite taxing to those who already suffer. Moreover, it is striking and, at times, incredible how much these "agents" are the ones most needy of reassurance and tending in forms ranging from, say, a regular serving of abstract hope in the future of humanity, to relief from guilt of their privilege, to conquest of the inscrutable, to stability in the stock market after a tragedy *somewhere else.*

It seems that the eager anxiety about the "perspective of the victims," whether in hearing their voices, forcing them to speak, or speaking for them, is indulged as long as it completes "my" knowledge, "my" picture, or "my" sense of justice. This scenario accords consolatory functions to sensuousness, speech, and representation not only, or even primarily, for those who suffer and are the plaintiffs but also for those in power when they demand that sufferers speak and act their suffering in certain, prescribed ways. There is no room here for the vast space between the said and the unsaid, the enacted and the undone, where those for whom speech is always a response persist. For many, even speaking for oneself is almost always a response whose burden is never felt by those who always get to interrogate and sympathize. This voice seemingly necessitated by suffering in turn polices the modes of suffering and subjectivity possible.

Harm and representation turn out to be reciprocal as the haunted negotiations between liberalism and democracy continue, rendering liberal democratic politics always in debt to suffering. This voice does carry, shaping the experience and the dominant aesthetic and political imaginations of people outside liberal democracies, to the extent that such voice becomes an index of their democratic desire insofar as those with the goods find it familiar. These forced familiarities severely compromise the fundamental experience channeled in this performance that could lead to different intimacies and alternative liberatory counter-discourses in the face of such scripted and mimicked desire to begin with.

For suffering to be allowed to live and desire differently, we must turn to those moments where its life and its becomings threaten an imperialist politics that moves predictably and swiftly to contain this living suffering. We may thus witness not only what liberalism does to its unwilling subjects but also what they do to it—and this may itself require a special capacity, and a new demand on our senses, not unlike the liminal shadows of William Hope's spirit photos.

My work here is thus charged with the arts and labors of suffering that vie for survival in different spaces under the current regimes of neoliberalism, neocolonialism, and imperialism, and in the mostly unrequited social and political struggles that comport their incompletions with honor. How living suffering survives amid dead suffering—suffering congealed into artifacts of liberal politics in the form of garrulous pain, legal harms, legible injuries, codified identities, or spectacular disaster—is the fact, miracle, question, and challenge that energizes the labors of this book. A cartography of living and dead suffering within and across ourselves and our societies reveals a complex economy of the production and distribution of suffering, kept in tact by the life that confronts dead suffering, sustains this deadness, and maintains its dominance, but often also defies it, asking, instead, for "more life."

In the chapters that follow, I am interested in addressing what this political and poetical economy of injury and victims *does* to those who suffer. A critique of liberalism is in order precisely in and through the moments where, as a philosophy and a program, it is most committed to a politics of redress through justice, law, representation, inclusion, and so on. To this, Part I, "Suffering Liberalism," is dedicated. One of the key premises of my inquiry here is that there is a fidelity between suffering and its many forms of presence that is much more elemental than the one on which contemporary notions of justice rely in academic or popular discourse. The familiar connection central to the legacy of liberalism is between suffering *as* harm and injury; politics *as* institutions seeking to redress it; and political actors *as* agents who make sure that both suffering and politics stick to their roles thus defined. In this triangulation, the mutually constitutive relation between suffering and representation is reduced to a passive, functional, and external one. One obvious challenge to this approach comes in the postmodern and postcolonial reflexivity about language. By espousing somewhat of a linguistic transubstantiation of victims into agents, and of suffering into power, much of this often serves only to lubricate the movement of political actors between suffering, domesticated as harm and injury, and politics, domesticated as the power to undo the former. The actual frame of this encrusted relation between suffering, politics, and representation thus remains undented. This relation desperately seeks (re)animation, and Part I of the book inaugurates this process.

I attempt to reinvigorate a corporeal, materialist approach to politics and normative struggles that is not simply submerged within the fetishization of the linguistic turn but works with it to challenge the limits placed on, and around, the human capacity to effect an expansive sensuousness, to suffer, remember, and still hope and transform (with) that suffering—a historical materialism if there ever was any. This is not a project that wants to hear the unspoken, or grant gratuitous world historicality to all suffering, as happens when alternative histories are written and transformative efforts reduced to assigning subversive meaning even when representation is rejected. It does, however, seek to subvert the privileged position of certain ways of writing about suffering, of a vocabulary of liberalism that is presupposed or naïvely reacted to in traditional liberal or postmodern, or even some postcolonial, writing. The work thus calls for an embrace of suffering consistent with a materialist politics as I understand it.

Marx's understanding of the historical nature of labor enables two analytical trajectories. First, that forms of suffering, representation, and politics are historical and spatially divergent. Second, that the distribution and production of suffering—and subjectivity—must be apprehended as moments of the same process. These analytic turns spur Part II of this book, "Recuperating Materialism." This half of the book is dedicated to the recovery of a materialism that refuses the subsumption of experience to abstract regulatory concepts that overdetermine prevalent notions of civil society, social justice, and democratic coexistence. In order to release it from conventional domestications into the pain, harm, and injury that frame many empiricist and idealist attempts at theorizing politics and practicing justice, I consider suffering more broadly as a correlate of undergoing one's sensuousness, which is, in turn, embodied time.[5] As suffering, embodiment, and sensing are so related, suffering has more than an external relation to subjectivity (as someone who suffers)—it also has an internal relation through the materiality that is given form, and *brought under*, in *subject*ivity.

My desire to locate suffering as the core of a transformative politics learns from Marx's regard for labor as both subject and object of theory and practice—as a living substance and what upholds, sustains, and nourishes its own death in capital. Any normal consideration of suffering as external object thus invites us to go beyond the externality—to see the suffering already framed and insinuated in the political method that makes an object out of the suffering in the first place. In addition, if we are to take Nietzsche for a credible genealogist and historian, then our treatment of suffering in the aftermath of modernity and secularism must go to the suffering that is the premise, origin, *and* source material for modernity and secularism. Together, Marx and Nietzsche inspire a form of fidelity in political practice that escapes the clutches of moral fervor and idealist certitude. My proposed politics of materialist objection, thus, does not object to redressal as such, so much as to its instantiation as an a priori or principle of exteriority. Part II works toward a materialist possibility that does not treat suffering as topic or object but regards its irreducible materiality as intrinsic, even immanent, to a desirable political method.

In the context of the global distribution of the production and redress of pain, the marginality of persons and groups in society is predicated on *how* they suffer, and how their modes of suffering confront, accept, and resist the proliferation of dead suffering—all on behalf of a desire to overcome the domination by dead suffering and to wrest a capacity to suffer out of the suffocating domestications of suffering in liberalism and capitalism. Any theorizing of a just, even revolutionary, politics in the present moment can find strength in the labors, the sufferings, the loves, and the hopes that remain marginal and illegible to dominant structures, eluding the sensual and political economy of liberal capitalism and other related ideologies. Based in a narrative of how we have suffered to suffer in hegemonic and privileged ways, this book seeks a politics of suffering that is less self-certain and exalted than theories based in empathy and sympathy that remain oblivious to these questions of living and dying. It is aware of the performatively discrepant nature of writing about excluded, obliterated sufferings and repulsed by most forms of inclusion, recognition, and presence available within this embarrassing but meticulous political economy.

Constituting a historical and materialist politics of suffering centered on the labors of those who suffer requires intervening on the side of the experience of suffering, before and beyond considering it merely an object of the agency that causes it or that solves the problem. In this process, the subjectivity of sufferers, their "health," their deaths, their presence, their absence, their love, and their hope all stand to be rethought in light of the continuing legacy of colonialism in the cartographies of global suffering and the gaping rosters of the wounded ranked according to the most valuable and visible injury. An understanding of compassion and hope that differs from reassurance, and is not served for the comfort of those in power, inflects this rethinking. The available forms of redress, then, would not appear merely as forms of apology or civic embarrassment in the face of suffering but would allow themselves to be contaminatingly composed of the same.[6]

PART I

SUFFERING LIBERALISM

CHAPTER 1

INCORPORATING THE VICTIM

THE ANTE OF AUTONOMY: LIBERAL PROVENANCE AND THE REALITY OF SUFFERING

One is hard-pressed to find a concept to match, let alone surpass, autonomy in its status as the crowning glory of liberal political philosophy. Variants of liberalism associated with its major thinkers engage in a drawn-out quarrel over how best to honor this amazing "invention" of autonomy.[1] This dispute is over the accenting of the *autos* or the *nomos*: the self as the giver of, or the given to, law; or the law, the giving or givenness of which makes possible the self. The former corresponds to a liberal politics invested in creating the potential "lawgivers" capable of valuing and deploying this right; the latter, to the premise of rights as ends in themselves prior to the virtues and capabilities of individuals.

Judith Shklar, a twentieth-century liberal, proposes that the popular, "happy" liberalisms that are able to indulge in this sparring are forgetful of liberalism's root commitment to abating human suffering.[2] By treating liberal politics as aimed either at securing and enhancing a set of individual rights[3] or at guaranteeing freedom as the good that enables liberal subjects to develop themselves and fulfill their goals,[4] these dominant liberalisms focus on rights and virtues rather than on wrongs and vices to which true liberals were always meant to attend. In various liberalisms, Shklar finds this forgetfulness manifested in prolific abstractions, neglect of moral psychology, perfectionism that seeks to create moral citizens, and a belief in progress that undermines social diversity. Her corrective to these liberalisms is a "liberalism of fear," based on the inviolable premise of negative liberty and the fear of cruelty, most faithfully inheriting liberalism's mandate with regard to the conflict, injustice, and suffering faced by a diverse populace. The liberalism of fear is "at its simplest, a defense of social diversity, inspired by that barebones liberalism, which, having abandoned the theory of progress and every specific scheme of economics, is committed only to the belief that tolerance is a primary virtue and that a diversity of opinions and habits is not only to be endured but to be cherished and encouraged. The assumption throughout is that social diversity is the prevailing condition of modern nation-states and that it ought to be promoted."[5]

The liberalism of fear insists that it is a political doctrine as opposed to "a philosophy of life such as has traditionally been provided by various forms of revealed religion and other comprehensive *Weltanschauungen*."[6] It is a *liberalism of fear* also because its main focus is on fear created by the state apparatus. It is a liberalism of *fear* because it is based in the lived experience of those subject to state power, is called to respond to immanent fearfulness and injustice, and endures its own dread of a society where this prevails. It is a *liberalism* of fear because it believes that the numerous inhibitors of freedom, including fear and favor, "are overwhelmingly generated by governments, both formal and informal," and are deadliest when "the agents of the modern state . . . have unique resources of physical might and persuasion at their disposal."[7] This is why the liberalism of fear is committed to freedom as negative liberty;[8] it is a project of guaranteeing against the use of political and administrative power to inflict public cruelty on individuals and groups. Shklar wants liberalism to be concrete by focusing on the ordinary lived experience of common people. She specifies that it should be "first and foremost based on the physical suffering and fears of ordinary human beings, rather than on moral or ideological aspirations."[9] She centers her project on curtailing and preventing physical harm and ensuring physical well-being; her empiricism seeks to put what she defines as physical experience back on the agenda of liberalism, so it gets accounted for in the costs of radical social change and utopian ventures.

Summoning the spirit of classical liberalism that predates Kant, and sharing the sensibility of Montaigne and Montesquieu, Shklar's argument does more than trump autonomy with an older obsession of liberalism. It clues us in to the forces within early liberalisms and their objects of concern that led to the concept of autonomy itself. Shklar's liberal ancestors of choice responded to religious bloodletting, the nascence of the capitalist body and soul, and the melting into air of things solid and such. She responds to the forms and channels of violence and aggression in the aftermath of ascendant nation-states.

These contexts dispose liberal thought to cringe at tension, conflict, pain, loss, and incertitude, and to be very sensitive to the anxiety and nausea brought on by excess, frenzy, and lack of exits. These elements contour how liberalism and its subjects have come to relate to suffering.

Shklar's account of liberalism does not strip liberalism of its crowning glories. Rather, she complicates the popular history of liberalism so that a celebration of liberal autonomy, divorced from its entrails, no longer seems fair to liberalism or acceptable to its subjects, since it actually discredits liberalism's labor of negotiating with the content and form of human suffering and with the experience of subjects and objects of a world coming into its own. Shklar locates liberalism's main justification in the human propensity to cruelty, from which follows the need to control human suffering. A response to the unpleasantness of real life in a "complex world in which every vice has distinctive political consequences and every virtue unavoidable costs,"[10] liberalism is obligated to keep its sights low and steady, in contrast to utopian theories that wander above and beyond.

After placing lives and suffering into compartments public and private, personal and political, interior and exterior, liberalism picks the battles that pertain to obtrusive political superstructures. It prioritizes the injustices, cruelties, and complicities that pertain to the political—narrowly understood in relation to the state and its laws—because it remembers the vulnerability and historical disposability of human lives in the face of the state's monopoly over violence.[11] Injury, with its connotation of human, or at least discernible subjective, responsibility in contrast to "evil," is the preponderant and fundamental frame for liberal justice. The interconnections between autonomy, subjectivity, injury, representation, rights, and justice repeatedly reveal that a sensibility regarding boundaries, opposition, conflict, pain, and despair permeates all relevant issues in liberalism to this day.

Given this, it is possible that liberalism's rational autonomous individual is more than a consequence of forgetting the horrors within which the ideology arose and within which it lives, as Shklar alleges. She provides clues to seeing this individual as product of a moral psychology distrustful of the body and its passions. Notions of choice, free will, and autonomy recast the state of passive reaction characterized by fear, tentativeness, and paranoia into a condition that is self-assuringly self-imposed. Perhaps the demon of pain would dissolve into the analgesic of productivity and progress.[12] Whose labor produces whose confidence, and whose suffering whose redemption, are questions left to be asked of liberalism.

Multiple logics orient liberalism to the reality of human suffering. First, is the universalistic domestication of pain and fear into harm and injury and the possessive individualism that frames our relations not only to our own injuries but to others' as well. The possessive individualism entails that suffering be alienable into injury and the injury be possessed. Liberal structures, whether utilitarian or not, share the conceit that a "natural" economy of pain and pleasure, and of suffering and activity, exists, and that their only role is managing their (re)distribution within society. A second logic tells of the key role of tolerance and impartiality in the relations that contain and nourish the political economy of injury. This economy claims, defines, and affirms its own scarcities (as does any economy). Third, is the logic that strings together the healthy autonomous agent with certain proclivities and capacities, political institutions understood as such agents, and the victim and agent as fixed and polar subjectivities. Fourth, a mixture of dogmatic idealism and empiricism actively sunders epistemic and ontic processes in relation to the body that needs, loves, suffers, and acts.

By working outward and backward from the key concerns of Shklar's liberalism of fear to other important moments in liberalism's evolution, these logics will be shown to cohere in the discourse of liberal modernity writ large, even when various relations shift and different factors impact each other to produce different complexions of liberalism. This coherence affirms suffering as the object of representation and action, as somewhat prepolitical and thus prerepresentation. These logics are at work in the various modalities of liberal justice.

Inclusion is one such dominant and pervasive modality, and it is my focus here. In its commissions of justice—even, and especially, as inclusion—liberalism is articulated with, and engenders a particular relationship to, suffering. The story of this relationship can be gleaned in the frames of suffering and modes of its presence in liberal discourse at different moments in history, as well as in the symbiotic relationships instituted between the who and the what of liberal suffering.

INCLUSION AND LIBERAL JUSTICE: THE SETUP

Shklar finds that when idealist notions of justice disavow physical experience to embrace either an abstract moral law or a limiting and static notion of actualization (however positive, like autonomy), they render both the state and the individual noncommittal. Opposed to these is her empiricist notion of justice, at once minimalist, negative, and protective with regard to autonomy, placing the state and its subjects in a concrete and immediate relation. The state is responsible for the forms of injustices and injuries that must be dealt with in order to ensure that subjects have the autonomy they were promised.

Shklar's justice is anchored in the principle and practice of inclusion, since it attends to the marginality and invisibility of injuries and injustices experienced by subjects of a liberal society. This is evident in the demand that this liberal justice *take into account* those parts of the body and the body politic, and their sufferings, that dominant liberalisms leave out. It is no accident that this will to include—*to admit*—suffuses a liberalism that takes it upon itself to cure the amnesia of other liberalisms. This is the logic of what I would call *justice as admission*.

Shklar's emphasis on the inclusion of the ordinary and the concrete, exemplified in her reliance on invisible but ubiquitous fear, has three key premises. First, human suffering is ubiquitous and is often unseen and invisible. Second, those who suffer are ubiquitous, unseen, and invisible—the masses and common people. Third, suffering and injustice must be viewed from the perspective of those broken and defeated. Not only does this centrality of the concrete, even raw, physicality of the experience of liberal subjects render Shklar a maverick to the forms of justice sponsored by the dominant liberalisms discussed previously, but it also offers an interesting lens into the question of inclusion within liberalism.

The terms of Shklar's own inclusion in the domain of liberal thought reveal the capacities of liberalism when it comes to its own near and dear, those who are already loyal to it, those who already claim its privileges. Where Shklar's voice fluctuates and performs the rites of the liberal genre, her rebellion and its limits are exposed. Opposing and disrupting some popular cosmetic attachments, she vouches for liberal fundaments and remains firmly ensconced within liberalism. Ultimately, instead of dismissing liberalisms that celebrate autonomy, she gives them historical validity. Shklar's relation to the ordinary and the concrete, and her attempts to push liberalism to be inclusive and just in a way that others neglect to do, reflect her own status as somewhat of an (acknowledged) outsider to liberalism. The moral commitments and methodological professions of faith that allow Shklar's work to be comprehensible to, within, and *as* liberalism, force us to think of marginality and inclusion more broadly. Her work draws special attention to the differential costs borne by the subjects, objects, and brokers of inclusion.

FROM FEAR TO INJURY VIA PROPERTY

Fear, as the dominant hue of the lived experience of liberal subjects, is one element of the violence that Shklar detects, confronts, and wishes to curtail. The diagnoses supply a definition of reality, as well as an interpretive framework for the nature of the fear suffered, the substance of the suffering itself, and how the suffering is processed before it can be treated. She writes, "Fear is as universal as it is physiological. It is a mental as well as physical reaction. To be alive is to be afraid. The fear we fear is of pain inflicted by others to kill and maim us, not the natural and healthy fear that merely warns us of avoidable pain. We fear a society of fearful people."[13]

The liberalism of fear conceives of politics as an activity of, and in, fear, whether its end is to abate fear, or to channel, control, define, determine, avoid, or even deny it. The fear that can be treated without endangering the sanctity of the private domain is of abuse of power, public disrespect, persecution, cruelty, and tyranny. Fear thus serves as the gist and grist of human suffering that can be legitimately addressed in the sphere of politics demarcated by liberalism. This focus recalls Thomas Hobbes. Beginning with Hobbes, the mechanist-materialist description of humans sees them as bundles of appetites and aversions that fuel our war against all.[14] The supreme aversion is to death, the material limit that confronts an already hurting, suffering being. This wariness of the persistent possibility, even actuality, of war and death is peculiar to the inception of liberalism. For Hobbes, argues Sheldon Wolin, "the desire for self-preservation [is] basic in the sense of being a response to the threat of violent death—physical integrity and not to his worldly goods or position."[15]

Hobbes gives a preamble for how liberalism comes to relate to fear and other suffering. Antipathy, repugnance, and fear are variations on a theme of suffering short of, and in place of, death. This active avoidance, when "translated into the driving fear of violent death, became the creative force provoking men to the rational decision of forming a commonwealth."[16] Once deemed characteristic of post-sixteenth-century human existence and sensory experience, fear is genetically connected to artifice in Hobbes's materialism. Fear becomes matter that can be sculpted into something else, such as the Leviathan itself. Following Hobbes, as the fault lines of the human "body" are defined in concert with the concepts of injury and property, the initial, merely corporeal, experience of fear originating in mortality also seeks ways of infusing ever-newer versions of incorporation.

With John Locke, the activity of labor and the creation of property serve to distract and displace fear.[17] As the self begins to permeate property and is also constructed through it—that is, when property becomes an expression of life, as well as a means to it—economic deprivation comes to have as much of an exterminating and annulling effect on the living being as blatant war and bloodshed had at the time that Hobbes wrote. When Locke tells us to own what we put our labor into, some convoluted things happen to pain, fear, and their connection to each other by way of the preservation of self and property. Private property and labor orient subjects to fear and pain, not least through the setting of terms for their admission into the political. In sum, the logic is as follows. First, the perpetual fear and the concern about preserving oneself are painful. Second, the way to discharge this fear is not the creation of a sovereign as a reserve and preserve of fear (as it is in Hobbes) but of labor; but herein lies the bind—labor not only discharges the fear but also creates more stuff to be protected. Finally, labor itself is a travail, hence painful. Thus, fear and pain are linked through self-preservation predicated on the labor of creating property, and this adds more things to the list of preserves. The catharsis of fear is the pain of labor. Then, the pain of labor may usher in the pleasure of property, and also the fear of losing it. The cycle continues.[18]

Consonant with Locke, Immanuel Kant's *Doctrine of Right* proclaims that without property, there is no injury. But there is more to this: without injury, there is no property. The sensitivity of the liberal individual gets channeled into appendages that are either the product of one's externalized labor of conquering nature, or of *someone else's* labor that could as easily become the source of one's self (via property). Things attain the status of "property" by virtue of how much injury they broker on our behalf. The injury to our property allows us to determine the injury we suffer.

In the beginning, then, is the pain of fear and the fear of pain—the threats are primarily physical, and pain and fear are experienced in a discrete and rather stodgy way, correlated with distinct objects. The pain and fear then morph into something more suffusive, more pervasive, and more capillary as they come to inhabit multiple registers and locations in relation to the living subject. This inhabitation is a peculiar one, since the sentiments slowly become more compatible with nerve ends that are, by now, both more alive *and* more dead. Their proliferation is the wonder of quantity since they are now found in so many more places: this chair, that goat, my woman over there.[19] The body in liberal thought bloats itself so much, and its sensitivity

gets so rarefied in that extension, that it can then only feel through
the circumscribed sufferings of these extremities. The form and the
content, and the thresholds and extents, of suffering are thus defined
and determined.[20]

Kant derives the condition for rightful, juridical property from the
sense of harm, injury, or wrong that occurs as a result of another person's act of using this property, attempting to use it, or entertaining
such notions. Kant also distinguishes between sensible and intelligible
property: the former perceivable by senses, and the latter requiring no
such condition. Since injury is the basis of property, the distinctions
Kant draws between sensible and intelligible property can be carried
over to the concept of injury as well. Injury can, then, be qualified as
sensible or intelligible, phenomenal or noumenal. Kant writes,

> The nominal definition of what is externally mine—that which suffices
> only to distinguish the object from all others and arises from a complete
> and determinate exposition of the concept—would be: That outside me
> is externally mine which it would be a wrong (an infringement upon my
> freedom that can coexist with the freedom of everyone in accordance
> with a universal law) to prevent me from using as I please.
>
> But the real definition of this concept—that which also suffices for
> the deduction of it (for knowledge of the possibility of the object)—
> goes like this: Something external is mine if I would be wronged by
> being disturbed in the use of it even though I am not in possession of
> it (not holding the object). I must be in some sort of possession of an
> external object if it is to be called mine, for otherwise someone who
> affected this object against my will would not also affect me and so
> would not wrong me.[21]

This last sentence suggests that ownership—or some sort of externalization or "extension" of the self—is necessary for injury to be
ascertained, felt, and catalogued as mere harm, on the one hand, or as
wrongful injury, on the other. In this way, property becomes a prerequisite to injury. In turn, property does not merely mediate between the
owner and the injury—it also allows for a second moment: the owner,
now victim, owns his injury, too. Property being a fundament of identity, the victim can be said to identify with her injury *and* locate her
identity *in* it. For instance, in the state of nature, the only injury that
can be perceived is what is inflicted upon the human body (the innate,
internal property). When the expanded sense of the "self" enters the
picture and brings with it claims on things occurring in nature, and on
one's "own" personality, a corresponding expanded sense of injury—
not restricted to the felt and the empirically inflicted—accompanies it.

It appears, then, that intelligible, abstract possession and intelligible, abstract injury necessitate each other.

Property's relation to injury does not simply involve a divide within external property but also a divide between internal and external property. This serves to install and affirm the separation of the realm of human contact with nature from that of human sociopolitical interface. This distinction is foundational to conceptualizing injury and right. The *Doctrine of Right*, being primarily concerned with the question of justice, is set in the realm of the interaction of human wills. The working notion of injury here refers to hurt caused by humans to other humans, sensibly or intelligibly, and not to that caused by nature in the form of calamities, ill fate, and so on.

In this formulation, the scope of human suffering and its control is already being determined. Right pertains to the sphere of humanity, which is articulated not in the relations of humans to nature (Locke has already taken care of that) but in the relations of humans to humans. What follows is the assertion of the preeminence of *rights*, possessed and asserted by their bearers, validated and respected by others who have the power to do so. This demarcation of the realms of suffering allows for human overcoming in one realm to compensate for the other: the power and assertion of the ownership of rights may make nature not seem so painful, and the pain of human conflict might be alleviated.

Kant presents the juridical postulate of reason that "it is possible to have any and every external object of my will as my property." Later, he adds that man's celebrated capacity to "conceive of something as an object of [his] will" (read, agency, autonomy) is predicated on a determination that this object is within his (physical?) power.[22] There is a correlation here between property as intelligible, on the one hand, and a judgment of potency having an empirical basis, on the other. This exemplifies the relation between experience and Kant's metaphysical method, shedding light on the nature of the empirical and the intelligible, not only in the notion of property, but also, following our previous discussion, in the concept of injury.

An initial broaching of the difference between the sensible and the intelligible, and of how the intelligible pertains to a doctrine of right (which is a doctrine of morals), happens when Kant deems experience to be constitutive of what he calls a doctrine of happiness but not a doctrine of morals. He explains that if the latter were merely a version of the former, "it would be absurd to seek a priori principles for it."[23] The former prescribes the means and the particular ways to seek happiness (or to avoid unhappiness), learnt and generalized from human experience. In the latter, "reason commands how men are to act even though no example of this could be found." This is why the doctrine of morals "takes no account of the advantages we can thereby gain, which only experience could teach us." Such a doctrine of right would "command for everyone, without taking account of his inclinations precisely because and insofar as he is free and has practical reason." On this view, the moral person will "not derive instruction in its laws from observing himself and his animal nature or from perceiving the ways of the world, what happens and how men behave."[24]

On one level, then, even the declaration of intelligible injury has to depend on ascertaining the nature of the injury in a sensible realm from which intelligible or "noumenal" injury can be abstracted and systematized. This is in the vein of an empiricist response to what could be deemed the absurdity of a priori injury. For Kant, the ideas of property and injury, not mediated or defined by, and in, human experience, exist outside of it and define experience itself.

On another level, however, while Kant's attempted reversal seems entirely formalistic, it significantly impacts the actual theorization of experience and the experiencing body. The empirico-liberal tradition is capable of granting suffering only a congealed reality to which everyone submits. Kant's substitution of the passive, empiricist, suffering subject with the active, autonomous, world-making one, in its mere reversal, is oblivious to an entire domain of the activity that (even) the empiricists could only relegate to the unavoidable, unexceptional, and inert domain of suffering. Even this new liberal subject fails to account for the fullness and "activity" of the "passive" experience of subjects anchoring the classical empiricist liberal project. The figure of the autonomous actor *could* have held the promise, in his proven relation between identity and injury, of allowing the domain of suffering to be incorporated in its naïve notion of being in, and suffering, this world, a notion purportedly more affirmative but, as yet, devoid of content. Had this happened, politics and law would be accountable to the sufferings that necessitate them, rather than turn citizens into supplicants who need their suffering validated by structures they produce. We might have recognized not only that there are strictures on the suffering admitted into the sphere of liberal justice but also that much suffering is produced inside it.

The issue of property lies at an important nexus. It is the paradigm case for conceptualizing injury in Kant and provides the terms in which the notion of *having* rights comes to us. This *having* allows us to imagine injury, property, and rights in a triangular relation. It also allows us to imagine a bearer who embodies the triangulation, tied together in a possessive individualist ethos that drives the political economy of injury.[25] This is the case not simply because these rights are *ours* but because the form and content of this ownership is a continuation of the logic and spirit of acquisition, private property, and exchange in a liberal capitalist system. Per the faux pas of allowing us to own everything, including our pain, the questions of whether the possession of this injury is suffering at all, and of who then owns the suffering of owning this injury, are elided. At the most basic level, despite its tenuous relation to the body, and despite the extension of selves into objects of ownership and desire, liberalism has steadfastly persisted in its assumption that "my body is different from yours, so I ought to know what my interests are."[26] It is easy to see how this leads to the core conundrum of representation being whether we can speak for others' suffering or only our own.

INJURIES, INTERESTS, GOODS

The relation between property and injury in liberalism upholds a possessive individualism of injury, whereby suffering can be owned as individuality insofar as it does not encroach upon the structures of liberal law, politics, and economics that permit certain modes of individuality and sociality. It follows that these modes allow suffering to be valued, owned, and exchanged for specified returns and often at unspoken costs. This relation to suffering is rendered universal, along with the form—injury—in which it is possessed and exchanged. This universality establishes commonality among suffering people by abstracting from the concrete, qualitative specificities of various sufferings and reducing them to their common denominator that is the source of the value of injury.

The institutions of injury and property are inextricably bound to each other in liberalism. A self that is owned and capable of being injured, and an injury that is possessed, together make possible a subject who can own his identity, rights, and interests—each of which sustain his potential to own, injure, and be injured. Alienable and exchangeable like property, injury resembles other products of our labor rather than only occurring in relation to (other) things we make and own. In the relation between labor and pain that gets articulated in the more advanced form of proprietary injury, the historical coincidence of capitalism and liberalism determines not only what, how, and for whom we labor and produce *but also* what, how, and for whom we suffer. Injury is the mode in which rights and privileges are demanded and fulfilled, and also the way in which life, experience, suffering itself, is produced in liberalism. It is a form that inhabits, and evolves with, forms of law, politics, economics, and society that get constituted in the historical development and consolidation of liberal contractarian relations.

While a detailed discussion of the collusion between capitalism and liberalism to render injuries (as representations of suffering) a historical form cognate with, if not analogous to, commodities (as products of our labor) will have to wait until the next chapter, it is worthwhile to consider an exemplary moment when injury *becomes* a good. This happens when, in the work of John Rawls, suffering as injury becomes fundamental to the formulation of primary goods, which is the starting point for justice as fairness. The goal of justice here is to improve the "worst possible outcome" for every member of the society as far as these goods are concerned.

In *A Theory of Justice*, Rawls explicitly posits the measurement and distribution of primary goods as an alternative to measurements of happiness featured in utilitarian conceptions. Primary goods are defined as things that a generalized political person would want more of than less.[27] They are "the various social conditions and all-purpose means that are generally necessary to enable citizens adequately to develop and fully exercise their two moral powers (capacities for a conception of the good and a sense of justice), and to pursue their determinate conceptions of the good."[28] Insofar as they are considered to be objective and generally applicable to the free and equal citizens of a society, these primary goods frame a particular attitude to suffering, its valuation, and its compensation by being strongly correlated with definitions of welfare permissible within this paradigm.

This permissibility is derived from Rawls's two principles of justice that "assess the basic structure according to how it regulates citizens' sharing of primary goods, these shares being specified in terms of an appropriate index."[29] The obvious privileging of income and wealth, for instance, is able to reward the material sufferings that conform to liberal possessive individualism and marginalize those that do not. It reduces suffering to economic factors that painfully simplify class struggles, let alone other desires, deprivations, and conflicts that at once ground, transcend, and disappear within measurement.

An "index" of attaining goods already incorporates suffering. It is perfectly at home in the valuation of suffering native to liberalism. If suffering is a state of being deprived of goods, avoidance of suffering becomes a good itself, affirming injury as value and a commodity for (or against) which we bargain. The right to goods (and injuries) is assigned value prior to entering the representation, consistent with the liberal regime of value-producing suffering. When an assembly of interest-bearing individuals is convened, the "positive" language of interests only masks the deep-seated betrothal of liberalism to the fear of pain and injury, and hence interests are real or potential injuries framed positively and acquisitively in happy liberalisms. The exchange of interests—in the form of primary goods in Rawls, for instance—is really an exchange of potential and actual injuries. Such material and discursive production of suffering as injury goes unseen and untended when the focus is on the distributive and redistributive modes of dealing with injury, whether in the courts or in the original position.

The calculated and consequential arbitrariness of what suffering is good enough to be injury, and which injury is good enough to be an interest—issues still within the more obvious domain of justice as distribution, redistribution, and recognition—remain to be addressed. The paltriness of political and legal vocabulary dealing with modalities of struggles that diverge from the logics espoused by liberal ideas of security, preservation, and peace as absence of conflict is one example. Consider the logic behind calculation of compensation for injury: centuries of slavery, the loss of a limb at the assembly line, the lives of war survivors, the aftermath of chemical spills, children's nightmares of bombs and gunpowder, unsatisfying cosmetic surgeries, all are weighed on the same scale, with clinical, mercantile accuracy. At the same time, it can be said that not all of them are weighed, that what we recognize as injury is predetermined. For instance, hunger and starvation are not considered injuries in the same way as a gunshot wound. Still further, victimhood is cheap and less "sticking" for those who can afford it, especially for those who set the terms and qualifications for the categories of victim and perpetrator. Recall here the "victimization" of global powers at the hands of terrorists, which is oblivious to the violence that created the new perpetrator in the first place. Old perpetrators are so quickly relieved of their title, while others are not able to wash their stains off for centuries.

FROM INJURY TO AUTONOMY VIA TOLERANCE

Liberalism's deepest grounding is in place from the first, in the conviction of the earliest defenders of toleration, born in horror, that cruelty is an absolute evil, an offence against God or humanity. It is out of that tradition that the political liberalism of fear arose and continues amid the terror of our time to have relevance.

—Judith Shklar, "The Liberalism of Fear"

The maxim of tolerance in liberalism not only manages, distributes, and controls suffering but also mediates its production and construction. Toleration has multiple cadences within the liberalism of fear.[30] Pain, fear, and cruelty have to be tolerated on the part of the sufferer; the verges of victimization and cruelty demarcate tolerability. Those driven to cruelty themselves work under limits of what might stir them to cruelty. These limits are confluent with liberalism's emphasis on indifference and imperturbability in relation to stimuli that may instigate the "tolerator" to act (in order to correct the situation). The discourse on cruelty prioritizes the agent of cruelty to the effective exclusion of the sufferer, and the discussion around toleration privileges the toleration of the agent who is cruel by agents who tolerate. The tolerance of the sufferer appears only later. So are affixed thresholds of cruelty and of suffering (as injury) that a society is willing to put up with. The act of toleration follows, delimiting what can be tolerated, a fact Shklar acknowledges when she criticizes dominant liberalisms for their tolerance of cruelties and injustices that are passive, unremarkable, and unseen.

Many liberal thinkers take great pains to distinguish toleration from unbridled license. As a liberal virtue, toleration is instated as an "allowance (with or without limitations), by the ruling power, of the exercise of religion otherwise than in the form officially established or recognized." This becomes more widely applicable as "the disposition to be patient with or indulgent to the opinions or practices of others; freedom from bigotry or undue severity in judging the conduct of others; forbearance; catholicity of spirit" (where someone even equates tolerance with charity).[31] Toleration then becomes a critical element of liberal pluralism, aimed at the coexistence of multiple viewpoints or ways of life without harm to anyone. Whether this goal is to be attained by being neutral and defying effect, or by actively struggling with that effect through deliberation, is left open. For either of these options to have any meaning, the relevant effect itself depends on pre-set thresholds or prejudged capacities on predetermined scales. The thresholds implied in toleration are grounded in liberalism's various divisions and dichotomies, including private-public, interior-exterior, personal-political, and so on.

It is hard to tell whether the interiority of the Kantian subject is the problem, since much of our truncated capacities to bear seem to be caused by the lack of dimensions of the thin, nonrefractive subject of liberalism. This does not amount to insensitivity to suffering per se but to a co-optation into enterprises of injury with preset conditions, thresholds, and terms of admission, not least about what injury means, what counts as injury, and what else in life is worth suffering. This inability to *suffer*, in an expanded aesthetic sense of the word, does not derive from a simple disembodiment or the inward "rational" propulsions of subjecthood. Instead, it is nurtured in a complicated economy of the mind and the body that can be simultaneously numb, amnesiac, and extremely fragile, and that can be ruled by reason as well as run about in a maze in a frantic quest *to have*.

This quest for possession, and the concomitant unleashing of choice by the autonomous possessive subject, is continuous with how autonomy, choice, and property work in liberal secularism and in relation to religions and ideologies. It is a paradox involving two central notions in liberalism: to *choose* to be *tolerant*. Toleration is central so that liberalism does not have to choose among specific religious or philosophical systems of thought. This means (appearing to) choose to forego a choice between systems of thought. The ability to not have to choose, or even an appearance to that effect, enforces the neutrality central to the liberal project—this ability or agency is possible only within the ideology of liberalism. So a victim who, by definition, is agency-impaired and structurally incapable of choosing does not get to choose tolerance and is therefore tolerant by default. In that way, toleration clearly renders us all "equally" victims, even if not equal victims, since those who choose tolerance are more of agents than those who do not choose it.

Liberalism installs a homogeneity of sufferers and suffering in the name of the equality that places us in a position to relate to other suffering beings. Fraternity, hence, is granted through an equality of the opportunity to be the injured and the injurious. Toleration suffers a similar fate as its object (what is tolerated). Its tonal relation to harm is unmistakable, especially in how toleration and harm together configure suffering and the enduring of it. Both the harm and its toleration rely on a definition of the tolerable that is the purview of dominant, agent-centered discourses. So even this excludes the effect of the activity of tolerating on its object and its bearer (if the object and its bearer are different).

Toleration strings together repression, submission, and endurance. Its insurance of our ability to make decisions without fear or favor serves to siphon off our desires into different domains. When one's wishes are liable to hamper someone else's ability to make decisions, they are redirected to seek fulfillment in the private sphere. Since the public realm cannot withstand these pressures, the private realm cannot stand for anything less than a capitalist ethos. This is the form that sublimation takes when desires suppressed in the public realm turn to our atrophied bodies that have no space to keep them. This siphoning off, this redirected repression, parades as endurance, even though it is a luxury of those who have desires they *can* fulfill, if not in one sphere, then in another. This luxury has people "injured" by limits on the freedom to have, to consume, and to be immediately gratified. The capacities to construe other sufferings and repressive challenges to liberty, and to attend to those who endure because they have no choice to begin with, are gradually eroded.

THE AGENT BECOME: HEALTHY, AUTONOMOUS, TRAGIC, SCARCE

That meaning and purpose do not reside as objective facts in the world of things was something of which, in fact, people were becoming obscurely conscious. There were a variety of reactions, however, to this breaking of the social and moral fabric. When purposes and values are knit comfortably into the great and small practical activities of life, thought and emotion move together. When this is no longer so, when action involves choosing between worlds, not moving in a world, loving and valuing, which were once the rhythm of our lives, become problems. Emotions which were the aura of what we treasured, when what we treasured was what we unreflectively did, now glow feverishly like distant feux follets, or have the imminent glare of a volcanic threat. The attempt to go on making a total sense of the social and political world, as well as acting in it, demanded a new conception of value which connected it with the character and affirmation of the agent.

—Iris Murdoch, *Sartre, Romantic Rationalist*

The object of this quote is not liberal modernity. Iris Murdoch is writing about the era of Joyce and the Surrealists, but her words illuminate the plight of liberalism itself, acknowledging how it sets itself up to deal with the breakdown of certain restful assumptions about life and being. Liberalism and other forms of hegemonic discourse can be seen to have within their sinews the misery of the disruption of the status quo. So if the modern agent, as we know it, is coeval with the unavailability of stable modes of knowing and is symbolic of a certain loss, then autonomy can be seen as a co-optation of tragedy in a dubious response to the changing world.

In crying "tragedy!" liberalism (1) commits to abating human suffering, (2) resigns to the impossibility of getting everything we want (what it calls the irreconcilability of choices), (3) draws up a balance sheet of pain and pleasure that can at best break even, and (4) deems human agentic action as central to the causing or courting of suffering, domesticated as pain. This centrality of human action ironically coexists with liberalism's insistent powerlessness in the face of the suffering it confronts. Liberalism's tragedy results from the irreconcilability of pregiven wills and choices, while its utilitarianism is perfectly at odds with a tragic sense, an aversion to suffering implicit here. The scarcity of choices that emerge in the redefinition of tragedy is mirrored in the scarcity against which mainstream liberal capitalist economics pits our needs. This scarcity is not always real but contrived. It may have to do with how the abundance and capacities within us are displaced and projected onto the fetishes outside of us, whether the state, or god, or other commodities. Religion takes charge of this scarcity by then letting its opposite thrive in the domain of charity and philanthropy, not to mention salvation and redemption. Privatized notions of suffering correspond to scarcities in human relations. Bounded individualities whose relationships are predicated on protecting themselves from violation of boundaries would fit Murdoch's understanding of interiorized scarcity. She writes, "Scarcity 'interiorized' leads every man to see his fellow as the Other, and as the principle of Evil." The individual and its other are reified in conflict on the basis of this scarcity.[32] Murdoch is not romanticizing a passive, nonagonistic harmony but lamenting these reductions: of conflict (and ultimately desire) to scarcity, of suffering to harm and injury, and of suffering for and with others to tolerance.

This scarcity and economy pervades tolerance and harm, concepts that affirm logics of separation, segregation and conquest, between one individual and the other, between the subject and the object of the tolerance, and between various realms of existence. Liberalism insists, rather assiduously, on the subject-object divide in the case of suffering—such that the only way someone else's suffering can be mine is if it is translated as a setback to my interest.[33] The agent and the victim, the sufferer and her other, are placeholders suspended within the constitutive strictures of liberalism that require property, injury, and the injurable property-owning subject. The liberal secularist separation between various realms of existence does not allow for the enduring of existential pain or angst to infect one's capacity to tolerate or to respond to the suffering of the nonexistential kind (unless, of course, one can somehow translate existential pain into harm). Any liberalism avowedly attuned to the ubiquity of human victimization and injustice should be asked how sufferers get divided between tolerant agents and victims.

THE CASE OF CRUELTY AND THE ACCIDENTAL VICTIM

The fear it [the liberalism of fear] does want to prevent is that which is created by arbitrary, unexpected, unnecessary and unlicensed acts of force and by habitual and pervasive acts of cruelty and torture performed by military, paramilitary and police agents in any regime.

—Judith Shklar, "The Liberalism of Fear"

The observation that all state forms are instituted on an economy of violence is not news. In that context, any government formed is paradoxical, perhaps self-defeating, if it tries to do "justice" (liberally assuming here that the need for justice arises in the suffering of subjects). The liberalism of fear recognizes this fact and is conscious of itself as a negative liberalism aiming to curtail excesses of any kind of violence.

In *Ordinary Vices*, Shklar defines cruelty as "the willful inflicting of physical pain on a weaker being in order to cause anguish and fear."[34] She gives a second definition in "The Liberalism of Fear": "Cruelty is the deliberate infliction of physical and, secondarily, emotional, pain upon a weaker person or group by stronger ones in order to achieve some end, tangible or intangible, of the latter."[35] Note the proviso that cruelty can flow only from the strong to the weak.

John Kekes supplements Shklar's definition by highlighting the assumptions constitutive of the concept of cruelty. First, being a victim of cruelty requires that one's functioning as a full-fledged agent is harmed through unjustified and excessive infliction of pain. Second, cruelty disposes the perpetrator "to delight in or be indifferent to the serious and unjustified suffering their actions cause to their victims."[36]

It requires habituation but not a conscious awareness of the meaning or consequences of one's actions. Thinking of cruelty as a disposition of human agents is consistent with Shklar's emphasis on potentiality. The vast human potential for unrealized and realized ordinary and extraordinary cruelty provides the key justification for the liberalism of fear. The fear of cruelty exists in those on the verge of suffering it as well as those on the verge of committing it. Shklar, Richard Rorty, and Annette Baier share the faith that cruelty is the worst thing "we" do.[37]

The three essential elements of cruelty, writes Kekes, are "the agent's state of mind, the agent's action, and the victim's suffering."[38] This implies that any "event" of a victim's suffering, if it is to garner the attention of liberals, must fill each of these taxonomic registers. The centrality of the inflictor, rather than the sufferer, indicates how liberal attention to human suffering qua cruelty is beholden to the cruel act rather than to the suffering. The reductionist universalism of fear featured in Shklar's liberalism is only matched by the reifications that result from designating cruelty the master template for dealing with suffering. One such reification results from the formalistic focus on the agency of the doer-subject. This is the case not only when agency is defined in terms of committing cruelty but also when victims are characterized as impaired agents. This is another instance of how Shklar's exposé of liberalism's reifications reenacts them, even as she wants to subvert dominant liberal tendencies.

Liberal conversations about victims and their suffering tend to revolve around the first two registers: the agent's state of mind and the agent's actions. In terms of actions and their effects, contemporary liberal debates on suffering fall roughly along the Kant-Hume fault line. Kantians stress the motive of the agent and his action regardless of the consequences, while Humeans center on consequences of actions (in this case, the victim's suffering as a consequence of the agent's cruelty). However, when it comes to understanding suffering, I find the divide between Kantians and Humeans to be inconsequential. In both iterations, liberalism fails to accommodate the real subject of its analysis, qua the suffering of the victims, and attends to suffering in a very limited, agent-centered way.

The invention of autonomy to which we have been referring is to Kant's credit and based in his departure from the dominant empirico-liberal tradition. It marks a morphological shift for liberalism by flipping the terms of discourse that enabled the theory of activity and labor nascent in Locke to surpass and frictionlessly overpower the passive, quasi-helpless, certainly unproductive character of human suffering and anxiety at the hands of nature and other humans. Kant's move disentangles activities of existence from their narrow focus on attaining happiness or abating unease and despair. In doing so, it jettisons the weight of consequences and effects and courts validation through more venerable and reliable avenues such as reason, the mind, or the noumena. Compared to the empiricists and the utilitarians, Kant proposes ways of engaging in the overtheorized conflicts of existence rooted in a relatively more confident and self-assured conception of the actor. While Kant's propositions allow for a new way of thinking about suffering, the apparent radical temper of the departure is sobered when the context in which this flip was effected is understood. Should his dialectics, even if idealist, not have made it clear to Kant how such tendentious flips do not really alter the terms in the relation?

The dizzying back and forth between professed Kantians and Humeans blurs the fact that, regardless of whether morality is anchored interior to the acting subject or determined by the effects of the actions of the subject as they play out in the outside world, the unit of analysis is quite the same. Thus, when touchy liberals desire better attention to the fact of human pain and suffering, they manage to talk about cruelty where, ironically, cruel actions are derivatives of cruel agents and the victim's suffering is just fallout.

Besides this shared inability to dispel the primacy of the agent and the perpetrator in favor of the sufferer of pain, the rift between Kant and Hume is deceptive in another way. In terms of historical evolution, the current status of cruelty betrays a fetish of the active agent. It is no accident that the terms "good" and "evil" require a focus on cruelty and its infliction, leaving untouched the suffering *of* cruelty. Moral psychology ends up being the psychology of cruelty, which is a moral question, and hence of those who cause it. In the same frame, suffering is never a moral, let alone political or legal, question *unless* a moral agent with a conscience has caused it. All sufferers automatically become victims in the eyes of politics and law when "recognized." Suffering is thus relevant as a political question only *after* it is a moral one, when it is embodied and located in a certain way, when it surpasses arbitrary thresholds.

It is one thing to claim that liberalism, whether empiricist or idealist, cannot overcome its subject-centeredness even in its moments of empathy for the "victim." It is another to understand the stubborn constitution of the agent at the helm of liberal justice and ask what makes it so incurable and headstrong and what the temperament of this stubbornness might be: is it pathetic, squishy, helplessly compassionate, humble, philanthropic, imperialist, venomous, neurotic, all of the above, or none of these? Not figuring out this pathos is bound to reduce all interaction with liberal assertions to one or another act of editing or "correcting" them. Inadvertently, all protests to liberalism tread a limited, predictable path and will be, at some point, incorporated within it. Liberalism's singular gall and violence is accessed every time a resistance to it is accommodated by liberalism. Think, for instance, not only of how often liberals affirm their clumsiness and mediocrity in speaking for the other's suffering but also of how quickly its antagonists—purveyors of many a righteous anti-representational politics—"make space" for the voice of others without challenging the (liberal, colonizing) structures that determine and distribute the suffering and speaking *self*, and the suffering and speaking *other*, to begin with. This protest leaves unquestioned what it means to speak *for* one's own, or others', suffering and whether there are other ways of speaking suffering that problematize these as the only options.

JUSTICE AS ADMISSION, THE LIBERAL METHOD, AND THE VICTIM CONSCRIPTED

The subjects to whom the liberalism of fear tends are those at the margins of public life and those considered potential victims of injustices. The injustices have been, and are being, committed; it is just a matter of time before anyone falls prey to them. Each person is, then, a potential victim of actual injustice and of the proven propensity of power to corrupt. Shklar calls for greater attention to the invisible, passive cruelty of those who do nothing to preempt the eruptions of injustice.

Shklar's emphasis on the everyday lived experience of people in a polity is refreshing, as is her attention to the ordinariness and ubiquity of injustice and to the people who suffer it. Hurting bodies serve as Shklar's template for political subjects that deserve a liberalism to be built around them. She reasons from "the standpoint of those who did not have the voice easily representable at the centre."[39] That they are to be considered as "not discursive and reflecting persons, nor friends and enemies, nor patriotic soldier-citizens, nor energetic litigants, but the weak and the powerful" only reinforces the torpor of subject positions pointed to previously.[40] While this attitude may certainly be born of sympathy, it leaves an entire range of manifestations and details open to question that go concealed in such care. For one, it is so centered on the person who is performing the inclusion that the included can be little more than "beneficiaries."[41]

Shklar's interest in the view "from the margins" and "from the angle not of what was visible at the centre of public life"[42]—and her desire to recognize the unseen without necessarily wanting to expose and name them—is touching, especially since this is something at which liberalism usually fails. Even in her more sensitive account, however, this willingness to see them immediately turns them into potential victims in liberal discourse. Whatever Shklar's intentions, this is *still* a conferring of identity, a naming with its own cruelty, and, hence, a determining with its own violence. Either Shklar is not aware of this or not bothered by it—ultimately, she keeps liberal legacy intact. This is mirrored in the magnanimity, through admission, with which Shklar wants to augment an already pretty engulfing liberalism. It also indicates Shklar's debt or affinity to Hobbes, in their shared politics of naming and representing what is unseen and, in doing so, perhaps reifying it. The ordinary, here, is equated with the physical experience of those who are either considered capable of ordinary vices, and thus susceptible to harming others through these, or regarded as the sufferers and always on the verge of injury.

An extension of the issue of *what* is made visible by the liberalism of fear is the issue of *who* sees and from *which* perspective. Shklar claims that the perspective of the invisible, powerless, voiceless victims is central to her liberalism. Much of this can be traced to her impatience with the weight that dominant liberalisms place on making claims. Most liberalisms either assume the claims-making individual or derive and produce one. The centrality of claims and their making bespeaks a philosophical rationalism that "focuses on what can be shared by all, on what is publicly defensible, or what can be articulated and defended in a public court of appeal."[43] The just society envisaged by the dominant liberalisms that rely on claims-making either presupposes or works toward "politically sturdy citizens, each able and willing to stand up for himself and others."[44] Both the presupposition and the goal are nonstarters for Shklar. She feels that such citizens can only be presupposed if the overpopulated margins are forgotten. These margins are home to those who are too weak and too defeated to even recognize injustice, whether on their own or as a community, let alone to put up fights and contestations of the sort that other, "happier" liberalisms necessitate.

The visible are thus not merely reliant for their legibility on those who are seeing but are logical extensions of them. Even in Shklar's work, "the perspective of losers" means little more than the observer or potential perpetrator tolerantly, even sympathetically, imagining the other and seeing their own position as merely accidental. This seeing is simply an extrapolation by the nimble subject. The losers, the faceless losers, are there, but when they are seen, the seers make sure they call out to them, and, in doing so, they merely confirm their own agency. Moreover, while Shklar is careful enough not to simply have these losers speak in their voicelessness, she does preempt their need to speak at all, patronizing them by granting a voice whose consolation is delusive.[45] The garrulous voicelessness and the identified namelessness persist in even the most earnest attempts at representation in liberalism, becoming key features of its narrative of human suffering.

The only way a person's suffering can enter the domain of visibility is if the suffering is represented as injury or harm, if the sufferer is a victim, and if the victim can tell a story of her victimhood. Ways to represent and own one's suffering are specified. Most basically, this is evident in the victimhood that is conferred on the sufferer once she earns the right to own her pain as injury. The terms on which this happens are structured around the liberal model of subjectivity and the centrality of the self, whether focusing on the agent's state of mind or actions (as in Kant) or on the consequences of the actions vis-à-vis the victim. One common thread is that the "self," whether the victim's or another affectee's, remains cogent and intact through the process of suffering injury—a self posited as outside, above, and ahead of time and space, certain of its content, and a devout disciple of liberal autonomy.

The ones to be recovered and brought back in are initially excluded qua victims by an inner circle of healthy agents. Given Shklar's stress on the ubiquity of invisible injustice and potential victims, she is in a position to dramatically question the terms of inclusion and exclusion. But she falls short of doing so just where the empiricism of her stance replicates the stasis of the idealist notions of justice she is challenging. The frames, empiricist or idealist, are uncannily similar. Whether the concepts contain material experience or abstract imperatives is rendered secondary to the mechanistic logic of their form. This logic does not admit of the dynamism that sees the capture by conception as a process itself. Nor does it factor internal relations between various frames of experience. The relations between what is "in" and "out," and across various dichotomies and separations, are not recognized since these spheres and categories are seen as self-consistent and unrelated to what they are either opposed or distant. This is how liberals adhere to a composite, rather than organic, understanding of language, subjectivity, and experience. This also fosters the luxury to draw and affirm boundaries without any thought of the materiality being divided up, and of the life that is bound to seep through and across the installed walls. Parcellations and amputations—imposed absences all—have a way of being present in their absence, of having a memory, of referring to that from which they have been severed, and so continue to surprise well-meaning liberals all the time.

Shklar's attempt to bring liberalism back to its basics (for her, the strongest case for liberalism's desirability) bespeaks an urgency to cure liberalism of its idealism through history, memory, and ordinary experience. Like earlier empiricist liberals whose professions of materialism go only so far, Shklar treats the body of the victim only as a static, congealed holder of some abstract, incontrovertible immediacy. In failing to account for the dynamics and dialectics of embodied experience, empiricist liberals bear a striking resemblance to idealist liberals. With empiricists and idealists both disaggregating matter and motion, any resort (or return) to corporeality is via stasis and coagulation, lodged in a body that wavers between absence and entrapment. This body—in experiencing, knowing, and bearing—is no more dynamic or complex in the empirico-liberal tradition than in the submissive servility conferred to it in the Kantian tradition.

Liberalism continually refuses to acknowledge or confront the processes that underlie and overwrite its needed abstractions such as subjectivity, victimization, ownership, memory, pain, injury, harm, and representation. When it does try to grasp the dynamic processes constituting experience, liberalism cannot do so without congealing them. In dividing up experience into suffering, injury, and injustice, it remains oblivious and insensitive to the internal relations between various registers of the experience it installs and shapes. By virtue of their shared formalism, idealist and empiricist liberalisms affirm each other's inability to recognize the spatial or temporal excess and residue of concepts. The word "admission" conveys this mechanistic logic, where subjects and their suffering are admitted into liberalism on preset terms, and where entry into a sphere or arena requires registering at the door with an assigned role, relinquishing any matter and materiality not relevant to the operations of liberal justice.

The problem is not passivity per se but the lack of respect both the idealists and the empiricists have for the body's way of suffering through the world. The inert woundedness in each case is considered inferior to the condition that puts the wounds to use, trades them, alienates them, or transcends them, with amputations, anesthesia, repression, denial, and amnesia. The idealist body, transcended, stays around as a tool for knowing, assessing, and doing. It becomes easily colonizable, with all ability to ask questions and pass judgment reposed securely in supposedly superior faculties. When liberals like

Shklar invest in their empiricism or materialism, the body is more present, but it is always already conscripted—at best, as the barricade at which these conflicts are fought; at worst, as one source of subjugated knowledge among others. Such materialism separates our ways of knowing, being, and confronting the matter and categories of experience; it is not dialectical. Any *return* to the body without a requisite disruption in these terms of relating knowledge, experience, creation, and destruction to each other, ontologically and epistemologically, is bound to only exhume the body in predictably vulgar and servile ways.

The victim is similarly redeemed by being corralled back to the center of a liberal politics that conceives of itself as having any fidelity to its founding. The word "inclusion," when used in conventional political discourse, still potentially misleads by suggesting that what is now being included or admitted was ever out. It is hard, though, to take liberalism at its word about when it excludes and when it includes—unless, of course, when each is seen in a relation to the other and to the conditions therein.[46] If the sufferer does not fulfill these conditions, her suffering remains invisible and illegible. When these conditions are enforced as the premise for suffering to matter and justice to be done, the violence, humiliation, and subjection that are conferred in this process are either not even sensed or are accepted as inevitable. Maybe when all is said and done, despite its steadfast adherence to a noble will to admit the excluded, liberalism has failed to earn any trust in it ability to sense absent presences and present absences—otherwise, why the impulse to hide one's face every time the curtain call sounds for the meticulously dictated performances of victims?

CHAPTER 2

THEATER OF THE ASCETIC

The domestication of suffering into pain and the translation of this pain into harm and injury starts off the process of admitting sufferers into the privileges of liberalism: the identity derived from this injury, the rights that compensate for the injury, and the interests that render injury fit for trade. Each stage of this process entails a series of translations, abstractions, and representations that are themselves suffered, not least when the sufferer self-represents as victim and when suffering that is not granted the status of injury within the liberal schema strikes back disoriented or triumphant.

Representation consists of the set of activities, processes, and goals in which the subjects and objects of liberal thought and practice interact to produce justice. The relation of suffering and representation has myriad iterations—in the representation of the suffering, or of the sufferer in relation to her suffering; in the self-representation of the sufferer in question or the representation of the suffering by someone else; in the representation of the infliction in isolation or in a context that allows interpretation as cruelty, injury, vice, or injustice. These are all activities of representation and suffering that purposively affirm and edify the political economy of injury in liberalism. Perhaps daunted by these multiple, overlapping activities, liberal procedures give the first hearing to the agent's activity that often speaks for itself, and the sufferer's subjectivity can be a poor and confused version of the healthy agent's. By the time sufferers figure out what to say, the suffering has become injury, and the injury has long become something else; the moment they learn to be victims and to speak the way they are told, their suffering has already been given a ticket to the marketplace of liberal justice.

What my narration of liberalism's relation to suffering, liberalism's own narration of our sufferings, and the spoken and unspoken claims of injury and victimhood all have in common is the issue of representation—of how something is made present and to what end. This is suggestive of at least two facts. First, representation is not merely one step or one activity among the procedures of liberal justice but has a more primordial and more intrinsic role in framing what, and for what, these procedures are. Second, the formal relation *is* a relation of substance and not prior or incidental to it. Aware of the burden of speech that arises only in response or relation to something, my inquiry is tied to representation, haunted as it is by the very question of how to speak of suffering as we suffer the act of speech, and what it means to speak for one's or another's suffering when representation has a role in determining what suffering we consider our own and what we consider another's.

Liberal narratives about human suffering determine the following: the form and content of suffering endured; the form and content of the claims made to redress the suffering translated into injury, harm, and injustice; and the relations between an actor, a sufferer, and each of their sufferings that are expected of them and considered valid. In the name of justice, when harms are recognized and compensated for, or when the excluded are given an opportunity to enter our world, representation mediates. The expectation is that certain individuals with a decent quantum of agency would be able to speak for themselves, or they will find someone to represent them if they fail to become agents themselves for reasons including (but not limited to) the lack of a language in which to express their wishes, desires, and pain to which the state, the courts, and other "caregivers" can respond.

Investments in representation ensue from and suffuse the core logics of the liberal approach to suffering discussed in the previous chapter. John Rawls is a liberal thinker who takes representation very seriously. His work engages representation at conceptual and practical levels, suggesting that representation's relation to suffering is more than an external and superficial one. Beyond its work to reduce suffering in the world, liberal representation shapes our experience, our realities, and the role of suffering in politics. Representation's attachments to subjectivity, voice, and experience need to be vetted in order to fully grasp its complicity in the problem of suffering. Simplistic dismissals of representation neglect, to all our detriment, its hardwired relations to suffering and subjectivity and the transformative potential of engaging these relations materially and politically.

Liberalism scripts performances of suffering toward the goal of justice. Examining Rawls provides insights into these performances that construct the subjects and objects of representation through certain modes of action, speech, history, and memory. His constructs of the "original position" and the "veil of ignorance" together convoke an *injury play*, and its featured actors and characters demand a sustained look—they are those whose speech, action, and constitution are relentlessly demanded by liberalism and whose performances channel life to the audience. This injury play exemplifies the *theater of the ascetic* that liberal societies ubiquitously stage and that they naturalize and normalize. This ascetic theater provides the substance and practices that affirm the philosophical self-conception of liberalism as a tragic genre where human wills and choices are concerned, and casts a different light on liberalism's broader dramatic affinities and the approaches to suffering, action, individuality, sociality, sensing, and knowing that they foster.

REPRESENTATION'S JOURNEY: FROM LIBERALISM TO MARX

Beyond being a subject or object of politics, law, art, and history, representation is a corporeal and sensuous practice. Many registers of representation weave into and overlay each other. These include—in juridical-legal and political representation—bearing witness, testifying, and self-representation, and the processes that construct victims, perpetrators, bystanders, enemies, allies, and interests. Other registers within which representation appears include the linguistic (the relation of language to reality and subjectivity); the aesthetic (in terms of literary and artistic representations of suffering but also more broadly speech, imagination, memory, and other corporeal articulations);[1] the sensorial-cognitive (related to capacities of perception, recognition, interpretation, translation—hence, an extended aesthetic); and the historical (individual, collective, institutional, structural memory, making "present").[2]

Hanna Pitkin argues that representation, however complex, has an identifiable meaning that has not changed much since the seventeenth century. This traverses, in large part, the evolution of liberal thought itself. Thus, her treatment of representation corresponds to the concept's typical situation in liberal discourse. In what she calls a meaning "broad enough to cover all its application in various contexts," representation is "re-presentation, a making present once again." She adds, "Except in its earliest use, this has always meant more than a literal bringing into presence, as one might bring a book into the room. Rather, representation, taken generally, means the making present in some sense of something which is not present literally or in fact. . . . In representation, something not literally present is considered as present in a non-literal sense."[3]

Integral to the descriptive and the symbolic representation that, according to Pitkin, does not "act for" is the act or activity involved in the installing of a descriptive representation or the creation of a symbol. Pitkin is interested in what surpasses the making of representations or symbols: the realm of acting for others beyond the formal representation, the substance of the activity, and the role of the representative. Her hinge is the notion of the representative as actor-for-others, and she firmly disqualifies all other ways of conceptualizing representation. She looks at many senses of "acting for"—the element of action, taking care or acting in someone's interest, substitution, delegation, and so on—to conclude that none can, by itself, adequately describe representation. Pitkin strictly separates representation as "standing in" (where she is able to entertain the artistic component of representation) from representation as "acting for."[4] Dispensing with the former as inanimate, she underestimates the stasis of certain actings for. The aesthetic element of a representation can be seen as an activity of a bringing to presence. Representations are not actually inanimate or static, and the two eventual referents—the animation and the activity—can work together to yield a more robust understanding of the possibilities and dead ends of representation.

Hobbes is smarter here. Most obvious in his work is his formalistic definition of representation in terms of arrangements that precede and initiate it—authorization, or the giving of authority to act.[5] However, his claim that *every* government is representative because it represents its subjects espouses a possibly "aesthetic" view when read along with his invocation, say, of the *body* politic. The Leviathan is, then, just one form of representation. Hobbes's aesthetic endeavors rely as much on making sure the Leviathan is composed of the bodies it represents, in the most accurate way, as they do on fixing signification and what words mean. Such is Hobbes's seeming dislike of metaphor, because of its inability to mark clearly what is included and what is not, that the Leviathan's representation of its subjects has to rely on a language that "define[s] and determines[s]" the representation.[6] This gives content not only to the representation produced but also to *what* is being made present. Hobbes's account of language and representation is cognizant and wary of the residue. Lost in ideological mayhem is the question of what exactly the residue is that is not captured by language. The standard legacy of Hobbes is that of the monument, the representation itself, ironic as it is since Hobbes thinks that it is not our memory per se that is distinctive about us humans but our knowledge that we forget. Given his understanding of representation, Hobbes provides crucial insights into liberalism's own beginnings and promises.

From one materialist to another, Marx inherits a Hobbesian inquiry into representation. He uses three different German words to refer to "representation": *Vertretung*, *Darstellung*, and *Vorstellung*. Taken together, they offer imaginative and critical formulations of the process and activity of representation.[7] Two of the most obvious companions to the forms of representation Pitkin and Hobbes raise are *Vertretung* and *Darstellung*. *Vertreten* comes closest to the common liberal legal-political sense of representation and corresponds to a standing for, substituting for, or proxy. Within the domain of juridical politics, perhaps *vertreten* even corresponds to Pitkin's expanded notion of acting and speaking for. *Vertretung* relies on liberal subjects who possess a certain set of interests transferable to someone who can represent and safeguard them.[8]

Darstellung, *re*presentation, refers to representation in the not immediately political sense, descriptive and symbolic, inclusive of the activity of creating those representations and symbols. Moreover, in the word *Darstellung*, "*dar*" is from the same cognate as "there," while "*stellen*" means "to place"; thus, the word may be translated as "placing there." With its closeness to the idea of proxy, this certainly seems continuous with *Vertretung*. Instead of having the sense of placement overwrite the aesthetic element of *Darstellung*, this continuity exposes the (aesthetic) work of re-presentation within *vertreten*. In her essay, "Can the Subaltern Speak?" Gayatri Spivak affirms, "In the act of representing politically, you actually represent yourself and your constituency in the portrait sense as well."[9] For instance, "class" becomes a descriptor of a parity of interests. Marx finds class to be an ineffective description if it does not emerge from an effort to construct and sculpt the merely identical interests into a certain unity. This is representation as an act of artifice, of *pro*duction, where interests themselves are creative constructs that claim to reflect a subject's needs and suffering. Following Marx, the face value of interests cannot suffice as material for the composition of a class; interests, as representations, are not reducible to the subjects who bear them, so bringing only interests together is not a bringing together of subjects. Class, in Marx, becomes a descriptor of a group of people who desire and suffer in ways that *may* be similar. This attribute of class forces our attention toward the actual process and the acts of its composition.[10]

However, the most peculiar iteration here is *Vorstellung*, and not merely because it enriches *Darstellung* through their proximity, given that the former is both more diffuse and more dynamic at the same time. Both these verb forms evoke a sense of re-presenting, showing, depicting, being, constituting, describing, giving an account, and portraying theatrically. *Vorstellung* straddles the boundary of imagination and reality, intellect and art, and can thus speak to a broader and more dialectical sense of material experience than can *Darstellung*. Translated in Marx's text as "chaotic conception," its other related meanings include "idea," "notion," "expectation," "mind," "imagination," "introduction," "interview," and "picture show."[11]

Vorstellung is the point of departure for Marx's method, for a journey undertaken to seek what is manifested in this chaotic conception, with the suspicion that the venture into the hidden abode of this representation would not leave unchanged the point of departure—the representation itself. This method does not simply remove a mask or veil but solidifies and adds meaning to the manifestation. Once the first moment yields the contents of the *Vorstellung* (in terms of simple concepts), the second moment constitutes the way *back*. Marx writes, "From there the journey would have to be retraced until I arrived at [the point of departure] again, but this time not as the chaotic conception of the whole but as the rich totality of many determinations and relations."[12] The journey, from representations such as injuries and victims, into the hidden abodes of their living material and back, straddles the realms of thought and practice, concreteness and abstraction, sensing and intellection.

At least two senses of the concept of representation emerge: first, representation as "making present" or "bringing into presence" by literal or symbolic artifice, and second, representation as "acting for," whether in Pitkin's classical political sense or in the theatricality and artifice of representation in Marx's usage. In each of these interpretations, the concept of representation spans the fact of presence as well as a way of making present that involves imaging, forging, and artifice.

The prefix *re*, in one sense, suggests repetition; in another, it suggests return. Together, repetition and return insert the issues of temporality and process into any analysis of representation. Representations happen in and over time. When partial to return, the process entails a less linear concept of time and history than is implied in repetitions approximating an original in successive representations. It also suggests that the journey alters what was departed from and also those who return.

Presence can be defined broadly, for now, as availability to the senses and to experience.[13] *If representations make present, then the process involves sensing and making sensible.* Representation can be seen as connected to suffering at a more elementary level than in the act of imaging it through speech or other faculties: *this* artifice *itself* requires a sensuous experience. So how we represent is related to how we sense. The representations themselves, as our creations, partake in the sensuous experience that produces more representations in that we sense them, interact with them, and produce with this material experience.

A liberal frame of representation is central even to those liberalisms that do not carry the explicit burden of cruelty and suffering like Shklar's and other empiricist versions do. A treatment of suffering as object is of a piece with representation understood as the conveyor of inert suffering and the tool for its redemption. Both suffering and representation stand to change by grasping the more complex, dialectical, and internal intermaterialities as embodied and sensuous processes. The intertwined activities of making, presencing, acting for, and acting as support my definition of representing as the process of sensing and making sensible. These activities are not temporally discrete, and neither are the positions of presenter, representative, and audience ever mutually exclusive. Representation is thus not merely a tool that acts on suffering. Even at its most procedural and formalistic, it already inheres an ontological and epistemological relation to suffering. Likewise, suffering does not stand outside of representation. An orientation to suffering is, thus, an orientation to representation.

Rethinking representation, as acting for, conjoined with a bringing into presence, can learn from the coexistence of *Darstellung* and *Vorstellung*. The imperatives of liberal representation render politics reminiscent of a theater with prescribed enactments, roles, and labors—importantly, in relation to the suffering whose recognition or redress subjects seek. The next step, then, is to examine the *Darstellung* of liberal representation exemplified in the work of Rawls, who is remarkably aware of the theatrical merits of his schemas. An analysis of this *Darstellung* as *Vorstellung* follows in order to discover the determinations and the relations it coalesces. In this journey, the purely formal procedures to which liberals such as Rawls are committed emerge as purveyors and substantive framers of subjectivity, action, and suffering.

JOHN RAWLS AND THE INJURY PLAY

Rawls seeks the establishment of a stable and well-ordered system of liberal government befitting a society within which multiple comprehensive doctrines of morality and the good coexist. He maps out this vision of "justice as fairness," focusing on the basic structure—the edifice of political and social institutions bound in a system—as the subject of political and social justice. The delivery of justice is an event both underpinned and preceded by stages of representation that yield the principles of justice. In his account of what transpires under the auspices of the device of representation, the "original position," and the "veil of ignorance" that solidifies this representation, Rawls exemplifies a liberalism aware of the layers of representation that go unacknowledged in liberal law and politics all the time. He compels a focus on the processes and activities that both necessitate and are necessitated by the constructions of suffering, sufferers, and their relations in liberalism. The processes of representing in order to reach principles of justice—summarized in Rawls's original position—are different from, and provide input for, the representations of suffering and sufferers that happen when the principles are put into practice through law and policy.

The original position is a stage that aggregates certain constructions, performances and representations. Rawls clarifies that the original position is not merely a place to begin aggregating, extracting, or polling principles for a well-functioning society—it is a thought experiment where these principles are formulated and embodied in certain implications and ethos. The product of this stage is more general and abstract than a government founded or a constitution written. This is because the inputs and outputs of the original position are hypothetical rather than historical or practical. The original position is thus a device of representation. The ends of the representation, in both cases, are (a) free and equal citizens, (b) the principles of justice, and (c) justice as fairness (a theory that can serve as a political conception of justice compatible with multiple comprehensive doctrines).[14]

Even in the move from *A Theory of Justice* to *Political Liberalism*—a move that narrows justice as fairness down from a comprehensive to a purely political conception (supposedly clean of metaphysical claims)—the role of the original position does not change. While it is fair to expect the limitation of inputs to alter the functions performed, the original position is steadfast. The original task of modeling certain valued behaviors and embodied principles is supplemented by another step. This is the "overlapping consensus" that seals the results of the original position, by providing a replacement for the glue that may have been lost when the mandate became purely political rather than comprehensive.[15] In this procedural split, the approach to suffering that is at work in Rawlsian representation is not compromised. Still informed by primary goods and still attuned to autonomy and justice in the manner discussed in the previous chapter, the ends remain much the same across this largely procedural move from metaphysics to "pure" politics. This clues us in to the exclusions and inclusions that are always already the condition of the most fundamental positing of ourselves as subjects—whether with bodies and histories or more like stick figures in pencil.

The performances of liberal justice within which Rawls's scheme fits can be likened to a *theater of the ascetic* that provides the substance, the bodies, the senses, and the orientation to the genre liberals narcissistically favor: tragedy. Some general features of the theater of the ascetic can be gleaned from aspects of Rawlsian representation that materialize an injury play. The following sections undertake this inductive task and provide support for seeing this ascetic theater as embodying the terms of the overlapping consensus of various liberalisms on suffering, representation, and politics.

A Play of Injuries I

Social contract theories frequently refer to a fictive or actual assembly of persons that convenes for a bargain: the sacrifice of some degree of freedom for protecting some interests. In Rawls's work, this fictive assembly takes a technical role of a thought experiment in which delegates participate in order to come up with the best approximation of the fundamental principles that guide the basic structures of a liberal society toward justice as fairness. The delegates, acting behind a veil of ignorance, actively represent citizens with certain attributes, taking on their personae and thinking and acting *as* them. There is a plethora of theatrical metaphors that abound in Rawls's terms and conditions for the performances in the original position. Repeatedly, Rawls talks about the original position's task as one of modeling, first, the kinds of norms and information that are to guide our political judgments toward justice, and second, the convictions of reasonable people, each of whom is responsible for the fundamental interests of a free and equal citizen. The required personae, veils, and modeling all conjure the image of a theater.

Rawls compares the performance of these actor-delegates in the original position to a simulation, and says that we can "enter this position any time simply by reasoning for principles of justice in accordance with the enumerated restrictions." He adds, "When, in this way, we simulate being in this position, our reasoning no more commits us to a metaphysical doctrine about the nature of the self than our playing a game like Monopoly commits us to thinking that we are landlords engaged in a desperate rivalry, winner take all."[16] At another point, Rawls compares the decision to put on the veil of ignorance as "acting a part in a play, say of Macbeth or Lady Macbeth." He thinks that this is not a call for unencumbered selfhood, just like "playing Macbeth (does not) commit us to thinking we are really a king or a queen engaged in a desperate struggle for political power."[17]

George Kelly recalls how "unmasking" comes to have two significations in nineteenth-century German thought: (1) the revelation of "happy consciousness" once the tragic actor in Attic comedy is unmasked and ordinary folk enter the play and (2) the "depersonification" of the subject of Roman property law.[18] Working backward from unmasking, then, the veil refers to the mask of the legal subject of bourgeois law that, in making a "person," reifies a particular subject. It also refers to the *removal* or excision of "ordinary persons" in order to keep the show going, as performance of prewritten scripts and preassigned roles, deeply connected to how the genres of comedy and tragedy in their original forms are themselves filial to certain structures of inequality, subjectivity, and privilege (more on this in Chapter 6).

The Genre

Theatrical genres articulate modes of relating to suffering; genres of action *are* genres of suffering. Liberalism's ascetic theater, instantiated in Rawls's injury play, not only coexists with but also thrives on proclamations of the tragic irreconcilability of choices and incontrovertible scarcities that have been discussed earlier, and to which we will return in the final chapter. This is important not because the injury play always technically falls into the tragic genre but because the performances demanded by liberalism coexist with its self-proclaimed philosophical kinship with tragedy. This coexistence is worth exploring because, in trying to favor and impose certain forms of action and suffering, liberalism reveals its desire for the comfort, however illusory, of known genres, completions, and predictable finitudes. These genres resonate with the strictures of the form and content of suffering broached in the previous chapter. As is its wont, liberalism subjects the messy reality of action and suffering to its preferred epistemological, and thus ontological, accommodations without regard for how this reality is deformed in this subjection. The marriage of tragedy and ascetic theater in liberalism is suggestive of the template of human action and suffering that gets patronage within liberalism, in tandem with the stories about those who suffer on which rests the vitality of liberal political and legal discourse.

Does tragedy learn from ascetic theater or does ascetic theater submit itself to tragedy? Maybe the relation is more mutual and symbiotic, if tragedy is seen as furnishing the philosophical self-conception and ascetic theater as supplying the political and sensuous material. This reconciliation is rather amazing, as it follows the familiar inclusive logic of at once triumphal and consolatory assimilation—its emplotment is tragic, the materiality is ascetic; its syntax is of tragedy, its semantics are ascetic. Because of the form of agency and asceticism by which liberalism makes the tragic legible, all other possible relations to our own and others' suffering are colonized and left unseen or rendered incomprehensible.

In a remarkable exposé of the imbrications of the aesthetic, the ethical, and the political, the body is what bears the injuries that determine the mode that liberal drama takes. Even the tragic heroes know only how to function within the crass materiality of an amnesiac and escapist individualism. This amnesia and escapism *harms* those who confront and suffer liberal pathologies of insufficiency and garrulity at the same time. Meanwhile, the fetishes in the original position who have already "willingly" checked in their senses, their suffering—and their sense of harm—to liberal capitalism, are those on whom the rest of us are, tragically, relying to convey our harms into the courts that might regard them. It is with these thoughts on liberalism's generic attachments, even promiscuities, that I launch next into an analysis of elements of the injury play that convoke the ascetic theater of liberal representation. These elements can provide insight into the aspects of health, ill health, and performed subjectivities that fix liberal society's relation to suffering and the roles of its constituents.

A Play of Injuries II

Before examining the representational content of Rawls's original position and the veil of ignorance, we can recall some of the representations that happen even prior to the mechanics of the original position. Citizens in a liberal society possess interests that are to be defended politically and legally—the protection of a certain measure of freedom is an interest, as is the protection of the subject from the exercise of another's freedom that may harm him. While liberalism defines injury as a setback to interests, the definition is rather circular: in this framework, there would be no interest without an injury, whether actual or potential. Suffering is the basis of interest in liberalism—superficially, because an interest is a good, the lack of which is injury; more fundamentally, because the interest signifies an abstract protection from suffering predefined as the lack of predesignated goods. As bearers of actual or potential injuries, citizens are thus represented as actual or potential victims on whom a fetish and ascetic character is imposed and whose acting requires certain objectifications, transactions, and translations.

The Plot

The agreement reached in the original position yields principles of justice to guide a political liberalism and involves those who do and will cooperate on the basis of the principles being yielded.[19] This theatrical enterprise thus has a self-fulfilling nature. The very entry on the stage and everything that follows is scripted. Rawls deems that, with all conditions of the original position met, it would be absurd not to have the two principles of justice as fairness emerge at the end. The original position suddenly seems to hold the key: well directed and well performed, the play will end the way it must. While informed by the noble content and egalitarian intention of Rawls's principles, the proceduralism is more than a benign following of rules in order to reach a mutually valued end; it hypostatizes the represented and the representatives, codifying their suffering by drastically abstracting from and erasing their particularities. If Rawls's trustees know what they are looking for, they will find what they seek. Rawls is quick to supply the attributes of those who are sought but chooses not to take up the more interesting question of what this finding does to how the citizenry is founded, whose sufferings he seeks to make present, at what cost to them, and for whose consolations.

In contrast to the notions of representation that privilege a version of knowledge or likeness in relation to the represented, Rawls's process happens under the auspices of the veil of ignorance. The veil is constructed to block out the chance inequalities of birth and rank. This veiling entails that representatives abstract from their particularities and commit themselves to drawing up the fundaments of justice that would apply to those free, equal, reasonable, and rational citizens whom they are modeling. The conditions of this "giving up of the self" are laughable in the privation they bespeak—not unlike a

Bentham whose only hope of holding on to his body was either by completely transmogrifying it into an abacus of pain and pleasure or by mummifying it. To be sure, Rawls flaunts no unselfing; rather, the self is conserved when supplanted by its proxy, the model citizen who is free, equal, reasonable, and rational with certain moral powers.

The veil of ignorance filters out the delegates' knowledge of themselves and of the particularities of those who they are representing without acting on their behalf. In *A Theory of Justice*, Rawls writes,

> No one knows his place in society, his class position or social status; nor does he know his fortune in the distribution of natural assets and abilities, his intelligence and strength, and the like. Nor, again, does anyone know his conception of the good, the particulars of his rational plan of life, or even the special features of his psychology such as his aversion to risk or liability, to optimism or pessimism. More than this, I assume that the parties do not know the particular circumstances of their own society. That is, they do not know its economic or political situation, or the level of civilization and culture it has been able to achieve. The persons in the original position have no information as to which generation they belong.[20]

The veil of ignorance acts not only on the objects of vision but also on the capacities of vision. Given that the trustees are expected to undergo this procedure for themselves, with the imperative to imagine others in the same way, the problem of representing the other can now also be framed as the problem for representing, speaking for, oneself. Rawls is a very unusual liberal, for the very fact that he problematizes this speaking for oneself allows him to raise the question of speaking as oneself, and thus, of speaking as others.

THE CITIZEN AS ACTOR, THE ACTOR AS CITIZEN—HEALTHY SUBJECTS OF THE ORIGINAL POSITION

In Rawlsian liberalism, citizenship is predicated on the "healthy" public attributes of freedom, equality, rationality, and reasonableness. By elimination, the only subjectivities that partake in this process are those that mirror these attributes; a lack of these attributes is a lack of health, keeping the subjects from being either the representatives or the represented in the original position.

The actors who physically perform the experiment in the original position *are* rational parties, trustees of citizens, one for each; this means that all citizens are represented. The actors may be elected or nominated as decision makers. These are the ones who wear the veil. They *are* reasonable and rational in the business of representing their fellow citizens. The relation is not a conventional principal-agent relation, posited in accounts of relations between elected legislators and their constituents—there is no accountability, no condition of knowledge, and no expectation that the legislators act on behalf of their constituents. The representatives are representing themselves and others as reasonable and rational, free and equal, citizens. The activity of these actor-delegates is akin to acting *as*, since they are not acting *for* their constituents in any conventional principal-agent relation.

In the original position, the delegates, trustees, or guardians act *as* those they represent. The represented are citizens of a country who have learnt the virtues of a constitutional democracy from their history of conflict and conflict resolution. There are problems, such as inequality and intolerance, to be solved, but the urgencies of these problems do not make the delegates any less diverse in their adherence to completely irreconcilable comprehensive doctrines.[21] With certain emotions, histories, and other particularities disallowed, no one enters the original position as a sufferer or a victim. The actors bracket their own peculiar judgments and experiences and represent suffering and sufferers mediated by the notion of primary goods.

The delegates in the original position are guardians or trustees who represent citizens without acting on their behalf. The people who are imagining the citizens they are representing are deemed free and equal, reasonable and rational, which, in the light of the discussion of autonomy in the previous chapter. makes a certain health and agency a qualification for participation. This health is iterated in the delegates in the original position who are "free" because they possess two moral powers: the capacity for a sense of justice and the capacity for a conception of the good. They also have "companion powers" of reason—the capacities for judgment, thought, and inference required for the exercise of the two moral powers and for the practice of the virtues.[22] These citizens are equal by virtue of having these powers to "the essential minimum degree" to be fully cooperating members of society.[23] The sense of justice, as a form of moral sensibility, involves an intellectual power since exercising it lines up the powers of reason, imagination, and judgment.[24]

Rawls's metaphysical claims in *A Theory of Justice* and his political amendments to them in *Political Liberalism* are cognizant of the multiple identities that constitute us. Rawls conceptualizes this constitution, however, a bit problematically. While he does not claim a nonsituated ego (like a transcendental self may be understood to be), he does think of an ego that is contentless enough to be separable from the rest of the "self" and that can extract itself or allow the veil of ignorance to sift it out from the remaining personae or identities as needed. In addition, the ego chooses which identity to deploy and when. A major assumption seems to be at work here, observes Peter Weiss, "that a normal, healthy personality can constrain her thoughts in such a way as to take on the position of an atemporal individual."[25]

Another dimension of this "healthy" subjectivity of agents is their compliance with the injunction that the only identity that matters is their unchanging identity as free people in the public sphere and that this is what allows them to be whatever else they want to be in other spaces. These citizen-agents are able to take on identities at will and do not need to attach themselves to any identity. The separations between the public and the private are resilient, even profitable, for them. This voluntarism in relation to identity distinguishes these agents from those whose very personhood, even humanity, is premised on the injury and identity seared into them. The separations between public and private may not map onto the nature, logic, and ambience of suffering of the injured. So, far from being profitable or liberating to these suffering bodies, the resilient separations native to liberal cosmology impale them. It is surprising to what degree Rawls has completely detached his free person from its hard-won, tortured history. He engages in nervous denial on behalf of all those whose tortured histories may not be over yet, and whose ability to claim these moral powers may have something to do with either the voices they are given or the voices that are rendered unnecessary and meaningless—crazy talk, really—without the "distortions" of history Rawls is so quick to remove.

The individualism and impartiality implicit in this discussion are of critical importance. The costs of impartiality are greatest to those who lack the privileges that Rawls's delegates flaunt; the luxury of impartiality is theirs whose "double-consciousness" is a matter of postmodern whimsy and not something that is confronted out of necessity and suffered everyday.[26] The original position is also picky about how healthy subjects participate. The health is indexed by a neutrality qua indifference that can only come about once we have all treated our pain in the private sphere as a condition of entry into the original position via someone else's imagination, or if we are just too exhausted or too vulnerable to flaunt our sufferings lest it drives someone away (looking ahead to the next chapter's discussion of *Angels in America*). Asking for justice and inclusion happens once the aspirants have worked through their pain and anger and have learned to speak in a "civil" manner, with no negativity and hurt making them disruptive, hard to hear, or worth abandoning.

The way the possessive individualism of injury reconciles with what seems to be the dispossession promised by healthy agency is bound up with the methodological pathos and insecurity of liberalism, whether of the empiricist or the idealist bent. For one, this apparent dispossession (more on this in the final chapter) is not property undone but property made absolute. Admittedly, delegates do not enter the original position with any of their injuries. But the very premise of extricating one's humanity from one's suffering could only derive from injuries being absolutely possessable and hence absolutely alienable (within capitalist notions of property)—like commodities. This makes possible the distancing from injuries that may be too threatening and unsettling were they to be explicitly convoked in the original position. The state of quarantine suggests a paranoia that can only result from a doctrinaire and confident attachment to the possessive individualism of injury and to the ontic presumptions of ascetic theater.

Sketching out what can and cannot enter the original position perhaps imputes a spatiality to it that may controvert the essence of Rawls's thought experiment. But even if the original position is material only in and to the liberal imaginary, it affirms liberalism's self-conception that always trumps time with space. Each of liberalism's pet notions, be it inclusion, tolerance, difference, diversity, or property, is shot through with a spatialist bias. Further, this imaginary posits inclusion into its space as a centripetal process, construing outsiders as always being let in by liberal justice. The circularity that is deemed a justification of this process is not subtle, even in Rawls. For instance, when *Political Liberalism* expands its reach to subject these principles to another step of justification, it is the *overlapping* consensus, visualizable as bodies overlapping and cascading with each other to fit within a space that has already been bound by the assumptions. In this step, citizens with different religious or philosophical views (or conceptions of the good) are asked to endorse the work of the original position to round it out, enclose, and secure it.

Rawls cognizes that the representations created in the original position index our own preexisting assumptions: "We can see what we have assumed by looking at the way the parties and their situation have been described. The original position also brings out the combined force of our assumptions by uniting them into one surveyable idea that enables us to see their implications more easily."[27] This applies to everything from the very nature and character of the individuals who participate to what is deemed healthy subjectivity. What emerges here is our implicit consensus on the meaning of health and its lack and on what separates an agent from a victim. Even victims who enter have to make sure they have done the work to imagine themselves in a certain way so that they have approximated and affirmed the visions the "healthy" ascendant subjects of a liberal society would like to have of themselves.

THE SENSING AND THE MAKING SENSIBLE

Working the Veil: The Repertoire of Affect and Injury

A veil is usually thought of "as a kind of straight curtain, opaque or translucent, which impedes normal representational vision or refracts it into a new mode of penetration."[28] The players behind the veil know the generalized laws of society but have no history of this knowledge. Both the subject and object of this knowledge are atemporal and non-situated.[29] This atemporality and nonsituatedness is the product of a series of treatments of experience that domesticate the varieties of experience and then abstract from them to yield timeless representations in the forms of traditions, habits, reactions, and interests. The kinds of feelings that are fostered and deemed necessary to the procedures and promise of justice are also defined rather insistently. Wolin writes, "Rawls does not pause over the possibility that 'strong feelings' and 'zealous aspirations' might be directly related to frustration on part of those social classes and groups for whom the rhetoric and processes of reasonable pluralism have been least responsive. Instead, he seems to look forward to the elimination of the passions generated by oppression and neglect, apparently forgetting his own insight into the intractable existence of significant inequalities."[30]

In addition to their freedom, equality, and reason, the persons in justice as fairness also hold some moral powers. A key player here is the capacity for a sense of justice that feeds into the reasonableness of individuals in their ability to relate to others' conceptions of the good. This capacity spans the capacity "to understand, at least in an intuitive way, the meaning and content of the principles of justice and their application to particular institutions; to understand, at least in an intuitive way, the derivation of these principles as indicated in the analytic construction; and to have the capacities of feeling, attitude and conduct."[31] No one without a sense of justice can ask for justice, let alone be in the original position as the principles of justice are being reached.[32] With no capacity for a sense of justice, then, we can be neither participants nor claimants nor beneficiaries.[33]

The sense of justice spans the chosen Rawlsian moral feelings—indignation (our reaction to the injuries that the wrongs of others inflict on others) and resentment (our reaction to the injuries and harms that the wrongs of others inflict upon us)—and the chosen Rawlsian natural attitudes—mutual trust and affection. The stated moral feelings are more central to the sense of justice, and the natural attitudes are channeled in a guilt response. In the absence of a sense of justice, no one would "have a ground for complaint" if cheated or deceived by another. Rawls writes, "The injured cannot feel resentment; the others cannot feel indignation. They do not accept the principles of justice, and they experience no inhibitions from principle guilt feelings for breaches of their duty of fair play."[34]

Experiencing resentment and indignation is a prerequisite for making a claim to justice here. Resentment and indignation are the forms that our feelings of anger and hurt must take in order to have any valence in the eyes of justice. In his suspicion of the empiricist whimsy attached to behavior, Rawls wants us to keep behavior and feeling distinct and to be able to explain our feelings.[35]

Guilt holds together the various elements of the analytic construction of the sense of justice. While seen by Rawls to be "simply a way of arranging what is said about the moral feelings,"[36] guilt testifies to, and validates, the presence of those natural attitudes of trust and affection that precariously hold the populace together in the face of everything that tears them apart. The sense of justice assumes that cooperation is to be striven for and that the basic moral relation is one between sovereign individuals whose love and fellow feeling is mediated and affirmed by guilt. The feelings of guilt, resentment, and indignation thus become indicators for trust itself.[37] Rawls goes on to say, "To feel guilty or ashamed it is often sufficient, however, that a person sincerely say that he feels guilty or ashamed, provided that he has the concept of guilt or of shame and that he is prepared to give an appropriate explanation of why he feels as he does."[38] Neurotic feelings must be interpreted as guilt if they are to enter the fray.

With regard to the memory of suffering and injustice, Rawls is engaged in a dangerous game of first owning the legacy of a liberal society that has relied on reducing people to their injuries, necessitating that their identity be known only in relation to their victimization. This is affirmed in the emotions, and relations to justice and injustice, validated and required in the sense of justice. Then follows a demand for precisely *that* history to be left behind in the original position. At core, then, the sense of justice espouses a menu of what it is we can suffer and how.

Our ability to apprehend what is present impacts, and is impacted by, what we *re*present (the object of representation in the sense of who we are representing and what we represent it as). It also has a bearing on the relations recognized or established between the subject and object of representation, how representation is done, and how the acting may impact the sensuous beings involved. The sense of justice and the representations reciprocate and necessitate each other, carving the experiential and affective domain of the subjects in the process. Rawls is not naïve about articulations being generative of capacities, and this is what makes his project so potent and dangerous.

Original Speech

When Rawls wants the delegates to wear the veil and resist the temptations of history enclosed in the scars they see on their own or other bodies, we see liberal justice (a) displace any sense of being responsible to, and for, another by rendering us all sufferers of guilt and *ressentiment* and (b) prescribe speech that redirects pain, now abstract and dislocated, into general currency, absorbed by the principles of justice via the notion of "goods." The limits on the seeing and sensing carry into limits on expression. The statements are descriptive, with no judgment. Since the knowledge here is also atemporal and nonsituated, the expression is supposed to take the form of noncontingent laws. Since knowledge takes the form of laws, it is to be available to everyone in the original position and applies equally to all. The result is "a pure and untainted corpus of knowledge."[39]

Such a role of the veil brings to mind language, a representation of something by veiling. The veiling function of language does not begin with metaphor; language is veiling through and through. Thus, the claim that the language of actors in the original position is altogether devoid of metaphor renders the veil imperceptible, not absent. The veil veils itself. An utterance becomes the spoken only because its accompanying invisible fabric of meaning is compatible with the sense of justice. Those sufferings, realities, and experiences that have no words in the dominant language, or those that were not translated into permitted sentiments and externalizations, will never be spoken. In his discussion of the relation between voice and suffering, David Morris writes, "Voice matters precisely because suffering remains, to some degree, inaccessible. Voice is what gets silenced, repressed, preempted, denied or at best translated into an alien dialect, much as clinicians translate a patient's pain into a series of units on a grid of audio-visual descriptors."[40]

Thus, language understood simply in its composite, verbal sense, and interested in a depiction of how things "really are," keeps short-circuiting the immense possibilities for giving voice to this deep silence. However, literature and art, understood in an autonomous and nonliteral way, "labor to make such silences 'speak' by extending our awareness of an irreducible, nonverbal dimension of suffering that can never be put into words."[41] Turning to language beyond literality and beyond games of conveyance of meaning also exposes the many avenues within which representation already happens before we consume it, showing how inaccurate the compartmentalized and formalistic understanding of liberal representation can be. The aesthetics of language can thus force a look beyond the dichotomy of speaking for oneself or others.

"The impossible project of giving speech to silence is important especially because it exposes how we simplify and betray suffering whenever we ignore its power to elude every linguistic and conceptual tool that humans can marshal to understand it," continues Morris.[42] The actors in the original position do not carry with them the experience of this voicelessness, given the demands to articulate the sense of justice. There is no confrontation, let alone engagement, of the problem of alienation central to suffering. Nor does this representation struggle with ominous silences. The problem with voice in the original position is not merely a lack of these lacks—it also includes saturation by forced, predictable, and scripted speech. The ascetic theater bids actors speak and also tells them how to speak. Failure to perform the script leads to much jetsam over the course of lifelong initiation as liberal subjects. Any representation not the result of the struggle with deep silences, whether one's own or the other's, already brackets the suffering that is constitutive of human beings and all activity that makes us human. What kind of suffering *is* the original position to begin with? If the suffering that *is* representation does not make it into the original position, then what of the suffering that necessitates the device itself?

Liberalism institutionalizes slave morality when it necessitates the economy of suffering and sufferers by insisting on injuries and victims: it is easier, simpler, and cheaper to treat all sufferers who matter as victims, and to ensure that these victims—disciples of the imposed sensuous paradigm that installs them as victims—act to affirm it. The traces of Nietzsche's slave morality in Rawls's account are not exhausted by the sense of justice (in its early, substantive formulations), colonized as it is by guilt and resentment. Beyond the content of the feelings that are allowed to matter is the imperative to externalize them in a certain way if they are to figure in considerations of justice. This acting entails an array of actions and passions consistent with the sense of justice, the latter serving as a benchmark. Suffering and other emotions, such as annoyance and indignation, are translated into those moral feelings that befit the sense of justice and can be explained in such language. The sense of justice projects itself on the principles of justice that will be produced as its closest representations possible. The principles are, then, symbols of the triumph of a liberal ascetic ontology and its preferred comportments in norms, laws, knowledge, thought, speech, and action.

Behind the veil, the actors work with a congealed internal ethos. This ethos is a reservoir of garrulous representations that further alienate and mask, often beyond recognition, the suffering that they claim to be appearing as, not to mention the suffering they do not even claim to represent. As discussed in the next chapter, these on-demand representations testify to the liberal incapacity for uncomfortable silences and for the suffering that evades instant accommodation into a category. Liberal capitalism's philanthropic garrulity is nervous, afraid, and betrays a dwindled ability to be compassionate in a manner that is not predicated on its knowledge and, hence, on its power. Elite philosophical, political, and legal discourses are complicit in rendering suffering—whether "natural" or "moral"—mute by insisting on a certain representation. The dominant and fixed representations of injury and victimhood in liberalism provide the images, the memories, and the words—frozen, selective, and verbose. The loquacity of contemporary liberal humanitarian discourse is silencing in precisely its reliance on a particular mode of representation that helps to alienate, define, and control suffering and how (much) it reaches us, what it calls us to, and how it assesses and harnesses our capacities and claims of humanity. Just a peek behind the a priori constituents of liberal justice will expose how liberal representation is most powerful and effective in its promise of protecting its privileged subjects from the messiness of suffering and laboring with it.

Nietzsche's Scenes and Senses of Suffering

The ongoing discussion of the embodiment and productivity of the Rawlsian sense of justice within liberal spaces necessitates a stepping back into Nietzsche's discussion of suffering and its sensuous imperatives. In *Daybreak*, Nietzsche talks about the knowledge acquired through suffering. In his enumeration of the benefits of suffering—"the intellectual benefit that accompanies profound solitude," "the permitted liberation from duties," and "the acquisition of knowledge"—he seems to be more pointedly referring to more *organized*, socially acknowledged ways of suffering (sickness, disability, madness, punishment, etc.), as it were, especially when he refers to the permitted liberation from duties and to solitude.[43] However, these particular kinds of injury and suffering illuminate the realm of suffering that would also include, referring back to my discussion of Kant in the previous chapter, what we might be *cautiously* able to call intelligible injury.[44]

Intense suffering allows the sufferer to view things in their true light, stripped of "the lying charms with which things are usually surrounded when the eye of the healthy regards them."[45] Here, Nietzsche talks about the sufferer looking "out," while she herself has lost the "color and plumage" that was perhaps once hers. In one way, we find Nietzsche saying that these processes are related and contingent—that something in the famous eye of the beholder has changed for her to apprehend things in their bare, not-too-flattering reality. Syllogistically then, when the sufferer suffers, she exits the "perilous" world of fantasy, not only with regard to the world outside her, but also within and of herself.

Nietzsche calls man "the sick animal," which, in light of the passage discussed previously, would mean that man is the sick animal *who suffers*. On a similar note, perhaps, he also calls man "the bravest of animals" and "the one most accustomed to suffering"—"he does not repudiate suffering as such; he desires it, seeks it out, provided he is shown a meaning for it, a purpose." This is where the idea of man actually suffering *from* meaninglessness emerges—of sufferers suffering from the meaninglessness of their suffering but not before they have been touched by the ascetic priest's promise or deception or illusion of meaning*ful* suffering. "The meaninglessness of suffering, not suffering itself, was the curse that lay over mankind so far—and the ascetic ideal offered man meaning. It placed all suffering under the perspective of guilt. Man was nevertheless saved, not leaf in the wind, a plaything of nonsense—the will itself was saved."[46]

It is this seeking a purpose and cause for one's suffering that leads the sufferer to seek an agent who is responsible for his suffering and is also himself susceptible to suffering? Nietzsche here locates the "actual physiological cause of *ressentiment*, vengefulness and the like." Here is where the sufferer starts thinking of relief as simply a deadening of pain and, hence, would go to any lengths to get there. This happens in the use of affects and defensive retaliation as reactive protective measures, almost like "a reflex movement set off by sudden injury or peril . . . in one case, the desire is to prevent any further injury, in the other it is to deaden, by means of a more violent emotion of any kind, a tormenting secret pain that is becoming unendurable, and to drive it out of consciousness at least for the moment."[47] There is, however, a way in which the priest effectively reroutes and deploys this pain, which is relevant to the discussion begun with Rawls's sense of justice, and to the question of the capacities and incapacities of liberalism to deal masterfully with the suffering it produces as injury and the suffering it cannot bear to recognize *as* suffering. The content of *ressentiment*, for instance, is not merely "the inversion of the value-positing eye" and a fixation on the doer behind the deed to the exclusion of the doer's subjection to the deed.[48] Rather, it entails the continual resuffering of the injury caused by the designated doer, with the meaning of the suffering ascertained precisely to avoid the "greater" suffering of the pain that does not lend itself to successful ascetic hermeneutics.

What Acting Brings to Presence

Great nausea and great pity, writes Nietzsche, are the two main human afflictions that do not allow for convalescence, ensuring that the madhouses and hospitals of culture remain populated. These afflictions "unite to beget the uncanny monster: the 'last will' of man, his will to nothingness."[49] It is the ascetic priest who gives the sufferers their last will because he gives them a target, an aim, or a goal for that will—however concocted—only in order to give a life to the very chimera that is *willing*. I find this to be Nietzsche's hint to the manner in which suffering is rendered productive and retooled for the institution of the healthy liberal subject.

Entertaining the notion that subjectivities are constructed through sense experience, and then taking Nietzsche's insight into the mnemotechnics of a "civilized" society that grants citizenship and subjecthood by decreeing a certain memory, it is fair to wonder which citizens enter the original position as representations of themselves and what they feel toward whom.[50] If being a citizen is itself a role—and a relation—with its set of sensings, performances, duties, and expectations, then those with sufferings that have not perfected their sense of justice, those whose sufferings do not fit into the regime of liberal mnemotechnics, those that have not met the test of ascetic character, and those without *ressentiment*, cannot enter liberal politics. In thinking about the roles thus played, Nietzsche is relevant in another way as well: for his ascription of different characters to the suffering as embodied by his figures of the ascetic priest (the champion of slave morality) and the tragic artist (Nietzsche's counterpoint to the former). Each exemplifies a mode of suffering, differing *not* in how much they suffer but in the form their feelings take *and* in how they embody, represent, and respond to, this suffering—aesthetic imperatives first, moral after.

We are told that the ascetic priest, in his role of the savior and shepherd of the sick and the suffering, had to have been sick himself. Nietzsche writes, "It cannot be the task of the healthy to nurse the sick and to make them well—the necessity of doctors and nurses who are themselves sick; and now we understand the meaning of the ascetic priest and grasp it with both hands."[51] The ascetic priest himself suffers, despite (or because of) adopting the role of the savior of all other sufferers. Nietzsche talks about the *art* of the ascetic priest, his skill at *representation*, at a few different places in the text. The very fact that he seeks out the suffering to claim dominion on is part of his art and mastery. His historical mission as savior, shepherd, and advocate stems out of his mastery of his suffering at all times. Not only has he been able to simply deaden his pain by subjecting himself to more, and effectively "reveling" in it, but he also has turned his *ressentiment* against itself, whereby he no longer seeks the answer, the agent, and the cause outside of himself. But this is accompanied by the notion of guilt and sin, with an immoderation that contradicts his labor, and an exchange of some illusions for others when the sufferer ceases to be intoxicated by fantasies and when suffering makes him apprehend the world in its not-too-flattering reality. It is at this point that, while the suffering is rid of the crutches of a contempt directed outward, the ascetic priest nestles his prescribed suffering in the crutches of contempt toward oneself, dissimulated by illusions and artifice. Nietzsche calls the ascetic priest "an artist in guilt feelings"[52]— the notions of guilt, sin, debt, suffering as punishment, all took form, were created, in the hands of the ascetic priest; they were the seeds *and* fruits of his labor. Furthermore, the transformation of the invalid into a sinner is the priceless and timeless masterpiece of the ascetic priest's art, to which the multitudes have constant access and of which, at the same time, they are objects.

It is this art that requires the ascetic priest to "evolve a virtually new type of preying animal out of himself, or at least he will need to represent it." The priest would need to represent (or *re*present, *darstellen*) "a new kind of animal ferocity in which the polar bear, the supple, cold, and patient tiger, and not least the fox seem to be joined in a unity at once enticing and terrifying."[53] Accompanying this is his confidence in his art and ability to dominate the suffering at all times. In a sentence that is decidedly the crux of Michel Foucault's Nietzschean lineage in thoughts on madness, science, therapy, and the exploration of the confessional roots of sexuality, Nietzsche writes, "He brings salves and balm with him, no doubt; but before he can act as a physician he first has to wound; when he then stills the pain of the wound he at the same time infects the wound—for that is what he knows to do best of all, this sorcerer and animal-tamer, in whose presence everything healthy necessarily grows sick, and everything sick tame."[54]

The shepherd exists so long as the herd exists, which is why the ascetic priest has to constantly combat anarchy and the threat of disintegration of his flock posed by *ressentiment*. This is where Nietzsche tells us that the priest's accomplishment of altering the direction of the *ressentiment* (a feat that Nietzsche deems to be the "supreme utility" of the ascetic's art and the only "value of the priestly existence")[55] is rooted not in some selfless love of mankind but in an artful and strategic act of self-preservation on part of the ascetic priest.

Here, three things loop back to themes put forth in this book's Introduction—and give us clues to where the secret of the health and longevity of liberalism and its privileged subjects reposes. First, there is an aesthetic component—both in terms of artifice and of sense experience—to the suffering of any subject in liberal society. Second, the seeming simplicity and "barebones" nature of the framework of liberal justice is stilted upon feverish negotiations of the meaning of life and death. As the following excerpt suggests, the affixing of the suffering god in the Greek drama foretells the liberal drama that replaces a democracy of suffering with the drama that features singular notions of suffering, life, and death in principles of justice, no less Apollonian in incarnation than the *late* Dionysus (the Dionysus of the *Twilight of the Idols* rather than the *Birth of Tragedy*):[56]

> We have now come to the insight that the scene [*Scene*] together with the action is basically and originally thought of only as a vision, that the single "reality" is the chorus itself, which creates the vision out of itself and speaks of that with the entire symbolism of dance, tone, and word. . . .
>
> The chorus sees how Dionysus, the god, suffers and glorifies himself, and thus it does not itself act. But in this role, as complete servants in relation to the god, the chorus is nevertheless the highest, that is, the

Dionysian expression of nature and, like nature, thus in its frenzy speaks the language of oracular wisdom, as the fellow-sufferer as well as wise person reporting the truth from the heart of the world. . . .

Dionysus, the essential stage hero and center of the vision is, according to this insight and to tradition, not really present in the very oldest periods of tragedy, but only imagined as present. That is, originally tragedy was only "chorus" and not "drama." Later the attempt was made to show the god as real and then to present in a way visible to every eye the visionary figure together with the transfiguring setting. At that point "drama" in the strict sense begins. Now the dithyrambic chorus takes on the task of stimulating the mood of the listeners right up to a Dionysian level of excitement, so that when the tragic hero appeared on the stage, they did not see something like an awkward masked person but a visionary shape born, as it were, out of their own enchantment.[57]

This excerpt brings to light two distinct currents I find intertwined in my relation to Nietzsche's work on suffering. The first includes his conceptions of the Dionysian and the Apollonian as they span his oeuvre, occurring together. The second involves the characters of the ascetic priest and the tragic artist that are developed more unevenly in different texts. It is difficult to do justice here to how I see these two currents evolve in relation to each other. Suffice it to say, for now, that considering them together is necessary for grasping Nietzsche's critique of *ressentiment*. There is no way to regard ressentiment as a moral sickness and a sickness of Christian and liberal morality without seeing it as a political and aesthetic pathology and a pathology of Western liberal politics and aesthetics. So, the next time the *Genealogy* inspires a defensive reaction on the part of all of us who are the "sick" and the "memorious"[58] within liberal capitalism, perhaps we must remember that the confessional is not the place to expel it. That is *not* where we will be saved. A real, honest look at the political economy of liberalism as embodied in liberal representation and its accompanying ubiquitous ascetic theater—where not even the Dionysian, as a redemptive impulse, is safe—will give us some clues to where and how the sins of liberal capitalism must be begun to be atoned for.

The "new" drama that Nietzsche talks about signals to how liberalism reifies modes of suffering and action via the ritual personifications, objectifications, and subjectivations that suffuse our sensuous existence and our attempts at imaging ourselves and making this world thus. This drama thus demands different sensuousnesses, different performances, and different submissions. But, importantly for my purposes here, so do resistances to it. Bachmann's *Todesarten* refer to the domain that opens up when the hegemonies of life and death, of health and vitality, demand us to be subjects in a particular way, where any challenge to these deaths can perhaps ultimately take the shape of suffering, and dying, differently. The ascetic's self-preserving self-abnegation is the only *undoing* of the *self* liberalism knows—as it passes for the victim of its own contrived pathos and tragedies, forcing the rest of us to rise to the occasion to save it every time it proclaims a threat to itself (forgetting very quickly that its very raison d'etre was that it would save us from each other and ourselves).

The ascetic priest combats suffering by placing a "monstrous valuation" on life, and it is his "evaluation of existence" that the priest demands obedience of in order for something to be *put right*.[59] Needless to say, the very notion of putting right by deeds or anything else assumes compliance with what life and its rightness would be. It is this ideal of life and existence that gives the impression that the ascetic labor is one that chooses life and affirms life, as is believed by those who revere it—but the fact that it chooses to value a life that opposes and excludes "nature, world, the whole sphere of becoming and transitoriness" is, for Nietzsche, the reason why the ascetic's labor is one rooted in the denial of life.[60] Nietzsche locates this ascetic ideal in the "*protective instinct of a degenerating life* which tries by all means to sustain itself and to fight for its existence."[61] Nietzsche thus terms the ascetic ideal "an expedient," and "an artifice for the *preservation* of life," adding that "life wrestles in it and through it with death and *against* death." The true substance of willing within an ascetic's labor is characterized further—"a hatred of the human, and even more of the animal, and more still of the material; a horror of the senses, of reason itself; a fear of happiness and beauty, a longing to get away from all appearance, change, becoming, death, wishing, from longing itself—all this means a will to nothingness, an aversion to life."[62] Since the ascetic priest's dominion rests on *so little*, and since his entire faith, will, power, interest relies on an ideal of merely existing and merely preserving, he does live fairly precariously but with hope! Regardless of his intentionality and sincerity, this denier of life willy-nilly ends up functioning as a life-conserving and "yes-creating" force. Any wonder, then, how, and on what terms, liberalism keeps preserving and renewing itself, and at what cost we preserve and renew ourselves as its willing, unwilling, wanted, and unwanted subjects?

CHAPTER 3

THE LIBERAL SENSORIUM

Recognizing the historical determinants of the form and content of our suffering is essential to the debate over the "right" location of suffering in politics and over the "right" legibility and, indeed, utterability, of the same. It is conceivable what the costs are of speaking *for* the others who suffer, whether to compensate or to liberate them. But when everyone speaking for oneself as such becomes the guiding principle of ethical and democratic politics, some of the issues of speech and subjectivity are rendered ahistorical and are thus ill-addressed. This confers a particular value to speech and self-presentation, and also domesticates and tokenizes those who, along with their wounds, make it to the table. This inclusion has a method, whether intentional or not, of isolating, excluding, and privileging. This happens when new maps are drawn and when a self-aggrandizing multiculturalism neuters and evacuates the politics of class, race, and gender. This also happens when philanthropic commitments render others visible in a way that makes even the master-slave dialectic seem optimistic; when our care constructs its objects monologically and only the speech that responds to us counts as speech; or when others serve as faithful illustrations of our moral conundrums or successes. It is assumed that if others do not speak or do not make themselves understood, despite the space given to them, then they either must not have anything to say or they need to work harder. Contemporary politics knows no better than to dishonor this speechlessness with its garrulity.

Liberalism fosters mechanistic and linguistic pathologies that distort and silence precisely what it is trying to in*voice*. Its well-crafted relation to language ends up supplanting sensuousness that would otherwise be demanded of a sensuous being responding to her own or others' suffering. Particular representations necessitate a certain sense apparatus and, in turn, a certain relation between politics and suffering. The liberal goods of redressal, recognition, inclusion, and empowerment are affirmed by a sensorium that furnishes and privileges an externalized relation to suffering as a condition for these goods. When a certain premium on representing suffering hammers both the suffering and the sufferer into a prescripted form, this representational imperative itself becomes an ascetic ideal that violates rather than honors, even in the most fervent attempts at justice. This consideration is lost to arguments between those who want to speak for us and those who want us to speak—*still speak!*—for ourselves. Suspicion of the modes of presence sanctified within these debates is thus requisite. These perverse attachments to voice qua speech betray a regimented objectification of suffering that buttresses them. This enables the arbitrary designation of the subjects and objects of politics outside of the negotiations over the material that gets sculpted into these subjects and objects. This misses a fundamental moment of the collaboration between politics, ethics, and aesthetics, and neglects imaginative possibilities of the scope of politics, political method, and political subjectivity.

The relation between suffering and making it present for political consideration is certainly a holdover of democratic aspirations within contemporary liberal politics. Voicing suffering, then, becomes a value in any version of the politics of representation, even when there are disagreements over who should speak and for whom. A whole range of critiques within democratic theory have further explored the conditions within which such speech becomes possible or not, enabled or not, valued or not. In light of the discussion in the previous chapters, a greater suspicion of the assumed relation to suffering as object and of the reliance on certain performances of suffering is requisite, since both are affirmed only to the detriment of an aesthetic-political experience that can allow us to locate suffering and its sensorial demands as intrinsic to political method, toward which the next part of this book gestures. Moreover, representation itself constructs the experience of the suffering subject and the very presence of the subject (both the suffering and the sufferer), thus configuring the range of possible relations between suffering and politics.

This chapter chances into some contemporary cultural texts to illuminate them with the discussion of the statics and dynamics of liberalism in Chapters 1 and 2, respectively. Common triangulations between liberal ethics, politics, and aesthetics that institute a very passive, functional, and external relation between suffering and representation in liberalism are threaded in the three meditations that follow. The first involves the collusion of ethics and politics in the liberal secular state's relation to suffering and need and how this sets up social relations writ large. The second addresses the premises of humanitarian optimism in the quantifications and taxonomies of suffering performed by policy makers. The third delves into the coming together of the moral and the aesthetic in responses to eventful suffering and the consequential sensorium and sociality particular to liberalism.[1] Some of the usual weapons liberalism wields that were identified in preceding chapters, including the separation between the public and the private and other comparable dichotomies, the centrality of the agent, and the neat economics of emotions and sense experience, reappear in each of these short meditations on some not-so-random encounters with suffering in liberal culture. The interlocked nature of many of these issues meticulously enables liberalism to privilege a form of presence of suffering, compromising both sensuousness and suffering and, ultimately, justice. In anticipation of the materialist approach configured in Part II of this book, these discussions may hopefully deepen our material grasp of how the scaffoldings of liberal representation are wrought, and where they can begin to be pulled apart.

NEED, SUFFERING, THE STATE, YOU, AND ME

Angels in America is Tony Kushner's critical history of AIDS and the escapades of the liberal state. For every masterful mocking exposé of realpolitik and religion presented to its reader, the play can be mined for its trenchant insinuations into the visceral economy of American liberalism and its routine maneuvers with human suffering. Reading the play this way is an exercise in honoring this suffering itself, without cold legalistic interrogation, since Kushner hides magic even in the most broken and defeated of characters without necessarily making their pain into something more palatable. Kushner allows us another angle on the kind of ordinary incapacities and weaknesses that characterize liberal subjects whose peculiar mixture of vacillations and certitudes is just a symptom of their evolved inability to suffer. This alone is a remarkable subversion of tried and tested encounters with suffering in contemporary culture. The play is thus an eloquent commentary on the political and ethical incapacities of liberal philosophy, the liberal state, and its subjects. The possibility of justice becomes inseparable from the ability to love and to not abandon in need. The question of politics, thus, is transformed into whether we are able to suffer the tragedy of justice and if we can still ask, as Prior Walter does, for "more life."[2]

The character Louis embodies the uncertain, garrulous, and pathetic nature of American liberalism. He talks a lot, is weak and uncommitted, is quick to feel sorry for himself and trump his pain of self-proclaimed powerlessness over the suffering of a *real* victim, and is clever enough to first know what he is doing and then to never be responsible for it. Louis's tenuous relation, as a homosexual man, to the publicness and privateness of the suffering of outsiders like him, conforms to liberal boundaries; he chooses having a "public" hope over "private" acts to corroborate it and then invests in this very discord as his redemption. Louis redeems himself by hiding his weaknesses behind the insistent priorities of liberal justice and its juridical politics. Soon we realize that liberalism's failure lies in, among other things, concocting for itself that very redemption, not comprehending the nature, consequences, and oftentimes unreality of separations between, for instance, the public and the private, politics and ethics, church and state.

An early scene in Part I of *Angels* finds Louis next to his grandmother's grave in conversation with a rabbi. Prior, Louis's boyfriend with AIDS, has just updated Louis on his sore count, with a fearful confidence that he is going to die.[3]

> LOUIS: Rabbi, what does the holy Writ say about someone who abandons someone he loves at a time of great need?

> RABBI: Why would a person do such a thing?

> LOUIS: Because he has to. Maybe because the person's sense of the world, that it will change for the better with struggle, maybe a person who has this neo-Hegelian positivist sense of constant historical progress towards happiness of perfection or something, who feels very powerful because he feels connected to these forces, moving uphill all the time . . . maybe that person can't, um, incorporate sickness into his sense of how things are supposed to go. Maybe vomit . . . and sores and disease . . . really frighten him, maybe . . . he isn't so good with death.

> RABBI: The Holy Scriptures have nothing to say about such a person.[4]

The play negotiates how the liberal commitment to managing human suffering is performed in the chambers of law and in the hallways where our friends desert or die. It also understands the separation between these spaces, and the meaning of this separation, to be either overstated or misconstrued. More importantly, the liberations or purifications these spaces grant each other by their professed distances are not equal for everyone. This inequality has to do with the suffering experienced by those involved, and the imperative to translate across their bodies, caught in a distance that may be liberating to everyone in some way but which still exacts a price for those who have to give an account of their sufferings across this distance. With their respective languages sealing one space from another, subjects and their bodies perform the mediations that maintain these spaces. While much postmodern theory imagines these mediations to take the form of gliding movements of hybrid border crossers, the reality is not so *play*ful for those who traverse vast deserts, make journeys in the wings of airplanes with bodies that have not been liberated from gravity, or press their wrists down hard on the barbed wires of liberal and neoliberal politics. The silences across the divides are more fearsome, especially to those in power, when liberal institutions are denied what they want to hear, even as they magnanimously ask us to speak. The rabbi's refusal to make the scriptures speak to Louis's demand is a pertinent and instructive one, interpretable as a recalcitrant silence in response to someone who keeps asking for translations but is ill-equipped to hear them unless they are what he wants to hear.[5]

A late scene in Part II of *Angels* marks an important follow-up to the silence the scriptures keep on behalf of those who suffer abandonment or the pain of translation—a silence that those in power ultimately may or may not be able to hear and a suffering they do not experience. This happens when, with his sores, disease, and vomit, Prior Walter makes it to the court of angels from all the continental principalities and asks for justice.[6] While the scriptures kept their silence on those who desert, Prior has opted for these words over prophethood granted by the angel. Prior appeals to the angels representing all the principalities of the earth to grant him "more life." Prior calls out to "He" who has left him to suffer, whether Louis, or America, or God, or what they share—not the ability to help or cure but the ability to leave someone in the time of need. Prior asks the angels for more life and to punish "Him" for betraying those who suffer. Prior also refuses to surrender to the denials of life accorded him. These denials often come with a shrug from those who not only deny life but also deny their own power in the face of another's suffering. This feigned powerlessness is especially shameless when dealt to those who clearly have no power. It is the luxury of being able to desert, and the very availability of a choice to do so, that is being challenged.

A crucial scene intermediating between these instances from *Angels* raises questions as to the history of liberal theory and practice. The scene is that of a conversation between Louis and Prior that shows us a more hope-inspiring side of Louis's garrulity. This potential is carried within his rare tentativeness that is vulnerable and searching, rather than self-vindicating, or dismissive of the pain of the other by way of abstract hope or contrived confidence.

> Louis: Jews don't have any clear textual guide to the afterlife, even that it exists. I don't think much about it. I see it as a perpetual rainy Thursday afternoon in March. Dead leaves.

> Prior: Eeugh. Very Greco-Roman.

> Louis: Well for us it's not the verdict that counts, it's the act of judgment. That's why I could never be a lawyer. In court all that matters is the verdict. . . . It's the judge in his or her chambers, weighing, books open, pondering the evidence, ranging freely over categories: good, evil, innocent, guilty; the judge in the chamber of circumspection, not the judge on the bench with the gavel. The shaping of the law, not its execution. . . . That it should be the questions and the shape of a life, its total complexity gathered, arranged and considered, which matters in the end, not some stamp of salvation or damnation which disperses all the complexity in some unsatisfying little decision—the balancing of the scales. . . .

> Prior: I like this; very zen. It's . . . reassuringly incomprehensible and useless. We who are about to die thank you. . . . You get too upset, I wind up comforting you. It's easier. . . . Tell me some more about justice. . . .

> Louis: Justice . . . is an immensity, a confusing vastness. Justice is god.[7]

At this moment in the play, Louis elicits the most sympathy that he ever will. On display is the intellectual radical type who has many words but no matching capacities to see the question of human relations to not be at odds with the questions of justice, or to see the irony of his own stance. His lack matches the system's incapacity to take care of those who suffer and to understand their suffering beyond the labels it needs. This incapacity underpins a proclivity to pronounce sentences of life and death without adequately understanding that the extensive realities of these words, along with their complexities, are themselves to be suffered. Those who suffer thus end up consoling those who cannot bear their suffering, no different from the burden of consoling placed on subjugated populations to assuage the guilt of the privileged, not sure whether they should have gratitude or regret for the inappropriate recognitions granted them.

The ability to abandon forces attention to the meaning of love in this play. The scriptural silence on this question conveyed by the rabbi to Louis at the beginning of the play can be read more suspiciously for its guilt, sheepishness, or complicity, rather than as noble, sarcastic, or dismissive, as suggested earlier. Maybe this is religion's "toleration" and tight-lippedness to match the state's garrulity, equally impotent at that, and ultimately collusive. Louis has no clue of what is being kept from him, shown in his hopeful, idealist ravings about justice in the scene just before Prior collapses for the first time. Kushner titled another of his plays "Only We Who Guard the Mystery Shall be Unhappy," but *Angels* has its own guardians of the mystery. These are Prior and Harper, and, in a more "practical" way, Belize in his power over Roy Cohn. The effective exteriorized scarcities of religion and the state have given up on love, sponsoring "interiorized scarcities" a la Murdoch in all relevant spheres of existence. Anything less scarce would be threatening to the institutions that religion and state together foster. They are the valid "providers" of such love precisely because the model of human relations they endorse sees love as a way of maintaining the power of existing institutions. Here, love is antonymic to conflict: it is bourgeois, institutional, instrumental, abstract, general, humanitarian, narcissistic, fetishistic, affirming of status quo, and unable to deal with particularities. When human beings fail other human beings, the state and religion pretend to save us, without regard for the fact that they already have defined their limits and the nature of salvation. They hold us captive by being oblivious to their own role in, and need for, rendering us destitute and victim in the first place.

Louis, and, for that matter, liberalism, can always take an exception to their betrayals and presumed impotence in various realms. They do so by hiding behind the shadows of the grandest of all betrayals: the departure of God from the state (or as religious conservatives would put it, our betrayal of God). In any case, there is a narrative of abandonment, the romance of which is shared by triumphant secularists and faithful antisecularists. Clues to the nature of departure are to be found in the state's definition of need and its promised relation to it. Betrayal means little without a prior promise to stay, even if the promise is not explicit. The liberal state would not, however, be amiss in resembling the lover who is beyond responsibility because he never promised anything more. The forced or amicable exeunt of God from the liberal secular state sets the precedent for this abandonment. In other words, if all sufferings pale in comparison to the suffering of Christ—and that is a suffering (and a betrayal) that we can never really match—all departures ought to pale in comparison to the grand departure of God.

Such a narrative allows both religion and the state the exceptions and liberties they would not have on their own. For all its sincerity of purpose, liberalism has not put religion away in order to get our sufferings back to the world. It has actually bailed religion out only because, like any ideology, it cannot gain any power without laying a claim on suffering or at least reserving for itself the act of disbursing the ability to claim it. Liberal secularism, then, is not a distribution framework without being a productive and consumptive one. When religion and state are seen as domains constructed in relation to each other, then the critique is not of the state that abandons or is abandoned by religion but of the discourse and the philosophy that foremost relies on God's departure to set up the state's departure. The state, under liberalism, can only break the promise of abating suffering and is constructed to fail. Playing the game of whether God is really gone, or how ineffectual the separation is, has gotten old. The liberal state's own affected burden of autonomy masks its comfort with, nay reliance on, departure and betrayal—stories that keep the state, and us, coming back, and forgetting the past in the desperate fluster and promise of contrived new beginnings.

One way that God was apparently expunged from politics was in the separation of suffering caused by nature and its elements from that caused by the actions of human beings. This radical move certainly laid the groundwork for revolutionary activity. But in limiting the scope of the natural, it also delimited the political, allowing a mechanistic liberal politics to arise precisely where certain human actions impede on certain other human actions. The *secularism* of suffering, ensuing from early liberals attempting to deal with grand natural disasters and great wars, has remained partial to suffering with agentic origin.

This setup is affirmed by liberal thought and practice. Our sensibilities continue to be impacted by the sundering of questions that are intrinsically related. The language of the origin and purpose of things that took off in this era (without God) ends up centering on responsibility and choice, to the gradual occlusion of the activity of suffering and the sufferer's experience of its materiality.[8] On the surface, secularism fosters the instituting of internal alienations, discontinuities, and autonomies between different spheres of existence—really, the division of life and its various labors. These institutions are in turn beholden to the separation between church and state.

Angels exemplifies many of these by broaching the private and the public in relation to suffering. This is one of the separations and discontinuities constitutive of liberalism, others being those between political, social, and divine sufferings, between injury and disaster, and between the political domain and nonpolitical or prepolitical ones. These divisions are of historical importance in that they frame the problems that can be solved by political conceptions of justice that never claim to address the entirety of human life. For liberals such as Shklar and Rawls, the distinction between politics and metaphysics is *the* crowning separation in liberalism's mandate of justice. The intended minimalisms of these proposed political conceptions of justice raise questions about the nature of politics and metaphysics in relation to each other. *Angels* takes up these questions by forcing us to take responsibility for placing politics in relation to what is seen and what is not. By placing in view the imagined locations of suffering, where diseases live, and what division of labor is at work when those suffering suffer the way they do, the play asks us to scrutinize these liberal claims. In doing so, it ultimately calls for an examination of how politics, ethics, and aesthetics are constituted, which parts of our lives they account for, and how they are related to each other.

Liberalism claims that its favored secularizations work together to install an autonomous political space and to deliver more secure individuals—safe from harmful language, from bloodlust in Hobbes's world, maybe even from politics. These subjects are also supposed to be more in control of their lives, with the work already done of determining what goes where. Excluded from this benefit are those *on* whom these divisions impose arbitrary presences. Consider someone whose suffering does not fit into a preexisting category easily interpretable by law or whose pain cannot be explained by any disease. Consider also those sufferings that are addressable only by being ripped out of their original spaces, such as where psychological distress caused by systematic social structures is either privatized as an individual pathology or publicized as a cost to the state in terms of loss in productivity. In each case, this inequality corresponds with the imperative to make suffering matter with their parceled bodies—when these binds and portions serve as the promise of security and protection to some but hemorrhage those who still have to perform their suffering to make it matter across these ruptures.

These functions within liberalism establish an essential relation between secularism and suffering. First, a secularism of departures and boundaries needs to be seen as a secularism of *suffering* by emphasizing, etymologically, suffering *made* worldly, and by rendering suffering as world making. The change in suffering as God departs is to be seen as more of a shift in *character*, its performance, its externalization, and for whom it will be voiced. On the question of suffering, then, liberalism just recodes the hallowed character as representations of various kinds, produced by the labor of suffering—the materialities borne and the materializations enacted by sufferers to make their suffering matter.

Second, they expose the partiality of treating suffering as the "natural" domain of religion that moderns and seculars are doing their best to deal with or as the outcome of processes of marginalization, exclusion, exploitation, and so on, that call on us to make things better. Suffering is not merely the object of these actions but constitutes them—the domains of religion and the state, for instance, are realms bargaining over the apportionment of human suffering. In this way, suffering stands to become the source and origin, and not merely consequence, of the tragic or farcical fights fought within and outside liberalism.

The historical guilt Nietzsche associates with Christianity's co-optation and operationalization of the suffering of Jesus is secularized in the liberal state that severs all its explicit ties with religion, "tolerantly" suspending judgment on the latter's claims and functions in the private sphere. To the modern state shifts the task of managing and rationing human suffering. Its subjects are required to separate the suffering caused by other humans and thus addressable by the state, from that with no explicit secular cause and thus irrelevant to the state. The *demos*, then, is somewhat a little bit more "empowered" when it comes to having their suffering matter and someone to account for it. However, these subjects are still supplicants, still captive to a structure that sets the terms of their suffering, and their godliness speaks in prescribed tongues. Hierarchies of good and bad suffering abide—and some of us end up being better rewarded for our suffering than others, given how we choose to suffer—the value linked to the mirror that our subjecthood and suffering grant the state. In other words, the debt to the suffering God is now refinanced through the liberal state, our payments coming in the form of allegiance to it, topped off with gratuity to the fallible state for its attention to our suffering and its ability to recognize, compensate, and redeem it. The most literal, legible, and comprehensible sufferings are also the promise of, and the condition for, the continued existence of the liberal state.

The unspoken collusions of religion and state, where both feign having nothing to do with each other—and perhaps often actually believe it (thus, this is less a story of deceit than conceit or a bit of both)—are evident in the continuities between the religion and the state on their interactions with human suffering as the primary way to garner and organize their subjects. Religion and its sense and power apparatuses—and the state and its sense and power apparatuses—are thoroughly historical and bound in a mutually and reciprocally defining relation with the psychic and sensual capacities of their subjects. The state and religion are forms historically contingent on time and space and their peculiar combinations, co-constructing each other in order to keep certain regimes of power in tact. This power acts on our bodies and communities, through corroborated, structural, and institutionalized determinations of need, suffering, and their dominant forms. Thus, the seeming oppositional dramas between the liberal state and religion, whether within the work of contemporary conservatives or contemporary liberals, Democrats, and Republicans alike, need to be seen with suspicion. I suspect Prior does not want to be Jesus in a Mel Gibson movie. Can we blame him?

This discursive and institutional collusion of the state and religion is not to be read conspiratorially, but as a necessarily ontological one, not because they are the same or form one indistinct whole, but because their material and locus is human life. It is no surprise that the secular state relies on particular constructions of religion, and that the kind of power religion as a familiar institution has in any given era has everything to do, materially, emotionally, and discursively, with the power of the state.

MORTAL SPEECH, MORBID SPEECH, AND INVOICES OF HOPE

The silence of the scriptures and Prior's representation to the court of angels speak to each other. In keeping their silence, the scriptures recognize that they are being asked to vindicate not merely those who do not know how to love and to be there in time of need but also those who set the terms of life and death for those who suffer. Prior's speech has to be considered not a violation of the rabbi's silence but an indexing and recoding of it. In asking for more life, he says what the rabbi could not. This is not because Prior has bought into Louis's definition of life and death. Rather, Prior's very survival, despite Louis, and despite Ronald Reagan, answers Louis's question to the rabbi with a question about the very definition of life. Prior, former drag queen, now prophet, simply has more ways of making silences speak than Louis's garrulity and the rabbi's inversion of it! Death, for liberalism, is a filler of silences, not the ultimate silence—because it is quantifiable, measurable, and enumerable. Prior's denial of death in response to the life denied him is a withholding of comfort that liberal structures desperately need. This is why—on behalf of those who are about to die and those who die in all the ways society inflicts death on them—Prior wants the question of life to overpower that of death. Both life and death are defined by liberalism in narrow, instrumental, and mechanistic ways, and beg a refiguring and reconstituting in the conceptual and sensible realm of liberal theory. So does liberal justice, which often cannot decide whether death is the ultimate suffering or the end of it.

This confusion about death—is it the ultimate suffering, or its termination?—is parlayed beyond the realm of gay fantasia satires on liberal justice into the actual workings of global institutions committed to the liberal project of controlling and abating human suffering. It is this confusion against which the domain of ethics arms itself. What could be more final, more incontrovertible, and more unambiguous than death? Moral imperatives follow, which work with the presumed finalities to cover up for the abundant ways in which finitudes and departures that are *not* death are suffered. In their book *Social Suffering*, Kleinman, Das, and Lock tell a story about how such issues are confronted by policy makers in the spheres of health and human development as they decide on the problems and areas to which resources will be committed.[9] For a long time, mortality rates were the mainstay of such policy debates, being "representative of the distress level of a society." With populations now living long enough to experience the suffering that *is* life, health professionals felt that mortality rates were unable to represent the distress, disablement, and especially the cost of these conditions. Mortality gave way to morbidity (the suffering from chronic illness) and a new metric was sought.

In 1993, the World Bank and the World Health Organization commissioned the five-year-long Global Burden of Disease Study.[10] The aims were (a) to create objective estimates of mortality or disability from a condition, (b) to quantify the burden of disease and injury borne by human populations in different parts of the world, (c) to facilitate the inclusion of nonfatal health outcomes in debates on international health policy, and (d) to quantify the burden of disease using a measure that could also be used for the analysis of cost-effectiveness.

The study produced a new metric: the disability-adjusted life year (DALY). DALY measures the "objective" burden produced by specific diseases and injuries in order to aid in cost-effective resource allocation. It brings together the impact of premature deaths and disabilities that result from the said diseases and assigns degrees of suffering to years of life and types of disability. In taking death at a given age into account, the number of years of life lost is evaluated by using the expectation of life remaining at that age for individuals in low-mortality countries. The focus is on disability (defined in terms of the impact of the performance of the individual) and not handicap (impairment in the context of the overall consequences that depend on the social environment). The formula for calculating DALYs takes into account the age at which the specific disease is acquired, the years of life expectancy lost (and the relative value of those years calculated in terms of human productivity), and the years compromised by the disability. Not all years have equal values: a year in one's twenties is worth more than a year in one's eighties. Wisdom and suffering go, ironically, unrewarded. The values assigned are universal, standardized across different societies, social classes, ages, genders, ethnicities, and occupational groups. Age and sex are the only nonhealth characteristics considered in this formula. Where a disease and its burden are placed, however, is up to those who make decisions. For instance, mental health problems that show up in tables to have greater "valence" in certain countries—suggesting that greater resources be applied to them—are arbitrarily placed in the discretionary category so that their burden does not fall on the state.[11]

An inscription at the beginning of a book on world rankings pronounces that statistics are signs from God.[12] C. S. Lewis, in *The Problem of Pain*, writes that pain is God's megaphone to rouse a deaf world,[13] which is reminiscent of the angel of America who brings the word to Prior. "The photographs are us," says Susan Sontag, in her work on how our imaging of the world tells us something about how we do or do not grieve and how we do or do not regard the pain of others.[14] These quotes together suggest that our senses and activities of speaking, hearing, and seeing may have something to do with the interpretation and translation of the sign and the word. This juxtaposition provides one possible way of inquiring into our capacities and experience of suffering as subjects of liberal capitalism and their implications for ethics and politics. Statistics and information, and our ways of knowing, interpreting, seeing, and listening, tell us something about how we attend to the world and about the content of our ethical life. They are those speech acts that emerge from, or counter, a discomfort with the silences that the rabbi pronounces and the silences that Prior rewrites. If statistics are the voice of God, need anything more be said?

One wonders, though, what is most intriguing: that we need these measures, that we construct them, or, still, that we are shaped by them? If, indeed, statistics are words of a language, or entire forms of speech, and if a subject is constituted in and with language, it is anybody's guess what sorts of commensurable and measurable—or, to use Nietzsche's language, "calculable, regular, necessary"—subjects of suffering (whether as sufferers or those responding to them) are produced with this language.[15] Certainly, we cannot just wish away these measures and their relevance to the usual tasks of policymaking, given (a) the condition of the large majority of the world's population, (b) the prevalent commitments to the notion of scarce resources, and (c) that even distributive justice of the kind these policies seek is still a worthy, albeit distant, goal. However, these statistics and solutions deserve a look beyond and under, into the processes involved in the creation of these decision inputs, which are continuous with the processes of defining life and death and the suffering of each.

Attention to these processes does not merely second-guess the expediency promised by these categories and measurements in working toward a just end; instead of detracting from the goal sought, it enriches it. The lofty goals of justice are inseparable from the representations of human suffering, such as the DALYs, and the concomitant production of subjects who suffer and represent. The processes that yield inputs for the most earnest schemes of justice *are* the subject of any politics that speaks of justice, and they must be recognized and dealt with as such. Prior's abjection knows that choosing not to suffer is *not* the quickest way out of suffering. This is why he is able to labor under the silence and to allow it to incarnate itself in ways that do not adhere to the specific voicings and enactments demanded by liberalism. When DALYs are seen as representations of suffering, they are not merely features of a story. Rather, they *are* the story that often silences other stories. As repositories of the struggle between languages in which different stories are told, they also tell the history of narrating and managing human suffering that collectively configures politics.

MAPS OF INJURY, AFFECT, AND NONSENSE

The statistics discussed in the previous section speak of how we grieve and whether or not we are the bereft. They bring up our capacities to suffer and our ways of relating to suffering, our own and others. These issues extend beyond sufferings graspable in these statistics to those limit cases where these measurements and quantifications fail. In cases of immense suffering—especially "natural" suffering—other forms of translation and sense making have to kick in, in order to mediate our experience of them. The regime of valuing suffering endemic to liberalism does not leave the sphere of this "readymade" suffering untouched. The arbitrary values placed on various sufferings also appear in the realm of grand disasters, their very definition flagging the thresholds—of political sensibility and of the ability to suffer—that emplot liberal discourse.

Any crisis, disaster, or injury comes to be within a sensuous machinery involving interpreters, translators, and sufferers. While statistics such as the DALYs exemplify the creation of an event out of suffering so that it can at least count even if only in this paltry way, the case of natural disasters or genocide—"events" first, one's suffering and another's medal for philanthropy after—liberal modernity does something importantly different. It shows off its specialty in readymade events of human suffering that can then be rendered productive. Both cases—of producing events and of rendering events productive—obscure and dislocate the suffering that necessitates the making of an event and the suffering that is caused by the sensuous pathology of liberalism.

Ways of treating suffering that define the terms of a disaster, and the terms in which a disaster is read, can also dysfunctionalize sense and mute other voices. One eventually just forgets to speak or speaks only to affirm or negate. Kant teaches us to talk about suffering only so far as it is caused by human action; liberalism's naturalized focus is on the injuriousness and harmfulness of human beings whose ownership of their bodies and their selves is predicated on their ability to be injured. This ownership relies on a separation of the domains of God and man, whereby suffering itself is secularized. When this happens, explanations are given in the form of who is responsible for the suffering in order to assess whether it is an injury that is addressable, or suffering that does not pass for injury, in which case it must be quickly shelved elsewhere (but never left unnamed and undetermined). So the secularism of suffering counters the nonmetaphysical claims of political liberals by clearly showing that even unassuming liberals cannot help but assume and operationalize a particular metaphysics of suffering as they, in the most basic way, determine the spaces where certain forms of suffering are allowed to dwell.

Unexplained suffering—as fact and problem—has often been christened "evil" in the history of Western philosophy, with the leading question of how a good God could create so much innocent suffering. Susan Neiman's alternate history of modern philosophy, written as a story of this concept, is instructive in helping us see what and how we make of disasters today.[16] Neiman talks about the two disasters that, for her, have marked the beginning and end of modernity: Lisbon and Auschwitz.[17] These two events are reminders of the unbelievable magnitude of human suffering, both allowing us to invoke the god that could possibly let such suffering happen in the world. Both betray, in turn, an overwrought emphasis on certain kinds of responses or certain kinds of speech. The concept of evil, historically deployed in order to redirect conversation from the stuckness and pointlessness of suffering, betrays the fact that knowing where suffering comes from is a condition of (knowledge and) speech about it.[18] Marx points to the abstractness of evil, even in a post-God world—it is a kind of fetish, composed of the remnants of religious thought that require a reason and justification for suffering.[19] The crisis that *became* the Enlightenment separates the cause and experience of suffering toward the eventual invisibility of the latter. Even when the condition of the visibility of suffering—that is, the presence of an agent who caused it—is met, the cause provides the frame for the visibility and finally stands in for the experience itself.[20]

A materialist cartography of a disaster, in time and space, has to contend with the constructed temporality and spatiality that has accompanied liberalism's treatment of suffering. Liberal modernity, through its peculiar ascetic ideals, requires suffering to be glorious and eventful since God is no longer around to overwhelm into submission. Mimicking the successive vulgarization of God, to which Feuerbach attests, wherein God is *real* only insofar as it is imaginable in a particular spatial-temporal moment—the sum total of our individual lacks and collective capacities as a species—the regime of liberal political economy leaves little to the imagination beyond a god that numerically and valuatively outdoes everything else.[21] Western philosophy is so infused in the notion of God that the aesthetic sublime overwhelms in the same way the divine does. In its original formulation, the sublime was what was deemed to be beyond empirical knowledge, using our experience of the unintelligible rather than our immediate sensuousness.[22]

The sublime can describe the largest natural disasters of the twenty-first century, for instance, the Southeast Asian tsunami or Hurricane Katrina. The sublimity has little to do with the naturalness of the phenomenon; the natural is not what is innate, occurring a priori a la Kant, but what is *made* natural through the growth and cultivation of our passions through education and constitution.[23] This illuminates the discord between regarding death by genocide and death by AIDS, on the one hand, as disasters that are unnatural and man-made, and the tsunami and Katrina, on the other hand, as disasters that are not.

Add to this the "representation" of the sublime (in the form of the number of deaths, for instance), which was supposed to be a non sequitur, and the scale of the hitherto immeasurable suffering becomes the condition of the possibility of redress. The liberal humanitarian internalizes this metaphysics of valuation just as the sublime mirrors the godly philanthropist who will soon, after confirming the suffering as sublime, want to feel better about it. There must be a difference between those for whom the sublime nature of suffering is a luxury or self-affirming, at least a protection, and those for whom it is a necessity and inescapable, who perhaps even laugh at the sublime, forcing it to get over itself. This is a critical example of the epistemological and ontological taming of the aesthetic and its potential for political sense and sensibility.

Maybe silences germinate in conscious response to, or as, an unintended consequence of suffering being diagnosed, interpreted, evaluated, sanctioned, and prescribed. This possibility is flouted by Neiman's elegy for an age that could be damaged in response to a disaster or crisis, the damage measured in terms of how compulsively and garrulously it can torment itself about the meanings of existence, God, and suffering. Insofar as she is wistful for the intellectual storms an enlightened age can brew (and sponsor), Neiman's sense of hope derives from mimicking the *philosophes* from the post-Lisbon scenario. She is quite nostalgic for, and reminiscent of, the Voltaire who, in response to Lisbon, raises questions about the rationality of providence, hope, and the essence of life on earth in terms of evil and happiness.

Neiman's quick containment of modernity between Lisbon and Auschwitz (which she sees as bookends of the Enlightenment) is very intriguing, as are the terms of speech ascribed to this age and its noted events. In bemoaning the loss of intellectual conversations and discourse about the meaning of life and our place in this world, with or without God, Neiman comes across as an apologist in a few ways: first, for the forms of hierarchies and privileges that the politics of this world has experienced for centuries, modernity having its own share of shame; and second, for what counts as speech in this scenario. She does not even entertain the possibility that the kinds of garrulity that do fill our ears about Auschwitz may be seeking to drown the conversation—not of some ethical-existential-speculative nature but of a substantially political one—of who *must account for it*. Could it be that those powers and discourses historically responsible outside of the narrow structures of blame are those who have become the saviors overnight, and even those who were the criminals are not begrudged when Europe stands righteous and strong, untainted in its power and its claims, with no crack in its armor? To the fray, we might add Kushner's Louis, whose professed neo-Hegelian hopefulness is yet another example of hope as an abstraction, a supplanting of the ability to suffer that allows suffering to be instrumental or not, meaningful or not, rational or not. It raises the question of whether this hope can lead us to have more tolerance of evil and other forms of suffering and whether it can distract us enough from the material suffering of another by trumping it. These insistences and diversions are consistent with the Mad Hatter–like dance of contemporary liberals who console themselves and fill the silences around them by repeating that cruelty is the worst thing we do.[24]

Liberalism may have ushered in yet another coming of slave morality in order to never be caught in its own act: where one can either follow the pied piper into fifteen minutes of glorious victimhood, or resist this accommodation by regularizing the pain so that the former is no longer tempting. This may be the only way the remainder, the excess of the discourse, protects itself. Or, to be hopeful for a moment, this could force another sensibility of suffering, obligation, and sympathy altogether, beyond the depleted senses of the colonizers. A materialist ought to be able to embrace finitudes and deaths, those of senses as well, when one's senses of damage have been damaged beyond damage, when suffering only matters when someone in power names it so. Maybe it opens the possibility of seeing the affluent enact their farce of petting their consciences so that any mention of human suffering immediately triggers a response to recite, for instance, how much private humanitarian aid has flowed into South East Asia or Haiti. There is an intimacy, a witness, in the silence that the rabbi keeps and that Prior Walter rewrites. Perhaps this closeness imposes a different expectation of how we suffer with, and for, someone. Liberal inadequacies in this regard also miss the fact of the how elite philosophical, political, and legal discourses are complicit in rendering suffering—whether "natural" or "moral"—mute by insisting on a certain kind of speech and translation. The way in which the question has forever been posed deserves only a very deeply felt refusal to speak.

CODA: SUFFERING POLITICAL DESIRE

The fundamental consonance between the moments discussed previously is that suffering is treated as topic or object of political, legal, or social inquiry and practice. This objectification of suffering is not benign, connected as it is to some most fundamental gymnastics with the meaning of, and the social configurations of, the living and the dead of suffering as well as the suffering of the living and the dead. This keeps us, at best, shackled within certain idealistic modes of ethics, aesthetics, and politics that flaunt their empirical prowess at will. It also betrays the constitutive continuities between these modes, acknowledging and harnessing what is essential to the life of the political, built by, with, and around those who suffer and their sufferings. The irreducible materiality of suffering as a subject of politics will have to be intrinsic, even immanent, to a method that writes such a politics and toward which this book gestures: a method that factors in those ordinary and ubiquitous experiences of suffering—even the experiences of subjection to an economy of representation and inclusion en route to liberal justice—that risk obliteration even by many well-meaning victim-centered politics.

Consider, for the sake of those who do not speak in the voice that liberal structures can hear, and whose suffering does not *matter*, with what this ill-rewarded burden of response and translation correlates. In a material and practical sense, it bespeaks, on part of those who are doing the listening, an atrophy of the capacity to suffer, to sense, to be subject to, and hence to *be* different subjects. Liberalism is tolerant of abundant speech as long as it does not have to take into account voices it does not understand. There is a need to address and fix the naïve investments in speech that do not seem to understand that all speaking is not the same, and that everyone's speech does not matter equally. We must problematize not only who speaks and what is said, but also who demands certain presences and absences and why. Even at its empiricist best, liberal sensings follow rather hardwired patterns when it comes to emotions felt, interpreted, and responded to. Liberalism's failures confirm that speech is not a sense, but the ability to withhold it, to hear it, and to sense its withholding is. Was there ever a confusion about whose ideal the "ideal speech situation" is, whom the nudity of the original position makes nimble, and whom it forces to seek cover?

The voices of those whose subjectivities do not necessarily hold sufferings immanently labeled as injurious or violating of certain *self*-certainties (and who therefore trail behind the liberal bandwagon) may still retain a promise of oppositional and liberatory politics in a state that "fails" to index and code these voices—it either just frantically avoids them or drowns them with its own stock garrulities. As such, then, a "failed" state is also an *incomplete* traitor—not yet the grand fetish that has sucked in all the love and betrayals to hold and dispense them at will. An outcome of this extraction is the privilege of declaring what right was violated, and of keeping a ledger of injuries that takes far more from those who suffer than from those who treat the injuries. If the validity of liberatory discourse, then, ensues from those who have "succeeded"—in this case, the West and the global philanthropic ruling classes because they have successfully accumulated all sorts of capital from *all* of us—it is worth historicizing the aesthetic and sensuous privileges that feed this accumulation. This can tell us which forms of suffering, passion, and the labor of making them material are being reified and which are being obliterated.

When the practices and politics of sufferers betray their complicities with the systems in whose mirror they practice their speeches to get them right (finally, this time), the scope and reach of the hegemony of the current political economy of injury becomes evident. The backdrop against which the production or distribution of suffering in the world should be examined can be expanded by looking at the discourses that span—courtesy of a history of colonialism and an ongoing reality of neoliberal imperalism—even those states that lack the basic "rule of law" and well-functioning institutions that are the hallmark of liberal democracy. One is bound to find remarkable continuities, and grounds for radical solidarities, between the experiences and political desires of those marginalized and betrayed along any avenue of global capitalism—including the well-functioning liberal-capitalist societies *and* the tragically oxymoronic feudal-capitalist ones.

The sensibilities, and the relations to suffering, that exist in the forms of marginalities people own and manifest everyday can push us to rethink and refigure the very collaborations between politics, ethics, and aesthetics that institute the political as a practical, ontic, and epistemic realm. They also force us to acknowledge that the casualties of democratization and liberalization are not merely, or most importantly, the exotic othernesses of different national cultures. Rather, the casualty of note is the sensorium, the molding of which homogenizes not only the performed desires for democracy and justice but also, and most crucially, the experience—the suffering and the everyday enactment—of that desire itself. If, as discussed in this chapter, voice is what indexes democracy in the negotiations between liberalism and democracy, then the roots and sources of this voice—in sense experience and in suffering—continue to be formalized within liberalism's own priorities. For these democratic hauntings to not be meaningless or farcical, the responses to these imperatives can be found traversing the senses and their everyday lived aesthetic work as sources of a reimagined materialist politics, a mandate that Part II of this book takes up.

PART II

RECUPERATING MATERIALISM

CHAPTER 4

THE LABOR OF SUFFERING

THE POLITICAL ECONOMY OF INJURY

The logics orienting liberalism to suffering, and the ubiquitous imperatives of representation that reinforce these logics, come together in an approach toward suffering that regards it as an object to be dealt with, targeted, treated, and managed. There appears to be a disjunction between the treatment of suffering in the politics of inclusion—where the possessive individualism of injury requires sufferers to identify themselves with their injuries and enter the realm of justice on this basis to make certain exchanges and enact certain claims—and in the original position, where our admittance into the material imaginaries populating it requires casting away any identities and injuries extraneous to the public identity of an autonomous liberal subject. This disjunction belies a deeper unity, in that the relation to suffering imposed in the former is presupposed in the latter.

Justice as admission is made possible by (a) the strictures placed on the form and content of suffering, (b) the universalized relation of possessive individualism to be had to it, and (c) the centrality of the agent for whom, and to *be* whom, this work is performed. The original position already factors human labor into a congealed, generalized sense of injury (via labor's attachment to goods and productivities that compensate or obviate injury). This sense nourishes an ascetic sensibility, upholding the circularity of principles given and principles reached. While justice as admission has us bear our injuries as conditions of the possibility of our identity and voice, the egalitarian liberal (such as John Rawls) demands that we bare ourselves. This is because someone like Rawls sees this relation to suffering to be fixed, universal, and immutable—and hence the only real, practical one possible—and tries to build around it. The pathology of voice endemic to the mode of justice as admission (with the costs and privileges appertaining) becomes an evolutionary feature of the original position. It gets sedimented in the deep materiality and the imaginaries of the delegates and in the figures they draw up in representing their fellow citizens. It follows that Rawls does not relieve us of tiresome speech but preempts the voicing unless it parrots the speeches already available to us, exposing voice as an object of faith of no consequence. In the original position, then, we have always already spoken. The upshot is that we also know what *they*—those in power, those who act *as* us, those who will respond to *our* voices in *their* heads—are going to say.[1]

The overtures to include, to recognize, and to deliver justice in the form of attention, rights, assurance, protection, and compensation, are emphatically distributive. There is a universal substance of suffering whose nature and value is ascertained, and justice demands that it be distributed in society in a fair manner: nobody gets more than a maximum share of deprivation and lack, and the protections afforded us from injustice, harms, and injuries are to be distributed within society to avoid extreme inequalities. The distributionist tenor recurs in the talk of granting recognition and when the issue of the equality of rights and opportunities comes up. For instance, rights are fought for on the basis of certain proven inclusions, and opportunities follow the logic of access to certain goods and foreclosure of certain ills (such as the protection from certain diseases or certain excesses of hunger, disease, or neglect). In these moments, the syntax of economics is not just a symbolic presence but provides the pattern for deeming resources, choices, goods, attention, satisfaction, humanity—at least the ability to preserve or guarantee them—scarce, informing society's deficient ability to prevent suffering.

The real or imaginary locales of liberal justice can be compared to a market where victims bearing injuries and rights trade them for admission and other, or more, rights. The knowledge that enters the original position is also remarkably resonant with the "free information" of the perfectly functioning market, if it can be read as information that is free *from* any particularity not already appropriated into the "equally" had, freely available, hegemonic, "common sense" of a liberal society. In the generalized understanding of suffering made objective (as in cruelty or fear) and quantifiable (as in primary goods), and in the presumptive value placed on its avoidance and on its inert yet productive nature (so that we either make it into something else or can trade it in), a market is invoked, with conditions for entry and exit met through certain performances of suffering.

If the market, conventionally understood, performs necessary distributive functions within the society, suffering is subject to this, too. An obvious example is the global cartography of suffering: the reality, necessary or avoidable, predictable or accidental, that certain people and places in the world suffer more than others and for different reasons. Then there are the concerns with how suffering falls along and across fault lines of class, gender, race, age, and sexuality. There are also the disparate forms of suffering assigned to different stakeholders in a liberal society. Bourgeois sensitivities that have disproportional recourse to the courts of law tend to be quite fragile but not vulnerable. The truth a citizenry is able to bear changes with how much they have to eat and what wars are created to overwrite which conflicts. The quanta of suffering we can, and do, count on from different segments of the same society, and for whom we legislate the thresholds of deprivation everyday, are a clear instance of how unaccidental this distribution is, let alone how drastically the value of death alters when we cross a man-made boundary. One can, in addition, also consider the distribution of liberalism's attention and the scope of its vision— that is, how it recognizes various kinds of suffering and sufferers and how it tolerates them.

The notion of distribution can be expanded to include not only the distribution of quanta of suffering but also of the modes of suffering. The "natural" disparity in the *ways* peoples, populations, individuals, and groups suffer can be seen as having something to do with the histories that suffuse them and those that they resist, and with relations different from the ones with which liberal thinkers enshroud them. The key questions change, for instance, from *whether* discrimination is injurious, to why, to what, and to whom it is injurious. This switch makes a difference when goals of diversity and multiculturalism are held in esteem with no regard for how some all-around useful and well-intentioned inclusionary practices do co-opt and neutralize the suffering that they let in.

In addition to the distribution of suffering considered through both these lenses—that of the quantitative distribution of suffering and that of the plurality of ways in which people suffer—the premises and predicates of this market and its distributive conceit must be addressed. We must consider where the suffering exchanged in the market is produced and how this production necessitates *and* is necessitated by this market. Then there is the suffering that produces, both within and beyond the confines of this exchange. Produced and productive suffering recalls the nature of labor in capitalism and suggests the usefulness of the notion of the labor of suffering mentioned earlier.

For now, the labor of suffering may be said to include the activities of representation undertaken to *make* suffering in prescribed forms, and of relating to and producing with this alienated, objectified suffering.

The modes of distribution of suffering in liberalism are inextricable from the modes of producing suffering in the form of injury as commodity. The production of suffering raises three practical issues to be addressed in a discussion of such labor. First, liberalism imposes a form and content on our suffering—by defining, permitting, and privileging certain affects and effects, it determines how and what we suffer.

Second, it also has a stake in the productivity of our suffering—what we produce with it, how we relate to the product, and what it costs. Thus, is my suffering good enough for a memorial, a reparation, or a trial? Does compensation effect a real exchange, so that the injury I surrender for exchange is no longer mine? What does it mean to call suffering mine versus another's? How and when does suffering become mine in the first place?

Third, liberalism is either handicapped or disinterested when it comes to acknowledging the burden of voice, representation, and victimhood it places on sufferers as it presupposes a particular hegemonic relation to suffering as injury. At best, it comes across as naïve about whom it serves and whom it taxes. What of the suffering that is not injury or not yet injury that exceeds or upholds it? It is in pursuit of these curiosities that a critique of liberal suffering needs to be directed at not only the liberal mode of distributing (and trading) suffering and sufferers but also the liberal mode of producing suffering in the forms of injury and harm.

Moving from the distribution to the production of suffering reveals how both moments are unified in the *labor of suffering* that substantiates liberalism's *fetishism of injuries*. These are categories of a political economy of suffering, human relations, and experience within a liberal, capitalist society; the labor of suffering is a methodological and substantial concept through which representation and suffering, and their connection to politics, can be seen differently. Marx's understanding of labor and commodities helps unravel this political economy by directing us to the living process of our suffering that is congealed in injury, and this understanding aids in theorizing how suffering is produced as injury and injury produced as suffering. The methodological proclivities of liberalism and capitalism show how ill-framed and ill-addressed the "problem" of suffering is when injury and harm are the key features. These retrievals, detailed in this chapter, are not to the end of recognizing the as yet unrecognized others and of extending the parameters of admission into the liberal framework but of imagining a different form of politics that emerges from within those whose sufferings either do not fit, or abide clumsily and restlessly, within liberal limits. These deformed sufferings may premonition a reframing of the ethical, the aesthetic, and the political in a manner that challenges the preeminence of the liberal approach to suffering. This challenge involves tackling the sensual economy that liberal capitalism bestows even on the very well-meaning alliances, solidarities, heraldries of newer than new subjects of history, as well as other fervors of radical and immediate politics. Approaches that continue to treat suffering as object, even as they reverse certain emphases, perform certain linguistic redemptions, and see themselves as "new" for doing so, cannot mount this challenge.

TOWARD A CRITICAL ETHNOGRAPHY OF LIBERAL CAPITALIST SOCIETY

Fervent readings of Marx as a righteous claimant of the worker's suffering and a rightful return on his expended labor expound on exploitation as not only an analytical category but also an ethical one, where capitalism is bad or wrong or evil because it intercepts the worker's right to the value he creates. While this is a useful certainty Marx can inspire in us, I am drawn to terms in his work of a different, more trenchant critique of capitalism—and its attendant defacements and paucities. Such a critique does not rely on the ethical judgments that scaffold capitalism's edifice with liberal culture, morality, law, and politics. Marx's critique of labor in capitalism does not operate despite or through liberalism but assumes and necessitates a critique of the liberal relation to suffering itself. It is insufficient, even counter to Marx's goals, to see him as fighting, in a liberal mode, for "reduced suffering for workers." He cannot be read as affirming the manipulative tendencies of an energizing deprivation. Bad, glib readers find Marx's dictum that workers of the world have "nothing to lose but their chains" to be a quantitative ultimatum rather than a qualitative one more consistent with his method.

The upcoming sections take two routes to a critique of the liberal approach to suffering. One channel is Marx's analysis of labor and commodities, as a guide to the production of injury in liberalism. The other plies the dialectical materialist method, analyzing, and redressing the implications of the liberal method for the life, death, and potentiality of suffering and sensuousness as human powers. Together they show a critique of the liberal approach to suffering to be fundamental to Marx's critique of labor in capitalism, and able to take us beyond it. In the move to the next chapter, these two strands and their implications entwine to yield a fetishism of injuries that accesses the issue of the subjectivity of sufferers.

Marx calls the sphere of ownership, distribution, and exchange of commodities, including labor, "the noisy sphere," and guides us on a trip to the hidden abode of production of commodities and of labor itself as a commodity. Injury is the key inhabitant of the analogue of this noisy sphere in liberal politics and culture, and it deserves an inspired treatment. To Marx, the categories of value, abstract labor, commodity, and capital "express the forms of being, the characteristics of existence . . . of this specific society, this subject and . . . this society by no means begins only when we can speak of it *as such*."[2] Moishe Postone finds these to be "categories of a critical ethnography of capitalist society undertaken from within—categories that purportedly express the basic forms of social objectivity and subjectivity that structure the social, economic, historical and cultural dimensions of life in that society, and are themselves constituted by determinate forms of social practice."[3] Any critique of liberal politics and jurisprudence that focuses primarily on the structures and categories of law, market, property, and so on—and does so without attending to the notion of labor that inheres in those categories—is bound to miss one of Marx's crucial lessons regarding the critique of capitalism, liberalism's cognate system. And this lesson is that labor plays a historically unique role in mediating social relations, and this mediation has consequences.

Relations between labor and other aspects of our existence, and the kinds of collusions that are nourished and necessitated between economics, politics, and ethics, are peculiarly totalizing within capitalism. Additionally, this regime of labor sees itself as transhistorical and beyond negotiation. The structures that affirm this self-perception—such as liberalism—also get to posit their framework, attitudes, and approaches as transhistorical and beyond negotiation. Consequently, injury, victims, and representation can be deployed as categories of a critical ethnography of liberal society. These categories rely on certain conceptions of labor and suffering that frame many aspects of our lives. These conceptions pretend to be timeless and permanent, and they provide the rather resilient material connections—between various aspects of our existences and various labors needed by them—that may not exist in any other mode of organizing human relations.

I will say a bit about the other route now. Inheriting Marx's irritation with the methodological antics of the idealist apologists for

science, capitalism, and the liberal state, I take on the deeply problematic ease with which liberal culture seeks to address the living with
dead processes. In the activity of human suffering, a life, power, and
potential can be found that gets brutally overwritten by the fatal certainties of categories such as injury and harm, posited as the conditions for the possibility of liberal justice—legal or "cultural," social or
political—and the basis for struggles for recognition or redistribution.
For Marx, philosophy, religion, the state, and German ideologues
supply these categories that occlude and overwrite layers of human
labor and contradictions—the material grist of our being. Values and
concepts are instituted to give the constancies to things that are not
constant and cannot be so; they serve as consolations and reaffirma-
tions of an order that relies on them for its survival. What is material
and heavy is rendered invisible, what is abstract and arbitrary is rendered concrete. Those subject to these concepts and their politics bear
not only the weight of what is not seen by others but also the burden
of someone else's consolations. These consolations continue to tug
at the labors of these subjects and pull them along, often unsensed
by, unknown to, and even unintended by, those others. It is important to remember that Marx is talking not to capitalists but to those
for whom idealism—whether through secularism or German philosophy—has become an end, in and of itself; his audience includes the
righteous, fervent activist who relies on the disruptions that only idealism can pull off.

Route One: Value, Labor, Injury, Suffering

The possessive individualism promised by the political-legal super-
structure of capital allows for the commodification of the worker as
the only means to the enabling and enactment of the labor-power
of the living individual. The sphere of the commodification of labor
and the circulation of labor-power is, for Marx, "a very Eden of
the innate rights of man . . . [where] alone rule Freedom, Equality,
Property and Bentham."[4] Marx famously explains,

> Freedom, because both buyer and seller of a commodity, say of labor-
> power, are constrained only by their own free will. They contract as
> free agents, and the agreement they come to, is but the form in which
> they give legal expression to their common will. Equality, because each
> enters into relation with the other, as with a simple owner of commodi-
> ties, and they exchange equivalent for equivalent. Property, because
> each disposes only of what is his own. And Bentham, because each

looks only to himself. The only force that brings them together and puts them in relation with each other, is the selfishness, the gain and the private interests of each.[5]

A cognate of this situation is the possessive individualism of injury, broached first in Chapter 1. It rests on the same assumption: that I can own my suffering as my individuality, insofar as it does not encroach upon the structures of liberal law, politics, and economics. These structures foster certain modes of individuality and sociality that, in turn, admit of only certain kinds of suffering in specified forms to be valued, owned, and exchanged for specified returns and at unspoken costs. Injury and property necessitate and reciprocate each other; victimhood requires property in injury, injury requires property in our bodies and in objects as extension of our bodies, and property itself requires the capacity to be harmed or injured. Moreover, interests and identities are owned and are themselves premised on the concepts of injury and harm. The relation of property to rights and subjectivity carries over into victimhood as identity and subjectivity, invoking exchange and distribution to the neglect of the production of injuries.

The act of exchange cannot possibly tell the whole story. In being "the focal point of individual economic activity" in the constructs of marginalists and utilitarians, exchange postulates the "calculating classless and apolitical individual, with a capital I."[6] Marx is interested in not only "what capital produces" but also "how it is produced."[7] He thus makes a move from private property to labor in the *Economic and Philosophical Manuscripts*, and a parallel one from circulation to production in *Capital*.

The Concepts of Labor

Labor is man's essence and species activity, involving dimensions of production, creation, and gratification. By the time Marx gets around to positing this, labor has already been accepted—courtesy Locke, Smith, and Ricardo—as a source and measure of value. English socialists have picked up on that and driven home the ethical implications for the worker, whose labor creates the value, asking that those who expend labor should be able to enjoy it, too. The element of gratification that Marx adds to those who were already convinced of labor as source of value is intriguing for two reasons. First, it provides a challenge to a simplistic dichotomy between work and play. Second, it is only by the attachment of this dimension to production and creation that labor becomes man's essence. This positing, in turn, enables Marx to claim two things: (1) that labor is not merely a source of value but is value itself and (2) that alienation in the production of labor must be understood to be contingent on all those dimensions of labor that make it a human essence, giving us a richer sense of what being not at home in the world may entail and why.

Marx engages with the views of labor prevalent in his time in at least two ways: he first deals with the nature of labor, and then with the nature of value, proceeding through the distinction between abstract and concrete labor.

First, in terms of the nature of labor, the *Grundrisse* reconciles the view that labor is only hardship and repulsive, asserting that human self-realization through really free labor would be either closer to play or effortless, akin to pleasure as imagined by crass empiricists. Marx argues: (a) that work that results in "the self-realization and objectification of the subject, therefore real freedom" is necessary; (b) that the activity of attaining this real freedom and of this attained real freedom is essentially labor; and (c) that an element of hardship resides in the freest and most self-enhancing of labors. This keeps the meaning of self-realization from being compromised by a childish notion of pleasure (as in Fourier) and, at the same time, prevents necessity and labor, pace Smith, from becoming only hardship, and hence undesirable, like pain in its domesticated forms.[8]

Next, is the distinction between abstract and concrete labor. This distinction becomes necessary only in the context of the creation of value in capitalism, when the distinction between living and dead labor forces itself. The specific kind of work that produces particular use values is concrete labor. As part of the labor force of society as a whole, concrete labor is considered labor in general, without reference to the particular characteristics or purpose, as with abstract labor. The production process in capitalism is, for Marx, one of the creation of value in the realm of both concrete labor (use values) and abstract labor (value only created in capitalism). Value creation in the context of abstract labor is twofold: it embodies the creation of the exchange value of commodities and the creation of labor itself as a commodity and as value. As a commodity, abstract labor is labor-power, because when a worker sells her labor, she is actually selling her capacity or power to labor. This power comprises "those mental and physical capabilities existing in a human being that he exercises whenever he produces a use-value of any description." In this commodification, the production process and the framework of market relations collude to make it conceivable, nay imperative, for a human being to put her labor up for sale, and to become, essentially, a bearer of herself as commodity.[9]

With the value of labor-power determined through what it takes to perpetuate and sustain the labor, it is not hard to imagine how capacities themselves result from the process that channels and converts them into productive activities of specific sorts. The domain of experience is reduced to certain privileged, productive activities, relations, and experiences that constitute the labor-power as capacity in the first place. Abstract labor becomes relevant in the act of exchange as a part of commodities or when labor is itself exchanged as a commodity. This latter reality makes abstract labor such a potent concept and allows Marx to distinguish living labor from labor in exchange. The concrete and the abstract are two dimensions of the same labor and are materially interrelated through the body that labors and that suffers the labor. Given that these labors exist in this duality through acts of production and exchange in capitalism, the distinction between living and dead labor becomes even more intriguing. Perhaps life and death call upon us to consider them as merely two iterations, two personas, of the same materiality and not the negations of each other.

Capital is dead or materialized labor. Its deadness—the accumulated, congealed labor that it represents—allows it to be "an independent social power" that "preserves itself and multiplies by exchange with direct, living labor-power."[10] Capital consists not in dead labor serving living labor as a means for new production but in living labor serving dead labor as the means of preserving and multiplying its exchange value. Marx hopes that materialized labor will liberate living labor, an event that may or may not involve freeing living labor from materialized labor itself. The call to abolish labor can then be seen as a call for the abolition of the domination of labor by materialized labor. It is suggested that materialized labor creates the conditions of its own undoing by creating its own gravediggers and by spurring recognition of itself as dead labor that opposes and unwittingly colonizes living labor.

In liberal politics and culture, there is the labor of suffering materialized in the form of injury, and then the living labor of suffering that lives in the shadow of the former without being completely subsumed by it. A relation of alienation exists between the living labor of suffering that cohabitates with the dead labor of suffering as they together enable the injury-form. The alienation that makes these dualities possible is a relation that sustains them as well, as two aspects. While these dualities of labor may be internally alienated from each other, or result from alienation, they are certainly not isolated or insulated from each other. Living suffering does a lot of work to survive amid corpses and to keep burying the dead, making room for their ghosts.

This dual character of labor is inherent not only in the commodity that is produced but also in the worker, the sufferer, who produces it. Alienation does not refer to the domination and exploitation extrinsic to that labor, but it is intrinsic to the labor itself.[11] It is not merely sensed as a static condition—it is a live relation and is lived. Thus, it is important to attend to how this happens—how the subject undergoes these multiple iterations, how the labor of suffering survives and negotiates between living and materialized suffering, and how it lives in between various spheres of determination, congealed representations, and the abstract capacity and need for materialization and recognition.

Marx's discussion of commodities and labor offers two distinct sets of insights into the labor of suffering. First, in the realm of liberal juridical politics, suffering becomes a labor, externalized and productive of injury, prescribing a template of human relations and expectations to match. The mechanics of the exchange value of the injury have a profound impact on its use-value (e.g., in rights, inclusion, identification, reparation). This involves regarding suffering as active qua productive, where this productivity is premise of the production of value; both use-value and exchange-value signal the alienation of the capacity and activity of suffering. Second, suffering in liberalism is not reducible to an isomorph of labor in capitalism. It is, rather, a capacity that is prior to and broader than labor itself. These issues are taken up next.

From the Commodification of Labor to the Commodification of Suffering

Injury's relation to suffering recalls the relation of commodities to labor, where commodities are products of labor in capitalism in the dual way of being produced by it and being predicated on the labor itself becoming a commodity. The language and relations of commodities and value creation extends into the juridicopolitical sphere through the commodification of suffering.

The labor process in capitalism subjects labor in two ways: as creator of commodities with labor and as commodity itself. Marx is concerned with the commodification of labor-power and with labor as a source of value, both occurring only under the auspices of the law of value that Marx discerns in capitalism. They bring to light parallel, and even deeper, processes in liberalism. In the first parallel, suffering is a sensuous capacity and a power that is alienated into "productive activity" under liberalism. In the other moment of this process, the activity of suffering becomes the labor of suffering, producing injury as value. The victim, like the worker, becomes a commodity herself.

With the capacity to suffer requisite to the experience of exploitation, it is conceivable how the diagnosis of exploitation forces us to consider how suffering can be rendered a *labor* once it is rendered active, external, and productive, in religion and secular liberalism alike. The *labor of suffering* is postulated in at least two moments: in injury as the yield of suffering rendered productive in order to be active in the market of liberal justice and, in this production, confirming suffering itself as a commodity that requires certain labors and their maintenance. In liberalism, suffering becomes labor that is valuable if productive, specifically in terms of the value it creates. Redemption and exchange speak not only to a simply productive nature of suffering and labor but also to a performance that enables them to fit certain criteria and spaces that are blessed by the consensus of religion, politics, and economics. Both the rendering of suffering as productive and the setting of abstract value and exchange as conditions for the redemption of this productive suffering must be questioned.

Marx responds to a discourse of production that, first, insists on framing productive activity to render our bodies productive in a very specific sense, and, second, instantiates the relations we hold to our products and also how we are related to them. In confronting the processes of our own production as subjects, the issue of what we do produce must be tackled, too. These productions are connected, not least in the extent to which our production of objects *and* our production as subjects are both deeply beholden to utilitarian precepts, allowing us to isolate not only the origins of our practices but their sources as well. Most fundamentally manifested in our relation to suffering, these are the orientations that carry over into all our other activities.

Marx's rebuke of Bentham is instructive here since it recalls that the question of production and suffering has to reckon with utilitarianism. The calculus of pain and pleasure, on the one hand, and the relation between an individual's work and the rewards of utility, on the other, must be comprehended as one question, mediated by the relation between suffering and production. The productive citizen who discharges his anxiety through work also considers suffering as productive in terms of rewards (whether in religion, capitalism, or liberalism). Therefore, a discussion of production in relation to suffering ought not to be limited to the production of injury; it must scrutinize the intersections between our relation to suffering, our practices as productive subjects, and our suspension in the regime of capitalist productivism. Any cogent attack on capitalist notions of production requires going to the roots of this productivism in utilitarian iterations of the work of the suffering body. While the notions of utility and exchange cannot (be allowed to) exhaustively characterize all suffering, they do fundamentally impact the labor that escapes their frame.

Creation of value by labor in capitalism and liberalism tries to encompass everything, equating value and labor, as labor becomes value's source. Diane Elson instructively and poignantly points to the fact that the "labor theory of value" would more appropriately be called the "value theory of labor."[12] Even if it is assumed that injury is composed in its entirety of the labor of suffering, this does not mean that injury captures the entirety of the labor of suffering—far from it. The labor undergone of making desirable and cognizable representations of suffering for the perusal of those in power is not all there is. The suffering that results from these representations becoming fetishes—when they forget the labor that created them and that their life demands constant sustenance from the sufferers—is part of no value or concept or injury. Injury creates suffering beyond the suffering it represents.

The key problem is with what value claims to be and what it does in the realm of representation. An exclusive focus on, and naïve trust in, value impairs our senses. This happens in two ways: first, when value claims to represent what it is derived from, such as when injury represents suffering, and second, when this representation has an air of self-confident totality to it, such as when value claims to represent all labor undergone in capitalism, and the codified injuries of liberal society stand for all the suffering that matters. Most important to a materialist, though, is the issue of what value *does* to what it claims to represent—that is, the impact of the commodity on the labor that creates it or the impact of the injury on the suffering that constitutes it. Marx writes, "The movement through which the process has been mediated vanishes in its own result, leaving no trace behind."[13] The response to the regime of value, then, has to ensue from a method that comprehends relations, activities, and processes in opposition to petrified, congealed, and static culminations and fetishistic representations.

In light of Marx's opinion that addressing capitalism requires understanding labor and value creation in a historical context, transhistorical notions of labor as value miss fundamental elements of his critique of capitalism. Accepting the relation that utilitarianism, for instance, posits—between labor and suffering, on the one hand, and between the labor of suffering and its products and rewards, on the other—as bearing the weight of transhistorical validity, has two problematic implications. First is a forgetting of the fact that other possibilities exist because other forms have existed at times different from ours. Second is a criminal oversight of the other relations and orientations to suffering that exist right now, in this temporal moment, in spaces different from ours. Consistency demands that if forms of labor, production, and subjectivity are not deemed transhistorical, neither must our relations to suffering and its constructions, especially when at stake is an understanding the work of the wounded and the subjectivity of sufferers that serves as the basis of many forms of liberatory politics.

The Powers of Alienation

While speaking of suffering becoming labor, the process of undergoing this alienation should also be considered. This necessitates reference not only to alienated labor but also to suffering the alienation itself. Labor is alienated because the objectification or externalization (*Entausserung*) of productive activity happens, in its corrupted form, as estrangement (*Entfremdung*). The labor of suffering, however, poses a different issue in terms of its alienation. Alienated labor of suffering entails the alienation of the capacity of suffering from the activity of suffering. This suggests that the precepts of externalization and objectification in suffering may be different from labor and explicitly productive activity. Given the demands and strictures of its productivity, suffering is alienated in two degrees. The first is the alienation of the activity from the capacity in clear contrast to the passivity or interiority, wherein suffering becomes secular, world making, and externalized, and then this productive activity is rendered a creator of value and injury.

The very ability to suffer the impact of *any* production process within liberal capitalism is at stake in how the alienation of the labor of suffering is understood. For instance, any moral or political purchase of the notion of alienation, even that of exploitation, relies on a body that is not merely the object of alienation or exploitation but subject to it. Only then can we invoke the body that labors—that endures the labor and its commodification. It is the body that suffers the domination of living labor by materialized, dead labor. Marx writes, "To mutilate the laborer into the fragment of a man, degrade him to the level of an appendage of a machine, destroy every remnant of charm in his work and turn it into hated toil, [and] . . . estrange from him the intellectual potentialities of the labor process in the same proportion as science is incorporated into it as an independent power."[14]

The systemic constraints of capitalism and liberalism determine whether, and how, living labor handles its domination by death and chips away at it. Here, the question of the social, and of relating to others as part of this claim to life, becomes relevant. If capitalism and liberalism organize how we labor and produce and *who*, what, and how we suffer and represent, then the sociality seems even more essential to suffering than to labor. The sociality of suffering is prior to, and the grounds for, Marx's claims regarding the social nature of labor. According to Marx, when we experience others as part of nature, we experience ourselves as part of nature and realize our "species-being." This is where the orientation to the world and to others coincides and subtends relations to our own and others' suffering. Species-being, as a concept and spectral materiality, is rather crucial to Marx's subversion of capitalism, given that one of the aspects of alienation in capitalism is the estrangement from species-being. Certainly, there is more than a random or accidental relation between different aspects of alienated labor that Marx identifies—being alienated from our productive activity is connected to the alienation from species-being, from fellow humans, from products, and so on. Similarly, being alienated from our suffering is fundamentally coextensive with alienation from our species existence and fellow sufferers. The argument tiptoes alongside Feuerbach's suggestion that God is the projection of our collective capacities, abilities, and skills, and our individual wishes that we could not bear. According to Feuerbach, religion is kept in commission only because humans do not realize this fact or because religion keeps them from attaining this realization.[15]

Capitalism becomes more efficient once we are no longer able to recognize our productive activity as part of nature, which we share with other beings like us. Just like religion, capitalism thrives on, and reinforces, such alienation of our labors. It follows that the great achievements of capitalism and liberalism have been possible because of our collective labors and suffering and because of the institutional and cultural prowess of these ideologies that court and surpass religion's ability to channel them.

In liberalism, victims enact their suffering by alienating it in the creation of injury as value and commodity.[16] The essence of injury, then, is the alienation of suffering. Following Lucio Colletti to see Marx attempting to defetishize commodity and recover our labors, it is a worthy aim to defetishize injury and recognize what constitutes the fate of suffering in injury: the destiny of alienation, congelation, and mortification in the fetishistic injury-form.[17] A more thorough discussion of what this may involve appears in chapters to come; for now, suffice it to state that this defetishizing does not involve demystifying or getting at some truth behind a fetish but is closely related to a recovery and redemption that involves rethinking presence and representation in terms of enactments of voice and memory.

Route Two: The Materialist Method

The role of labor in capitalism and liberalism validates the dialectical and relational materiality of the various dimensions of our lived existence—such as the aesthetic, the ethical, and the political—and the judgments native to them.[18] It is precisely the terrain of the body that bears the weight and consequences of claims of autonomy or indifference. The body is also the organic, living domain that gets implicated against its own will and the, perhaps benign, will of those who confidently believe in and affirm secularized and compartmentalized life in liberal capitalist society. The suffering, laboring body testifies to the fact that the various spheres into which philosophy and politics divide our lives are not immune to each other.

"Healthy" agents with "healthy" bodies can perhaps posit and sustain this immunity better, not least because they do not have to translate and represent experience in one domain to another. Ironically, the very imperatives to translate and represent experience seem to be predicated on the idealistic and categorical separation of bodies and experiences. Without these imperatives, the healthy agents need never run into the material limits of those bodies who cannot disown their raw vulnerability, and must, in the name of sanity, embody it in "authentic" ways to make it present for the courts, the media, and other licensed caregivers. These healthy bodies, never asked to faithfully enact their stories of injury, also do not bear, rationalize, or accommodate the inconsistencies of a life whose performance may never match its reality. Encounters with integrity, integration, and the daunting task of giving form to the irreducible materialities of suffering are thus hardly experiences of health and agency popularly understood. They are bound up with the suffering, marginality, and the not-yet-thereness of incompletely evolved liberal subjects.

On my part, there is a practical, material, and real investment in modes of subjectivity that are ill-understood as patterned on the form of healthy subjects. And, this is not merely a moment of pluralistic tolerance of many kinds of suffering, since this only invites the problems of admission as the mode of inclusion discussed in earlier chapters. Plus, if the question (as will become clear in the two final chapters) encompasses how people enact their suffering, this focus on pluralistic tolerance may be a practical and moral impossibility, given the reality of, say, thoughtless destruction of self and other, of self as other, or of other as self (think suicide bombings, terrorism, wars, and arguments against healthcare). The challenge here is to imagine a materialist politics that preambles determinations of morality and the worth of life and also of why life is worth fighting for or with. My aim here is to avoid the quick and limited move of agent-victim to agent-agent, especially if this "agent" is the same across the two dyads.

The labor of suffering may invite us to take *time* seriously when it comes to the activity of redemption and salvage. This would be a move toward understanding a subject-subject relation in a way that changes something significant in our grasp of the sufferer's subjectivity. This requires considering suffering, the relationship of action to suffering, and the relation of action and suffering to subjectivity itself more patiently and *relationally* than liberalism inclines us to in our most urgent moments and our own righteous states of exception. This can, hopefully, result in a different practical relation to those who suffer and to those who cannot claim injuries within liberalism and neoliberalism—whose tragedies either never get voiced or get voiced as bombs, and for whose honor and ordinary heroisms there is usually no room or time.

Relations

Methodologically, liberalism adheres to (a) concepts and categories of experience derived from empiricist epistemology and (b) utilitarian framings of what Daniel Brudney calls the "fundamental relation" and "fundamental orientation" to the world and to others. The fundamental relation to the world refers to the kind of connection an agent has to the world qua human being, a relation to the world essential to one's nature specifically as a human being. The fundamental relation to other human beings, Brudney gleans, is "some central way (some basic description under which) we are, qua human beings, connected to other people." Brudney continues, "How one relates to the world is a psychological matter (in a broad sense); how one *is related* to the world is not . . . I call the way that one relates to (as distinct from being related to) the world (or others) the way that one *is oriented to* the world (or others)." A fundamental orientation is more of an attitude, an abiding sense of how one is connected to the world, where we are in the world, moving in it rather than standing outside or transacting with it. An example of the difference between how one is related and how one is oriented is obtained in social roles: being someone's daughter, sister, or lover is the fact of relation, not the same as being oriented *to* someone *as* their daughter, sister, or lover.[19]

A fundamental orientation is a practical notion but is not necessarily geared toward action. It is not the same as a sensibility. Brudney further suggests that the orientation carries a bit more of an active tenor than sensibility but less than that of externalized activity. On the other hand, it is both more dynamic and more ontic than a set of beliefs or a picture of how the world is, from which one can then stand back and decide what is most worthy of adoption. Brudney clarifies, "One's fundamental orientation goes beyond that. . . . It has to do with how, day to day, one lives with respect to the world or others, and presumably that is not a matter of choice."[20]

When it comes to suffering, then, the fundamental relation can signal to the way our daily lives, consciously or unconsciously, transact with and in sufferings (seemingly) autonomously, and are connected to various objects, institutions, and structures out of will or necessity. The fundamental orientation is our active relation to these connections and dependencies, who we are as people who lay people off, who sue for damages, who claim unemployment, who assert power when it is completely unnecessary, and who call out the pettiness of this act. The fundamental orientation is, then, the way we relate to fundamental relations. For example, Brudney says that one may change their belief in the fundamental relation to others without a change in fundamental orientation.[21]

To follow Brudney's terminology, the materialism invoked here provides the tools for a critique of the liberal's fundamental orientation to the world, and to others, and gestures toward a different orientation (not all uses of relation and orientation in my writing, though, follow Brudney's definitions, unless I refer specifically to fundamental orientation and fundamental relation). My specific variant of materialism, derived from Marx and Nietzsche, allows for categories and the processes denoted therein—such as injury and its concomitant activities and labors of suffering—to be intrinsic to each other and hence to be considered together. It is marked off from other approaches to suffering by its priority to a self-reflexive yet not self-centered understanding of, and relation to, suffering, by its capacity for other ways of suffering as well, and by its investment in making matter those sufferings that exist but those that we are unable to sense, unable to suffer with, and unable to represent and act with—yet.

Sense and Sensuousness

The Feuerbach of the 1840s declares man to be a suffering being. Later that decade, Marx says "to be sensuous is to suffer."[22] Both suffering and sensuousness are ordinarily considered passive processes (suffering as an adjective means "passive").[23] It is clear that Marx finds Feuerbach's materialism too passive—an improvement on the empiricists but still beholden to sensation rather than to sensuous activity. It is intriguing, then, that a materialism that finds its locus in the *activities* constitutive of our material existence will render sensuousness, first, the central definitional category of existence, and, second, inextricable from, entailing, or equaling suffering.

The materialism channeled here via Marx does not collapse activity and passivity but rather suggests that matter that is active and living acts *and* is acted upon.[24] This recalls Feuerbach's quarrel with empiricists who rely on impressions: for an impression to occur, was it not necessary that something be impressed (upon)? Feeling, willing, and thinking are the three "existentials" Feuerbach finds constitutive of being. A sensuous being who suffers is, by definition, in receipt of objects through her senses, which is why the perceiving subject "cannot be exclusively active vis-à-vis a passively existing reality."[25] At the same time, suffering is undergoing and an "activity" that semantically necessitates passivity that, for Feuerbach, is dependence and need.

Feuerbach inaugurates "an activity-oriented, practical account of sensation, in which the identity between sensing and what is sensed is the material identity effected by a bodily process."[26] He also renders the human being herself as constituted out of the natural world by her own organic activities. Marx picks up these strands, except that he finds it needful to subject this constitution, organicity, activity, and sensing to a thorough historicization. He is informed by the suspicion that the modes of these ontic constants may have differed across history and may have been shaped otherwise within other systems. He comes around to say that if human relations are so critical to how the human being is constituted, then the subject's own concreteness needs to be historicized with the change in the configuration of relations themselves.[27]

In his wish to tweak Feuerbach's notion of sensuousness by making it more active, Marx is perhaps more interested in the origins and production of idols rather than the ways in which silent energies are channeled for existing idols to remain intact. The privilege of activity in Marx needs to be explored in relation to suffering. With perception, orientation, and appropriation as simultaneous elements of his "relational concept of reality," activity can be interpreted and historicized in a multi-layered way.[28] While Marx certainly talks about the activity of the suffering being, the undergoing of this activity itself varies in history.

How can suffering be characterized as a sensuous activity that does not require an objectification or externalization in the way Marx thinks productive activity does? This requires unsettling the active-passive dichotomy but not rendering all passivity active; if all passivity were made active, then this would affirm the privilege afforded to activity within dominant modern sensual and political economies, and would keep us squarely within the discourse of work and productivity. The wish to always make something out of someone's suffering is an overdetermination, as is the unspoken imperative to externalize amid the limited options granted by power structures within which this externalization may mean absolutely nothing. Each takes suffering to be an activity that is productive (often just for the sake of it) rather than a practice more richly considered.

In an early manuscript, Marx writes,

> Only through the objectively unfolded richness of man's essential being is the richness of subjective human sensibility (a musical ear, an eye for beauty of form—in short, senses capable of human gratification, senses affirming themselves as essential powers of man) either cultivated or brought into being. For not only the five senses but also the so-called mental senses, the practical senses (will, love, et cetera), in a word, human sense, the human nature of the senses, comes to be by virtue of its object, by virtue of humanized nature. The forming of the five senses is a labor of the entire history of the world down to the present.[29]

Bertell Ollman elaborates that, for Marx, the words power, faculty, function, and capacity are interchangeable, and they all suggest "the potential, the possibility of becoming more of whatever [they] already [are]." Thus, Marx's historical account is an account of these powers in the process of change.[30] The species powers Marx attributes to man are denoted by the term senses, and these powers are also one's needs. (Ollman says that natural power and need, while not equivalent, are cognate concepts for Marx.) A list of species powers would include "seeing, hearing, smelling, tasting, feeling, thinking, being aware (*anschauen*), sensing, wanting, acting [as practicing, not activity], loving." Ollman also throws in willing, procreating, copulating, knowing, and judging as species powers. The term "species power" encompasses what are generally considered to be physical and mental senses but also expands what human existence is considered to entail.

"What Marx calls mental senses in some places are labeled as practical senses elsewhere; and mental senses and physical senses together are also referred to as human sense, or man's human relations to the world."[31] Thus, the function of the senses already implies a relation and already implies enactment, not limited to activity of externalizing and objectifying—however they may function.[32] Marx explains,

> Just as *private property* is only the perceptible expression of the fact that man becomes *objective* for himself and at the same time becomes to himself a strange and inhuman object; just as it expresses the fact that the manifestation of his life is the alienation of his life, that his realization is his loss of reality, is an *alien* reality: so, the positive transcendence of private property—i.e., the *perceptible* appropriation for and by man of the human essence and of human life, of objective man, of human *achievements*—should not be conceived merely in the sense of *immediate*, one-sided *enjoyment*, merely in the sense of *possessing*, of *having*. Man appropriates his total essence in a total manner, that is to say, as a whole man. Each of his *human* relations to the world—seeing, hearing, smelling, tasting, feeling, thinking, observing, experiencing, wanting, acting, loving—in short, all the organs of his individual being, like those organs which are directly social in their form, are in their *objective* orientation, or in their *orientation to the object*, the appropriation of the object, the appropriation of *human* reality. Their orientation to the object is the *manifestation of the human reality*, [For this reason it is just as highly varied as the determinations of human essence and activities.—*Note by Marx.*] it is human *activity* and human *suffering*, for suffering, humanly considered, is a kind of self-enjoyment of man. [Emphases in original.][33]

Sensuousness can thus be seen as encompassing the active elements of the "passive" process of perception to which sensuousness and, not surprisingly, suffering, has often been relegated. Suffering, it follows, includes the processes of undergoing and enduring, and of relishing and embracing, both individual and collective sensuousness.[34] Sensuousness fits into the category of things of which there is coming into being—things that cannot *be* without *coming to be*. This introduces a temporal context in two ways: to see the activities of sensing, suffering, and representing without an end that is external to them, and also to see them as varying over time. Thus, it can be said that in the exercise or expression of one's "nature," a certain change occurs. This is what Marx means by the humanizing of senses. This is also what allows Feuerbach, and then Marx, to talk in a normative and as yet incomplete way about how a human eye and a human ear will see and hear differently. The question of time must apply to the evolution of capacities and not simply to their being discharged through action.[35] Brudney may have already addressed the substance of this potent liminality in his discussion of fundamental orientations and relations, in his attempt to separate not only the theoretical and the practical but practice and action, too: "Subjectivity and objectivity, spirituality and materiality, activity and suffering, lose their antithetical character, and—thus their existence as such antitheses only within the framework of society; we see how the resolution of the theoretical antitheses is only possible in a practical way, by virtue of the practical energy of man."[36]

Doing Matter

When materialism posits matter and motion, the body automatically becomes a collation of matter that is alive as long as it is in motion. Motion includes voluntary and involuntary, visible and invisible, processes entailed in occupying a particular spatiotemporal moment. Suffering, in this orientation, could be understood as the undergoing of these various processes; and as the enduring of passion, joy, sorrow, hope, imagination, and memory. This materialism sees human perception and confrontation of the world as the relation of matter to matter and of nature to nature. When these embodied processes are enacted, this materialism sees us, and the organic matter involved in these processes, as both subject and object. By recognizing the labor involved in making reality and in struggles that stake our sensibilities, this materialism can provide the philosophical basis for ethical, political life that can better bear the burden of bodies that think, create, experience, obsess, doubt, believe, struggle, remember, and forget.

Brudney offers an interesting characterization that adds detail to this materialism. In his reading of Marx's famous eleventh thesis on Feuerbach, Brudney proposes a distinction between the *feedback model* and the *simultaneity model* of interaction with the world. Both are "live candidates" among different ways of making sense of Marx's "injunction to change as opposed to merely interpreting the world." Under the feedback model, Brudney writes, "The injunction is to engage in an interaction of cerebration and concrete action. One needs a theoretical analysis to act effectively, but (a) one's ultimate goal is practical change, not knowledge (the relevant analysis is about how to change the world), and (b) one's analysis is to be continually reassessed, refined and perhaps altered in light of one's practical experiences."[37] Under the simultaneity model, on the other hand, Brudney states, "For human beings, the fundamental relation to the world is that of an agent continually changed and being changed by it, and a correct understanding of this fact is to be attained in and through the process of changing the world."[38]

Marx endorses the simultaneity model of interaction with the world. This further goes to show how the nature of production, whether of labor in capitalism or of the labor of suffering in liberalism, is problematic for Marx, starting with the fundamental way of interacting with the world it affirms. The feedback model sees "the world as already there, fully formed and waiting to be manipulated," hence its resonance with the versions of "old" materialism Marx finds lacking, all the way from Democritus to the French materialists.[39] A certain instrumentalism, even utilitarianism, is evident in the feedback model, wherein the world (including nature and others) is manipulated to satisfy one's needs, desires, and goals. Sensuousness here is understood as the *site* of practical activity rather than *as* practical, human-sensuous activity.

Marx claims in the tenth thesis on Feuerbach that his new materialism has the standpoint of "human society" or "social humanity."[40] Corresponding to the simultaneity model, sensuousness engages with the world not in merely a goal-oriented way but suggests an active, organic harmony with the world, where nature "appears to be an end in itself," as it would be under communism. The question of being is thus inseparable from that of doing, engaged as they are by activity itself. The fetishism of commodities, and of injuries, under conditions of alienated labor, not only thrives on a feedback model but also actively forces the extant simultaneity-oriented interactions with the world to surrender their form to feedback-oriented interactions. In terms of the activity of the senses, both Feuerbach and Marx take issue with a composite understanding of the human being wherein unity is only thought of as surrender or subsumption—of the mind into the body and of the body by the mind. For them, corporeality and thought (in Feuerbach), and perception, appropriation, and orientation (in Marx), are unified not in the abstract but by the activity of which they are part. How we suffer, then, is how we act.[41]

As a key category of a materialist political method called for by the political economy of injury in liberalism, the labor of suffering is found in the materialities, materializations, and enactments involved in the processes of representation that install injury as a value, commodity, and fetish, and in the negotiations between these fetishes and the sensuous beings who bear this fetish presence. It is interstitial to multiple commodifications and multiple dominations in liberal society. Visible in the suffering that installs and endures the fetish, the labor is internal to our incarnate memories and the imperative to imagine and create out of and despite them. Once it has produced injuries and harms, the labor of suffering then suffers the tyranny of such abstractions and the sociopolitical structures they support.[42]

Making liberalism's domination more thorough and more malignant, even where it is "absent," is the fact that its key categories and forms are produced and upheld by the labor of suffering extracted and divided within and across societies in submission to these forms, extending into many of those spaces that are not under the specific rule of liberal law and politics. This is cognate with labor being the key to capitalism's wide and intense influence on spheres of human life outside the economic, and on regions not technically, contractually, or totally under capitalist ideology. This abstract, but real, domination determines not only what people suffer for but also how they suffer and how they suffer labor itself. The representation that makes hubristic claims of encapsulating or "speaking for" the entirety of suffering remains in an ongoing conflict with the suffering that continues to evade congelation and determination as injury. There is no simple resolution of this agonism, nor must we declaim a resolution only when the former subsumes the latter. All the suffering that defies the liberal schema of representation can actually be seen as performing a desire not for an escape from its materiality *as* suffering (that liberalism wants to readily put forth) but for *materially* undoing the undesirable historical forms to which suffering, and action, have been relegated. The final chapter forays into a politics of the possibility of such acts only after the next chapter breaks down the question of action as conventionally put to liberalism's victims, making room for a fresh consideration of suffering and action in the subjectivities of sufferers.

CHAPTER 5

A FETISHISM OF INJURIES

An inquiry into injury as value and commodity, and the attempted recovery of a materialist method that can speak to the laboring and suffering body in liberal capitalism, converge to reveal some of injury's fetish qualities. Injuries as fetishes are products of the labor of suffering—the processes of liberal representation that mediate between our sensuousness and our ability to count and be valued as liberal subjects. When injury is installed as a form that allows our suffering to be visible and to count, it becomes a representation that only grants us solidarity as an afterthought. Injury fashions our suffering and our perceptions of others' suffering in its image.[1]

Injury is a fetish because it is dead suffering, valuable in its deadness and its detachment from the life and particularity of the sufferer but at the same time *actively* defining the sufferer's identity. Under the fetishism of injuries, suffering ceases to be a sensuous life activity because it can only be experienced in the mode of injury and recognized in its value-creating mode. Suffering counts only when it takes this abstract form of injury, equalizing many kinds of abiding inequalities in the abstract. The suffering that comprises the injury, on the one hand, and the experience of that externalized injury by the sufferer and by others, on the other, seem to be independent, unrelated, and unmediated processes. The relation between these alienated sufferings stands in for real, material social relations between individuals. These relations and their experience drop out of vision and are replaced by social relations between interests and injuries to them.

The crux of fetishism is in how production and consumption *appear* to be independent, unrelated, and unmediated processes that they are not. This feigned indifference arises from the fact that social relations between individuals and the relations of production on which they rest drop out of vision and are replaced by social relations between things. The worker's "external" relation to her product is not the key or sole problem. The space between production and consumption may even be where the liberatory potential of capital reposes.

Fetishism, however, encourages replacing the appropriation of productive activity (in a Marxist sense) by private property in things. Other obligations and virtues get supplanted. Fetishism is problematic not because it merely renders one's unmistakably individual labor as indistinguishable from everyone else's labor. The issue is that fetishism makes my labor *appear* private and individual, and that it does so by alienating, beyond recognition, its social character and my irreducible socialities and contingencies. The injury itself becomes an autonomous, fantastical object that is oblivious to the real material relations and the labors that have produced it. This autonomy is from history and perhaps even time itself, so the fetish starts to believe it always was, always has been, and always will be.

Fetishism is a broader and more trenchant concept for my purposes than, for instance, exploitation, for a few reasons. Despite the concrete ethical effectivity of Marx's "scientific" concept of exploitation, it has no structural safeguards against victims turning fetishes. In exploitation, the perpetrator-victim distinction is necessary, even if not framed in terms of the autonomous willful individual subject. More importantly, in order to make its injustice claims, the concept of exploitation relies on the existing mode of valuation and value creation that suffering (and production) follows in liberalism (and capitalism). Fetishism, though, sees subjects suspended within elaborate, suffusive, and subtle relations that make the language of exploitation possible in the first place. It thus forces us to confront the incorporated laws of value and representation and the economies of sensuousness and subjectivity in relation to our own and others' suffering. Fetishism and exploitation differ in the labors of suffering and the work of victims that they allow to be made visible and, ultimately, the very kinds of existences they posit as real and imaginable.

The modes of personification, identification, memory, and voicing that are fostered within the ascetic theater of the fetishism of injuries together call attention to how representation's purposive sensings and presencings occasion certain forms of subjectivity from sufferers. If representation is seen as involving sensing and making sensible, memory and voice are codependently intertwined in this labor (which also fuels Rawls's injury play). The labor of suffering and its many instantiations within liberalism thus bespeak life channeled to sustain the fetishes of injuries and victims. At stake within any response to liberalism is, then, the honoring of the reality and potentiality of other modes of suffering and valuation beyond liberalism. A befitting response to liberalism must necessarily traverse these components of the labor of suffering and challenge liberalism's undialectical understanding of them. This requires going beyond recognition of injury and victim as fetish, to addressing the categories and relations internal to liberal representation and the fetishism of injuries.

SUFFERING AND ACTING

In order, therefore, to find an analogy, we must have recourse to the mist-enveloped regions of the religious world. In that world the productions of the human brain appear as independent beings endowed with life, and entering into relation both with one another and the human race. So it is in the world of commodities with the products of men's hands.

—Karl Marx, *Capital: A Critique of Political Economy*

A product of labor that becomes unrecognizable as the product of any labor, a fetish is a representation oblivious to itself as representation—manifest labor that is more valuable dead than alive. Ironically, it is this embodied amnesia and this alienated life (a forced inanimateness) that allow it to be the supposed bearer of inherent, natural, magical powers, worshipped as if animated by a spirit. The amnesia entails the fetish's obliteration of all traces of what it is and how it has come to be that results in it being oblivious to other temporal and spatial iterations of the labor that constitutes it.[2] As for the alienation, if we take it to be an active and transitive concept (and if Marx is a materialist true to his word), then it must be acknowledged that a fetish is kept alive by the life activity of its creators discharged to it.

The fetishism of injuries provides an inlet into the political-cultural practices that emerge and get affirmed in liberalism and that are generalized by its omnipresent theater. For Marx, sensuous, productive activity and suffering are limited to humans. While fetishes are products of this life activity and are alive through their effects, they are not alive in a complete way—that is, with a memory, with sensuousness, or with an ability to suffer.

Marx's analysis of fetishism insists on the inextricability of the questions of production, distribution, and consumption. Injuries as representations-turned-fetishes are not static and lifeless but active, not least because they derive their life from us. Just like our products were to be mirrors for each other (for Marx), it is entirely plausible that we may not even begin to know our own powers and labors of suffering without investigating what forms of life they produce and which they forbid. The labor of suffering needed within the fetishism of injuries speaks of the activities, experiences, and materialities that exceed and dwell within the fetish formations we adopt and nurture in liberal society.

The injury form, in its representative role, cannot help but exclude the suffering that is not quantifiable or representable in numbers or speech.[3] One key aspect of the fetishism of injuries is that suffering only matters if it takes this form—a sufferer has to be a fetishized victim, representing and acting in prescribed ways, in order to be recognized and included. The labor of suffering produces injuries as fetishes that equalize and render abstract, exchangeable, and consumable the suffering that it seeks to abate. Importantly, since fetishism works at the deeper levels of social relations, it brings with it more than the static presence of a hypostatized representation. Fetishes actively relate to other objects following the imperatives with which their "character" imbues them. In discussing commodity fetishism, Marx writes, "The character of having value, when once impressed upon products, obtains fixity only by reason of their acting and re-acting upon each other as quantities of value. These quantities vary continually, independently of the will, foresight and action of the producers. To them, their own social action takes the form of the action of objects, which rule the producers instead of being ruled by them."[4]

Just as capitalism bestows on products of our labor a fetish character that renders them commodities, representations of suffering in liberalism adopt this character as well. Jean-Luc Nancy's thoughts on characterization may be helpful in understanding this character. He talks about a characterizing "not only in the strict sense of the word (to typify a property or an essence) but even . . . in such a way that the character (the stamp, the seal) is somehow inscribed on the thing itself and can no longer be detached from it, or at least without some loss in the substance of the thing." He adds, "Not just the commodity as the fetish—as if this were one of its traits or one approach among others—but rather the essence of the commodity revealed as fetish, so that the fetish character would remain once the approach was shifted or the 'secret' of its 'mystical character' was revealed."[5]

However, a character is also what a novelist or dramatist creates— "a personality invested with distinctive attributes and qualities" and, importantly, "the personality or 'part' assumed by an actor on the stage."[6] Representation already involves, as discussed in Chapter 2, a sense of acting for. The notion of character also involves artifice in line with a given set of attributes, and remembers their "given-ness" as well as their source. So this embodies both senses of representation: acting for, and making present again.

Finally, character significantly complicates the meaning of presence. A character makes present a person as much the figment or conjuration of someone's imagination as something that emerges from within the actor. Marx says that commodities are "social things whose qualities are at the same time perceptible and imperceptible by the senses."[7] More needs to be said here regarding how presence is regarded as perceived or perceptible. Is it a reflection or a construction? Is it an engagement with a truth that is discoverable, or an experience that works in a different epistemic and ontic register than that of information and reproduction?

Fetishes must act in order to know what they are; their sense of themselves is purely through their repetitive acts. The work of bearing a fetish, and then becoming one in order to be admitted into liberal justice, requires the sufferers to continually rehearse a given script. They gain their sense of themselves as victims by following the script; without this, neither their suffering nor they themselves can participate in the politicolegal marketplace. Victims bearing injuries are rendered fetishes as they are interacted with and represented in reality or in imagination (for instance, by actors in Rawls's original position), or when they have to produce their own representations in keeping with certain requirements, including that of interacting with others who suffer and those who deliver justice.

VICTIMS AS PERSONIFIED INJURIES

The Fetish Character

Following Chapter 4's discussion, labor as value implies that labor not only creates commodities but also becomes a commodity. Thus, labor as a commodity also takes a fetish character. The worker, whose worth is reducible to the value of his labor, becomes a commodity. In turn, the worker performs not only as a commodity but also as the guardian of a commodity. This provides clues for thinking of victims who are deemed reducible to their injuries without recognition of the fact that their own work involves, beyond the suffering that is being represented, enacting their assigned fetish character and negotiating the fetish character of the injuries they carry. What Marx has to say about the actions of commodities, and of those who bear them on their way to the marketplace, may help us reconstruct the script—for the injuries and for the victims who bear them—performed in seeking and delivering liberal justice. This would also allow a gesture to the elements of acting and representing that surpass the script's injunctions. Marx opens up the interpretive possibilities thus:

> Commodities cannot themselves go to the market and perform exchanges in their own right. We must, therefore, have recourse to their guardians, who are possessors of commodities. . . . In order that these objects may enter into relation with each other as commodities, their guardians must place themselves in relation to one another as persons whose will resides in those objects, and must behave in such a way that each does not appropriate the commodity of the other, and alienate his own, except through an act to which both parties consent. . . . Here the persons exist for one another merely as representatives, and hence owners, of commodities. . . . The characters who appear on the economic stage are merely personifications of economic relations; it is as the bearers of these economic relations that they come into contact with each other.[8]

The cognate of this process, in liberalism, features victims as possessors *and* personifications of injuries that are themselves the products of the relations and processes of representation that comprise the labor of suffering. The relations implied by the fetishism of injuries ensure that the possession takes the form of personification. In other words, the bearer of an injury absorbs into her personification the relations that injury as value and commodity signifies. Her performance in the market of liberal justice is in line with the precepts of injury as commodity. Personified in the victim, the injuries act out in the market for liberal justice. Marx goes on to say,

> In their difficulties our commodity owners think like Faust: "Im Anfang war die Tat." ["In the beginning was the deed."–Goethe, Faust.] They have therefore already acted and transacted before thinking. The natural laws of the commodity have manifested themselves in the natural instinct of the owners of commodities. They can only bring their commodities into relation as values, and therefore as commodities, by bringing them into an opposing relation with some one other commodity as the universal equivalent. . . . Through the agency of the social process it becomes the specific social function of the commodity which has been set apart to be the universal equivalent. It thus becomes— money. "Illi unum consilium habent et virtutem et potestatem suam bestiae tradunt. Et ne quis possit emere aut vendere, nisi qui habet characterem aut nomen bestiae aut numerum nominis ejus." ["These have one mind, and shall give their power and strength unto the beast." Revelations, 17:13; "And that no man might buy or sell, save he that

had the mark, or the name of the beast, or the number of his name."
Revelations, 13:17.] (*Apocalypse.*)[9]

Marx suggests that the fetish character is impressed upon, especially
when he says that relations between men "take the form" of a relation between things. This "appearing as" and "form taking" happen
together in the acting that is underway. So when we represent others
or ourselves as victims with certain capacities and desires, suffering
takes the form of injury, injuries appear as our suffering, and social
relations take the form of relations between injuries. Here, all representation tries to approximate an acting as, forgetting and even oblit-
erating the relation that may enable an acting for. This is what Marx
means when he says that commodities, as fetishes, have "absolutely no
connection with their physical properties and with the material relations arising therefrom."[10] In fetishism, appearance and form-taking
converge, removing the space between the material and its form, and
resulting in the process that makes one into the other.

Seeing victims as personified injuries within liberalism takes us back
to ascetic theater and to the actors of Rawls's injury play, bringing up
an interesting aspect of the acting as. These actors are representations
of actual beings and of their actual or potential injuries, reducible to
the abstract equality posited not only by the injury-form and its fetishism but also by the veil's impartiality.

In Rawls, the actors are personifications of "injury as value" without being victims. Injury becomes radically generalized, universalized,
and abstract because the performance has left the body of the sufferer.
It is as if Rawls has paid his dues to production in convoking the original position and overloading it with these productive, representational
tasks so that his idealized society has no memory of the production at
all. And when we come to the market for justice, we no longer know
if we had a suffering to speak for. Recalling from Chapter 4 the kinds
of subsumption that persist between labor and suffering in capitalism
and liberalism, Rawls can be seen as taking the next step from brokering our injuries to rendering them currency, or something more like
futures speculations, like never before, completely skipping the labor
and the suffering as mediators of this value to some degree. This resonates with the move of financialization, endemic to neoliberalism, as
it retires the labor theory of value altogether and recasts its fidelity to
classical liberals.[11]

Given Rawls's strictures on voice, memory, language, and
embodiment that enter the original position, one wonders whether
any knowledge or personality at all can be had by individuals in the

original position.[12] This dubious less-than-humanness of actors in the original position recalls the in-between, part perceptible, part imperceptible nature of commodities as fetishes. Fetishes know themselves through repetitive acts—in this case, their role-plays. The images they see across the veil are their own but are never recognized as such, since neither they nor others know or remember who they are (rather, they know, remember, and replay the dictates of their congealed ethos). Recognition here requires an imposed similitude, a making of the other in and through one's own image; the images are then enlisted in the ascetic theater as lost souls, made available to the senses of the fetishes in the original position.

The impact of the literalization of pain, the annihilation of poetry and metaphor in the original position, and the bracketed memories of those who make it inside the original position, must be seen in light of how this enactment disables and enables other enactments and other roles played. That these fetishes are life forms that act in conformance with the requirements of the ascetic theater of liberal politics recalls Nietzsche's notion of ascetic morality and its manifestation of "life against life."

> *The Primary Function of Ascetic Morality.* It will be immediately obvious that such a self-contradiction as the ascetic appears to represent—life against life—is, physiologically, a simple absurdity. It can only be apparent. . . . Let us replace the usual interpretation of asceticism with a brief formulation of the facts of the matter: the ascetic ideal springs from the protective instinct of a degenerating life which tries by all means to sustain itself and to fight for its existence . . . life wrestles in it and through it with death and against death; the ascetic ideal is an artifice for the preservation of life.[13]

As discussed in Chapter 2, there is a fundamental connection between an ascetic ideal and the form of injury, for there would be no ascetic ideal without ascertaining injury and injurer. The ideal, here like a fetish, is nourished by a resuffering, *ressentiment*, of the injury by the sufferers. It is kept alive by a redirection of the life that the *ressentiment* entails, by a searing into memory that freezes the meaning of the act that injured. Precisely so, ascetic ideals and fetishes seem to be very similar—in their paradoxes of life, memory, and suffering. They are kept alive by memory but are amnesiac about their sources and origins; they are kept alive by imposing a stasis on the life of the sufferer as their resuffering shortchanges the ability to suffer life in general. Here, Nietzsche gives us further (performance) notes for the fetish character, and the life it furnishes and is furnished by, as it plays out in liberal ascetic theater:

> How regularly and universally the ascetic priest appears in almost every age; belongs to no one race, prospers everywhere, emerges from every class of society. . . . An ascetic life is a self-contradiction: here rules *ressentiment* without equal, that of an insatiable instinct and power-will that wants to become master not over something in life but over life itself, over its most profound, powerful and basic conditions; here an attempt is made to employ force to block up the wells of force; here physiological well-being itself is viewed askance. . . . We stand before a discord that *wants* to be discordant, that *enjoys* life itself in this suffering and even grows more self-confident and triumphant the more its own presupposition, its physiological capacity for life, *decreases*. "Triumph in the ultimate agony": the ascetic ideal has always fought under this hyperbolic sign; in this enigma of seduction, in this image of torment and delight, it recognized its brightest light, its salvation, its ultimate victory.[14]

Bodies, Interrupted

My endeavor to retool the relation between suffering, representation, and politics keeps its faith in moments when the apparent analogies between commodities and injuries and between workers and victims break down. The difference between victims performing their labor of suffering to produce injuries and sanctioned voices, and workers alienating their labor to produce commodities that replace human relations, is especially crucial when the alienation and objectification involved in both processes is considered. On the one hand, we find the regime of embodied injuries to be prerequisite to the conferral of identities with political value; on the other hand, we find the erasure of certain identities at will, such as when the American worker seems to have no memory, no history, no injury that can even converse with, let alone trump, any number of preferred, privileged codifications and conscriptions of suffering. This is not an exception to liberal capitalism but essential to it.

Phenomenally, then, the body of the bearer of injuries and commodities, and the differential performances and demands made therein, fruitfully complicates the said analogy, if only to address (a) why the worker's selling of his labor is stuff of amnesia, and how the project of rethinking the politics of suffering has to be a project of rethinking the politics of labor itself, since both require a return to the labor of suffering methodologically and not merely as object; and

(b) the contemporary charm of immediacy inherent in brokering our injuries and identities in the marketplace of justice and the arbitrary "planned" obsolescence of this charm.

Both these issues inform one another, and may force a return to representation as a necessity that can interrupt the defacing trajectories of simplistic and humiliating identity politics that sufferers traverse without even being asked to, and then say and believe they did so willingly and were empowered by it. This should bring the focus on the aesthetics of this bearing to the capacities of the bodies to hold, speak, act, and perform their sufferings in ways that are rendered invisible or irrelevant by the unquestioned allegiance to liberal justice as a marketplace of injuries. These performed sufferings also, incidentally, continue to make liberalism very uncomfortable and paranoid. Efforts to redeem victims that do not understand the life of fetishes cannot unsettle the modes of acting and suffering that are manifested in liberalism; they cannot honor—and may actually violate—the work of the wounded.

In seeking other modes of redemption, or at least trusting the possibility of those, I turn now to the temporality of suffering as embodied in victims as fetishes, and to time as a key element in a methodological reclamation of suffering as the subject of politics and representation.

TIME, SPACE, AND THE WORK OF THE WOUNDED

Fetishes and time are genetically related. The clearest instance of this relation is the labor—the unit of which is time—that produces commodities in capitalism and injuries in liberalism. Time's lack of particularity, and its reduction to an abstraction as a unit of measured exchange of the material body of the worker, is noteworthy. It is in the "nature" of injury as value to lack a dynamic temporality and dialectic, since time, in capitalism (and liberalism), allows the exchange of labor (in commodities and as commodity) by rendering it congealed and redirecting its life away from life. Thus, a logic of distribution can only see things in the logic of exchange, possible only when something is rendered "calculable, regular, necessary."[15] The conversion of suffering into this sort of a labor enables and necessitates such exchangeability.

As far as commodities embody our material powers, they embody the time in which these powers get developed and manifested. Their character as fetishes entails a forgetting of this history and gives us, as it were, an "eternal" experience. This is why planned obsolescence and technological advances in capitalism take the form they take: time itself comes to disavow its relation to material powers and the fever of innovation betrays an indifference to, and disregard for, history. In its implied disabling of the experience of the product and of our selves in the product, this speaks to the alienation from products and productive activity. Whether this mindless disregard of history is taken to mean nothing beyond itself, or is seen as a depletion of the capacities to endure and experience, questions abound regarding liberal capitalism's relation to memory and history.

A fetish is a representation that makes sensible in a way that imposes certain conditions on the memory and senses of the fetishes. Historicizing fetishism thus historicizes sensuousness, a move to which Marx repeatedly alludes in his discussion of the becoming of senses and, more importantly, when he deems the sensuousness of the fetish worshipper being as historically specific an occurrence as the value-creating "nature" of human sensuous activity.[16] For Marx, the fetish poses the problem of amnesia as a problem of time itself.

This ranges from seeing suffering as a discrete and spatiotemporally bounded event that obliterates the suffering that has no such limits, to forgetting other possibilities in other times and spaces. If the removal of the fetish takes the form of the removal of its violence only in the sphere of possessive individualist exchange, there is the danger that the critique of the timelessness of a fetish works to contradictory ends: that, when the fetish is removed, the suffering will be deemed undone too, skirting the more difficult and abiding task of working on the amputated and decayed form of life revealed. Inserting time back into the equation must not, therefore, stop at undoing the essentialist congealing of the victim, or the universalist congealing of all victims in the same mold. It must also stand opposed to getting rid of the signifier too soon: what about the victims of Bhopal whose lives and sufferings stretch far beyond what an injury can measure? What if, per the logic of possessive individualist exchange, we presume the erasure of suffering in dismissing the fetish of injury? Confronting the fetish without addressing the labor of suffering precludes addressing the timelessness of the violence of injury itself—both the pain it marks and the pain of its hard-earned, cut-and-dried recognizability. This keeps at bay the recognition, let alone the revivification, of the life of the living-dead injury and the living material of suffering.

The role of time and history in the fetishism of injuries directs attention to the fetish character of liberal universalism on the whole. In encompassing the production, consumption, and distribution of suffering, fetishism does not simply speak to the reification of a certain mode of suffering within the confines of an advanced liberal society and its beneficiaries (as Rawls is careful to draw his boundaries). It also dictates the terms for the excluded and the wishful. In liberalism, victims as fetishes act among themselves, and with others, in order to install and affirm modes of sensuousness, suffering, subjectivity, and solidarity. The productions of the ascetic theater feature the structures and enactments that have to be affirmed and performed in order to sustain the political economy of injury wherein injuries and victims are produced as commodities. In light of the globalized burden of liberal notions of voice broached in Chapter 2, Rawls's claim that his play is limited to societies with a significant history of successful liberal constitutionalism is questionable precisely when we pay attention to the fetishism of injuries and victims. Liberal representation creates the whole world in its own frozen image by the acts of fetishes who look from behind the veil of ignorance at those who *do* fulfill the conditions of admission in justice as fairness—and at those who *should*.

Critiques of the ahistoricality of liberal universalism and essentialism stand to sharpen by appreciating the role of time. Universalism is not merely enacted in the external activities of the fetishes—it is embedded in their constitution. The ahistorical element inheres in the manner in which, for instance, Islam, Islamic countries, and especially the term fundamentalism are hypostatized as if they are "outside history": the same since the time of the Prophet.[17] Chandra Mohanty discusses how many Western scholars—and, in my view, many self-avowed Third-World scholars as remarkable vindicators of the reach of the fetishism of injuries—see these terms and their referents "evolving in nonhistorical time," frozen in time, possibly speaking a different, distant language.[18] Mohanty also attacks the discursive and subjectifying power of universalism that, in any attempt to speak for the whole world or even different worlds within one big world, flouts all historical processes. Her premise is that the universal is stable and misrepresents the fluidity of experience. However, this universalism's supposed stability and power is hard-earned, and its upkeep is the responsibility of its subjects: the petrified amnesia of a fetish is sustained by the life activity of human beings subject to it and subjects of it.

Part of the power of the fetish is its quality of encrusting certain characterizations in political and legal discourse, excluding other actual and possible configurations of relations and power and preempting any change in the existing ones. Its (feigned) ability to concentrate and localize its material may delude us into thinking that it can be easily removed, amputated, or traded, with no residue and perhaps not even a scar. Linguistic idealisms and merely linguistic materialisms end up succumbing to this notion, inspired by promulgations of linguistic turns that suggest that since language brings into being, it brings into being only in language.

Exposing the inconsistencies and contradictions of the fetishism of injuries and the politics it sponsors (a) opens up to visibility injustices rendered mute and invisible and (b) gestures to other, newer forms within different times and spaces. This recalls Marx's claim that secular freedom is but a farcical effigy of real human emancipation; an exposé of the invisible unfreedoms of a free society, his work is premonitory of a form of human emancipation not yet seen (partial to different times over different spaces).[19] Dynamic, temporal relations to given forms shape the space that *is* sensuous subjectivity, where suffering, joy, hope, and fear happen. The matter of whether the space constructed is individual or collective, proprietary or irreducibly social, is not presettled; liberal politics engenders only one version of this time and space, captured in its orientation to suffering.

I now turn to three instances in which the fetish character of injuries is normalized, not only in liberalism but in critiques of it as well. These instances will recall issues (raised in previous chapters) including: the emphasis on the agent in the attention to injury and the subsequent objectification and romance of the victim's voice; liberalism's self-perception of being attuned to the victim and of embodying the perspective of the injured; and, finally, the implications of dealing with this injury as value. The specific mode of this objectification that ties these three together in the sensual and political economy of liberal capitalism is commodification.

CONFRONTING FETISHES

Merely Victims, Hardly Agents

There is a fundamental reciprocity between how sufferers represent themselves, or are represented, and the way in which their subjectivities and those of the injurers are theorized in various political programs. Together, they determine the form of agency that is granted to the victim within any paradigm. In many theoretical attempts at redeeming victims, the work of the wounded remains attached to an imputed aspiration for agency modeled on the "health" of the agent qua perpetrator, bystander, and rescuer. Seeing the wounded as agency-impaired affirms the definition of victim as inadequate subject. There can be no justice done to the experience of suffering in its particularity if the only choice is to define it in relation to—even when only as the antithesis of—normalized healthy sovereign action.

Critiques of liberalism that build on responses to orientalism and other colonial discourses are suspicious of the mechanics of the identification of victims. For them, the victim status precludes any status beyond that of the object of an action, necessitates powerlessness, and imposes slave morality.[20] An inevitable result is the object's own resignation to its "assigned" lack of subjectivity.[21] In these criticisms, the question of naming becomes inextricable from representation. It follows that the need and validity of *representing* the victims, the oppressed, the third world, is doubted and, finally, rejected.

However, these challenges still remain attached to a relation to health as agency and to agency as health. An example is the call that victims and agents are not mutually exclusive—something to the effect that victims can be agents, too. Mohanty, for one, tells us of cottage-industry working women in Narsapur who "are not mere victims of the production process, because they resist, challenge, and subvert the process at various junctures."[22] What is implicit in the "not mere victim" reaction? It brings to mind Martha Nussbaum's claim that victimization does not preclude "agency."[23] Clearly at work in Mohanty's account is a defensiveness that ends up condoning and affirming the dominant notion of agency it opposes. Occupying very different locations on the philosophical spectrum, Mohanty and Nussbaum seem closer in their gut reaction than their avowals would suggest. Why is a victim *merely* a victim? What does it tell us regarding how we understand victimization? These reactions betray an inability to factor in the mode of practice that *is* suffering, which may spurn the redemption of the victim on the terms of health and agency, liberal style.

These thinkers highlight how voice and representation are so frequently framed in terms of agency, where agency itself becomes linked to representation: the victims or nonagents need representation, and they are redeemed by obviating representation and granting a voice all in one fell swoop. In my view, this link between agency and the authenticity of voice is a dubious one. It is on this suspect convergence that Spivak makes an important intervention. In "Can the Subaltern Speak?" she concludes that the subaltern cannot speak, an answer that, in dismissing Western intellectuals who "make space" for the subaltern to speak, reinstates a project of rethinking representation and the victim's experience. Spivak's analysis is more nuanced than Mohanty's, which rejects the very need and validity of this representation. Spivak takes issue with Foucault's wish to let the subaltern speak "in their own voice," which does not take seriously the notion that they have no voice as yet, and that this speechlessness is what defines the subaltern. She saves the notion of representation by arguing that, in the absence of a language of their own, there is no alternative but to represent the subaltern in a way that is sensitive to their silence.[24] As I argued in Chapters 2 and 3, the fetish of voice itself must be subject to a suspicion, since it serves those who thrive on its consolations more than those who are bid speak and must do so in order to write themselves in.

This is not to say that that the "victim"—its discursive and material reality—does not need redressal in a liberatory politics. Far from that, one can see it as a representation—a *Darstellung* and a *Vorstellung*—that has to itself be a subject of any social theoretical endeavor that is materialist in its imperative to make conditions (for the possibility of change) out of necessities. Liberal fictions and power structures need victims; unwittingly or not, they sustain them as they are themselves nourished by the latter's surplus suffering. Interestingly, the same Nietzsche who inspires a suspicion of the agent is also someone who forces a consideration of the material history, weight, and imperatives of agency, and of the terms and labor of its overcoming. It is more than a coincidence that Nietzsche's transition from the slave revolt in the first essay of *On the Genealogy or Morals* to the story of guilt, *ressentiment*, and punishment in the second essay, involves the myth of the doer behind the deed.[25] This transition is about suffering. Nietzsche's views on subjects and subjection suggest not merely that there is no doer but that the core of human existence is the suffering *of* that doing—that the subject is, in any case, subject to itself and its deeds. (As far as the fictive nature of the subject is concerned, Nietzsche drives home the very brutally material nature of fictions—are fictions ever *merely* fictions?)

The centrality of the agent in liberalism's focus on suffering is manifest in the necessity of an agent as the cause or remedy of suffering. This raises the question of which fiction is more enduring in the liberal framework: the agent who causes the injury or the victim who is injured with that agency? In both cases, liberalism's attention is clear. In its keenness to see as good for liberal justice only the suffering that can be traced to a sanctioned agent, it makes victims into objects of the action. While neither of these options exhausts the possibilities in reality, they do necessitate each other. This is why the agent looms so large, even in the imaginations of critics of liberalism, that it holds the promise, in its potential idealist-linguistic overcoming, of the undoing of the stigmatizing victim identity it spawns. However, the sufferer subjected to the fictions of agency and of the production of injury suffers these fictions through her labors of sustaining *and* unwriting them.

The Perspective of the Injured

One of liberalism's originary claims is its commitment to the fact of human suffering and to the victims of public harms and injuries. Shklar's reformed liberalism of fear, for instance, insists on the need for liberalism to go back to its roots and fulfill its promise of bringing in the perspective of the victim, by honing itself and its senses to fully apprehend cruelty and to see invisible injustices and invisible victims. Chapter 1 raised the question of whether this was actually a perspective *of* the victims instead of only being a perspective *on* them. Even this explicit attachment makes the liberalism of fear no different from any other liberalism that, in avowing to attend to victims, only goes far enough to regard the agency that causes injury. In Catherine MacKinnon's view, the problem is exemplified in the fact that "the injury of rape lies in the meaning of the act to its victim, but the standard of its criminality lies in the meaning of the act to its assailant."[26] Richard Bell elaborates. "Also, little credence is given to the *dignitary harms* in court because . . . '[They] are nonmaterial [and] ephemeral to the legal mind.' Given how the deck is stacked in the social and legal situation, the possibility of change in the direction of justice seems virtually impossible. We have not even begun to look at the 'injustice' in this case. We have failed in giving it proper attention."[27]

Liberalism's conceited, or deceitful, avowal of the perspective of victims has been famously brought into question in Wendy Brown's trenchant critique of the politics of *ressentiment*.[28] She finds that despite claiming to be a righteous concoction from the perspective of the injured, this politics detracts from the pursuit of freedom by relying on simplistic notions of blame and responsibility and reducing justice to punishment (the causing of a certain amount of pain to the injurer to avenge the injury). In light of our earlier discussion, is Brown's suggestion—that liberal politics is imbued with a righteous perspective of the injured—to be taken as ironic? I doubt that she thinks that this *actually* is a perspective of the injured, when in fact it is merely concocted and declared as such. However, her own opposition to liberalism does not clearly make this doubt overt, since while she is worried about the implications and consequences of this claim to a victim's perspective, she does not question its veracity, substance, or logic. Her more explicit concern is with liberalism's quickness and sloppiness in assigning blame and responsibility by affording an unfounded agency to the injurer. While the target is an economics of *ressentiment* and responsibility that traps the wounded in a never-ending cycle, the expediency of this critique is a bit suspect to the materialist in me.[29]

Brown's mechanism is intriguing. It seems to suggest that the way to take care of liberalism's claim to the victim perspective can be expunged once we sufficiently smudge the fictive category of perpetrator that necessitates the fiction of the victim. That way, we can begin to approximate the promised (*also* fictive) liberal terrain of rough equality in order to get beyond it. In other words, Brown gives us a choice of liberal claims to be taken seriously, to chosen strategic ends. So it is either that Brown acknowledges that no righteous perspective of the victim is possible, or that she recognizes that liberalism's perspective of the victim is no real perspective of the victim at all. It seems to me that these are two different critiques; I think she leans toward the former. The latter is a step toward the former, in a way, and is important at that. In any case, her focus on unsettling responsibility and blame addresses only part of the problem.

When a critique of liberalism focuses only on complicating and challenging notions of blame and responsibility, it seems like a convoluted way to reprimand and correct liberalism for its disingenuous claim to a victim's perspective. There is certainly a need to reconfigure responsibility and blame but not without effectively altering the concomitant attitude to the human suffering that necessitates these notions in the first place. Single-handed challenges to these notions affirm the liberal mode of agency and responsibility when victims are often allotted much of the agency as if there were not already a spate of qualitatively different labors that they perform outside those categories. This replaces liberalism's paternalistic and patronizing attitude with a different sort of paternalism and patronage.

Thus, if the central issue with liberalism is taken to be that it adopts the righteous perspective of the sufferer when it should not be trying to speak for anyone, the problem is being misplaced. Liberalism, in fact, does *not* take the victim's perspective. Its own internal structure and assumptions allow it to construe representation as an ahistorical and congealed notion of speaking for the experience of suffering. Furthermore, this is an experience liberalism misunderstands through categories and filters that predate an actual confrontation with the suffering. Even when liberalism sees the victim, it sees in her a suffering caused by some action; if that cause and will are not discerned, the suffering is as good as absent. Especially since injury is defined as harm to agency, the discussion remains within the purview of the perpetrator, and is really not focused on the injured at all. To mimic Brown, then, one way out is to remove the perpetrator so that it stops haunting and engulfing the process. However, the problem is an inarticulate commitment to the sufferer that never materializes except in removing the consolation of a cause. In doing so, it does not get at the suffering that demands justice, whether or not a cause is fictive or real, and regardless of whose desire for justice is affected very meagerly by the presence or absence of the doer.

Wounded Redemptions

The defensiveness of the likes of Mohanty is of a piece with an inability to cognize the fetishism that MacKinnon and Brown, in their own ways, do confront in their respective critiques. On the spectrum of conceptual proclivities that see capitalism and liberalism share certain approaches to the body, its labors, and its products, MacKinnon fully harnesses the concept of value and exploitation, while Brown's analysis factors in rights as fetishes.

MacKinnon's work is full of parallels: sexuality is to feminism, as labor is to Marxism, as suffering is to liberal law. Beholden to these parallels, then, such an account considers the labor theory of value a truism rather than a critique. In a way, MacKinnon wishes to overload the category of value in order to *make visible* via a certain kind of exteriorization as injury. This making visible and making present—indeed, representation—is the first step in redeeming the suffering: all suffering needs to be recognized as injury and all our labor subjected to the law of value. MacKinnon is willing to indulge the logic of value creation to make the law aware of itself, en route to the system being torn asunder by overload (not unlike Marx's story of history and the collapse of capitalism in the *Manifesto* and *the German Ideology*). In this, she pulls an Arthur Rimbaud, radically taking on language to its exhaustion and eventual overcoming rather than unquestioningly accepting the given structures of political emancipation.[30]

I can appreciate the logic, but I remain skeptical of such indignant (what Brown would call resentful) totalization. I recognize its rhetorical and symbolic value but with a condition. This effort has value only if we remember the excess of this effort and are aware of the prison this attempt is creating. Structurally, liberal capitalism does not have space for such a subvertible recognition, given its engulfing of excess and overage in order to prolong its own life. More victims just give liberalism more to stand on. MacKinnon is able to recognize suffering only as the labor that ought to get its word out on the market and be granted its fair (if not just) share of value. Thus, she is working at the level of the alienation of sensuous activity already understood as productive.

Third-wave and later feminist critiques of MacKinnon urge that we disabuse ourselves of universalistic categories that are oppressive despite themselves. The unbearable weight and "creativity" of history and its relation to injury is central to Brown's fights with the demons of liberalism and colonialism. She undertakes an "exploration of the ways in which certain aspects of the specific genealogy of politicized identity are carried in the structure of its political articulation and demands, with consequences that include self-subversion."[31] Brown wants to salvage collective struggle for freedom from the throes of this inverted dialectic that manifests itself in essentialist and inescapable narratives of these subjectivities, and she also renders these subjectivities immutable and abstract like mathematical identities. She is seeking the point where politicized identities would realize the need for "forgetting" the history that created and legitimized them—a forgetting in the pursuit of an emancipatory democratic project.

Brown talks about rehabilitating the moment prior to the wounding of desire, which can be construed as a move to reconceptualize injury. Forgetting, as a Nietzschean version of agency, counterpoints the task of representation as being akin to remembering, recollecting, or perhaps *reminding*. While Brown is not exactly talking about remembering in order to forget, hers is still a notion of selective remembering. Following the potential of perlocutionary speech acts,[32] Brown is trying to pry open a space for reinterpretion of the act of speech so it does not so easily wound. Perhaps this is a space that might be open to remembering in order to forget?

The fear in this case is that the representation is seared into the represented in a way that it becomes impossible to forget—a befittingly Nietzschean allergy, which I share. But I find no reason to link representation and *ressentiment* so tightly unless a representation is a fetish, like injury in liberalism. What if representation contributes to forgetting in a way that representation is remembering and a necessary step before forgetting? A premium on forgetting may be rightly placed, but I am wary of an accompanying imperative to be less wounded, or to at least act as if we were less wounded or immune. Hopefully, we would begin to internalize that over the injury. All of this assumes that there is something about being a victim that calls for being let go before *real* agency can step in. The redemptive reliance, in the work of Brown, on a perlocutionary act focused on preempting the wounding runs the risk of being a less than benign neglect of the victim's experience. Why could a wounded attachment not be nursed, instead, by a perlocutionary act that aims not to preempt the wound but to embrace it in a more singular and open-ended way? There ought to be other ways of conceptualizing the work of a sufferer; already the victim is the one responsible to escape the injury—to forget, to laugh, to have grace, to act honorably—in response to an ideology whose focus on the victim always takes the form of focusing on the *causing* of the *pain*.

Brown resolves "wounded attachments" by supplanting the language of "I am" with "I want," marking the overcoming of victim identity by reinstituting the desire prior to wounding.[33] This act of wanting, this mode of externalizing the injury, sabotages Brown's critique. It clearly belies an inability to understand the activity of suffering outside of the imperative of certain kinds of enactments, utilities, and productivities. *This* "radical" desire, in its reaction to the "I am," is consistent with the paradigmatic, narrowly productive way of making the suffering matter.

While Brown confesses an understanding of the dangers of fetishism here—she does see rights as fetishes—this does not carry into injuries as fetishes and to their material form and content.[34] It turns out that it is hard to find any significant difference in how Brown and MacKinnon understand the core activity of suffering, and thus the *labor* of suffering, which is why replacing "I am" with "I want" is rather inconsequential; under the law of value in capitalism and liberalism, "I am" and "I want" are the same. While a critic like Brown recognizes the system of value as itself oppressive, she is unable to see the problem with value as a fetish that emerges from, and dynamically impacts, the labor that creates it, in the end doing little more (if not actually less) than MacKinnon. Leaving out the fact that injury is suffered and that the suffering of injury lies beyond the suffering that comprises the injury, her analysis does not have the much-flaunted perlocutionary space for recognizing the suffering and its labors, articulated or not, that will be rendered unsensed once we turn away from the injury linguistically. When the multiplicitous and unsettled nature of subjectivity is presented as antiontological in critiques of identity politics, it often paradoxically also removes any ability to talk about the embodiment and enactment, beyond mere playful theatricality, of these personae. In more ways than she intended, Spivak's admonition—about intellectuals disowning with a flourish a circumscribed task that has to be performed—rings true for these critiques that also disown the labor already at work.[35]

It is in the relation between value and labor—highlighted by Marx's observation that the production process is dialectical and inheres all moments, even subsumption—that the incompleteness of these critiques shines through. Marx does not wish to simply assure and console us that *labor* creates value. He wants to make us uncomfortable about labor creating *value* in capitalism. He inspires confronting the Janus—that the very act of creating a world, willfully or not, is an act of instituting homelessness.

MacKinnon affirms the value-creating mode of suffering (inviting my charge that her materialism becomes undialectical the moment that it embraces a certain utilitarian legal frame). Brown apprehends only the fetish and fails to see that a more complex response is required to the coincidence of abstract and concrete labors of suffering in the same sensual apparatus. Brown's inability to bring in the victim save as the one with special powers (agency) to forget and to overcome is either a liberal hangover, or it corresponds to a limitation she professes in a footnote. There, she claims that neither materiality nor discourse is enough on its own, and that the next step forward from her analysis would entail addressing the dialectical relation between the two.[36] Materiality, for her, as with many linguistic materialists, is discursive materiality, coupled with materiality assessed in terms of one's position in the social order. (Put together, discursive materiality—the dialectical space she finds—corresponds to positionality in the linguistic order). While that is a huge step, the dialectical moment seems to have been amputated of its real flesh and blood, where not only the making of subjects but also the suffering of the subjectivity and our material activities of sensing and being need to be addressed.

Getting rid of value does not go far enough. Maybe Brown resolves the wounded attachment and sends us back to the moment prior to the wounding of desire too quickly. By not accounting for the time or the space of this suffering, she perhaps falls prey to a certain lack of history herself. After all, a great deal of life activity nourishes the fetishes that may hold the possibility of recognizing ourselves as species-beings bound together through our labor. Theorizing suffering has to be cognizant of the relation between injury and suffering, and between the fetish and the activity of creating it. It does not suffice to think of suffering either as pure activity of a productive kind that creates value or as activity that is maimed in the fetish it creates (which can thus be overcome by razing the fetish). The mutilation and obliteration are live and lived conditions and need to be recognized as such.

Both Brown and MacKinnon raise crucial questions and identify critical shortcomings of liberalism, but neither seems to be keyed into the labor of suffering endemic to the fetishism of injuries that their nemesis perpetuates. MacKinnon's adamant and accurate questioning of the victim's absence from liberalism and the law must be brought together with an ethic of destabilizing injury as fetish inspired by Brown. This requires a differently historical and materialist approach to the suffering that both MacKinnon and Brown want to make visible and present in their own ways. To this is devoted the next, final chapter.

CHAPTER 6

THE TRAGIC ART OF
HISTORICAL MATERIALISTS

The extent to which the solution of theoretical riddles is the task of practice and effected through practice, the extent to which true practice is the condition of a real and positive theory, is shown, for example, in fetishism. The sensuous consciousness of the fetish-worshipper is different from that of the Greek, because his sensuous existence is different. The abstract enmity between sense and spirit is necessary so long as the human feeling for nature, the human sense of nature, and therefore also the natural sense of man, are not yet produced by man's own labor.

> —Karl Marx, "The Meaning of Human Requirements,"
> *Economic and Philosophic Manuscripts of 1844*

The tragic spirit is a dangerous one, and its power is in the chorus, who do not interpret the myth for the audience . . . but, as the votaries of Dionysus, lead the audience into it, and in their enchanted state see its reality, rather than only the performance of the actors. True tragedy is a ritual of healing, which can turn "fits of nausea [at the meaninglessness of life] into imaginations with which it is possible to live."

> —Anonymous, with quote from Nietzsche,
> *The Birth of Tragedy*

To the finest communications we only lend a silent ear. Our finest relations are not simply kept silent about, but buried under a positive depth of silence never to be revealed. It may be that we are not even yet acquainted. In human intercourse the tragedy begins, not when there is misunderstanding about words, but when silence is not understood. Then there can never be an explanation.

> —Henry David Thoreau, "Wednesday,"
> *A Week on the Concord and Merrimack Rivers*

Challenging the purely instrumental and external relations between suffering, representation, and politics must involve rethinking the subjectivity of sufferers by way of addressing the internal relations between temporality and sensuousness, and between memory and voice. The forms and economics of subjectivity, voice, and memory sponsored within liberalism (and retained in many of its contemporary detractors), affirm suffering as topic or object waiting to be treated or dealt with, utilized or redeemed, and understood or rendered irreducibly other. In this scheme, the work of interpretation, translation, representation, and justice begins once this suffering has happened.

The labor of suffering does not affirm this temporal or ontological autonomy and sees its constitutive materialities, materializations, and representations as being continuous with the experience of suffering and occurring within the ubiquitous and ordinary struggles over its meaning and conscriptions. It recalls the necessities that these fetishes impose on those who live, suffer, remember, hope, and act—the life that these fetishes extract from those who suffer within and under them. It also brings to mind the modes of action and the relations to suffering implied in these available modes. This chapter proposes some pathways for a return of politics to suffering by remembering the forms of subjectivity and practice, sensing, and presencing that survive within, and despite, the fetishism of injuries and its congealed, dead labors of suffering. In this remembrance reposes the possibility of imagining forms of justice that do not sacrifice suffering to the external principle of redress but which see the struggles to make suffering matter to constitute a richer sense of justice instead of being in an external, apologetic, instrumental, vulnerable, even embarrassed, relation to it.

The spurs for this remembrance are found in the labors of suffering that cannot be judged or comprehended along the modes of presence and performance that appease liberal structures, and are deemed urgent, utile, practical, effective—and yes, "concrete"—by those allies of the injured who frame their politics within those structures. These labors predate and postdate, transcend and subtend, the politics made intelligible by forms of inclusion, voice, and corporeality sponsored by liberalisms, happy or fearful, passive or aggressive, optimist or minimalist, procedural or deliberative. They also do not quite map onto the contemporary versions of vulgar materialisms. Often operationalized in the return to the body and its affects, such materialisms collate objectification, narcissism, self-exoticization, fetishism of immediacy, and endlessly monologic reflection over a bloated self (even when this self, and its naïve equation with the body, is brought into question). The divisions of suffering and of the labor of suffering within and across societies point to the incompletely liberal subjects, those who remain somewhat unevolved in the modes of passive and active subjectivities sponsored by liberalism. This incompleteness involves resisting prescriptions of what we must feel, for whom and why, when we should speak and for whom, what is deemed harmful and injurious, what it means to own our suffering, and at what cost we should trade our suffering away. These concerns beg theorizing the subjectivity of sufferers beyond the liberal logics that conscript and occlude the work of the wounded, just as they grant inclusions by rendering suffering legible and intelligible.

The theater of the ascetic, on the one hand, and liberalism's proclamations of tragedy, on the other, together point to the dramatic inclinations and performative substance of the fetishism of injuries. Constituting these enactments is the labor of suffering that straddles the realms of politics, ethics, and aesthetics and shapes their mandates in turn. The injury play of Rawls's original position, an exemplar of the ascetic theater, furnishes the principles of justice that are then executed by liberal institutions—in ordinary life, the courtroom, in policy—that see themselves as tragically prone to not being able to do all the justice they would like to; the institutions address the advanced stages of the process of liberal justice that is said to begin in the original position. If any bodies perchance happen to drop out on the way, weary and fraught, they are already part of the tragedy before the final act. Enter Septimus Warren Smith, our unnamed and unsung "hero" from Virginia Woolf's *Mrs. Dalloway*.[1] Whether some tender their everyday refusals, or Septimus finds his way out the window, liberal society is relieved of its burdens since its modes of acceptance and inclusion are life-denying beyond what liberalism knows to *be* life. If society's sense of composure depends on convincing itself of Septimus's well-being through provisions of the liberal state (not unlike the philanthropic consolations discussed in Chapter 3), his departure from this scene is a vindication of suffering, of its life, and life itself. Septimus is not alone, nor is his the only refusal, vindication, and vivification.

The performances of memory and suffering required by liberalism do not exhaust all the ways that people do, and can, enact their labors of suffering. These labors inhabit different avenues than those mapped by liberalism—even if they always live in the shadow, and even if they always have to navigate the hegemony—of privileged sufferings and representations. The continuities and tensions between ascetic theater and liberal tragedy are points of departures for my attempted articulation of a *historical* and *materialist* imperative that can counter the fetishism of injuries.

The journey Marx loved to undertake is a familiar odyssey: begin with the given and the concrete, travel far and wide, deep and beyond, to find its determinations, and return to the concrete, having, in some important ways, transformed it through the journey, exposing its abstractions, and being transformed oneself. This was the charm of the hidden abodes into which Marx followed Virgil, Hegel, and Feuerbach, sharing their loathing of the stubbornness of the "empirically given reality" and its refusal to accept or declare its whences and whithers. Maybe that is where liberating justice from injury and harm to incorporate a different sense of suffering enters the picture. A richer conception of justice can learn from the methodology and travels of historical materialism. This could, in turn, approximate the sort of coming together of circumspection and execution, love and politics, ethics and aesthetics, that contemporary writers like Tony Kushner and Iris Murdoch are trying to provoke into existence—an impulse familiar to Hegel, Feuerbach, and Marx.

In the spirit of Marx's method of departure and return, the return journey from the hidden abodes must be tracked to see how the concrete—what this suffering is, where it lives, how people suffer and for whom, what people do when the modes of sanctioned suffering render their sufferings invalid, and when the modes of speech granted make them not want to speak—transforms upon return, as does a politics accountable to it. This chapter attempts this in two movements. The first section begins with a story of failed revolutionaries, as told in the *Eighteenth Brumaire*. This foregrounds sensing, presencing, and the dialectical unity of memory and voice (issues that emerged as hinges of the previous discussion of representation and victims). Marx's discussion of the making of history disrupts the oppositions of suffering and action, passion and production, politics and *poiesis*, and notions of agency privileged by way of these oppositions. This prefaces a treatment of the question of theatrical genres, as featured in the *Brumaire* but juxtaposed with liberalism's own favored genres, to see what they contain and what they leave out. These include, in the transition to the second half of the chapter, elements of a relation to suffering—one's own and others'—that can be gleaned from certain forms of enactments; and the subjectivities of sufferers that evade definition in relation to the healthy autonomous agency that started off Chapter 1.

Toward an articulation of a politics that is premised on these subjectivities, the materialities of necessity, hope, and sensuousness become hinges for an alternate approach to suffering. The second section of this chapter traces these elements, parsing out how they insinuate themselves in a rethinking of suffering and representation and in the positing of a materialist politics that honors the labors and the lives of those who suffer.

WOUNDED ENACTMENTS

Failed Revolutionaries, Historical Materialists

Men make their own history, but they do not make it just as they please in circumstances they choose for themselves; rather they make it in present circumstances, given and inherited. Tradition from all the dead generations weighs like a nightmare on the brains of the living. And just when they appear to be revolutionizing themselves and their circumstances, in creating something unprecedented, in just such epochs of revolutionary crisis, that is when they nervously summon up the spirits of the past, borrowing from them their names, marching orders, uniforms, in order to enact new scenes in world history, but in this time-honoured guise and this borrowed language.

—Karl Marx, *The Eighteenth Brumaire of Louis Bonaparte*

The writer of the *Eighteenth Brumaire* is a loser. He writes about failure, from within failure, to recognize it as such, understand it, and interrupt the moment and the self-fulfilling prophecies accompanying it, with much in the way of such recognition. He also writes for, and to, the vanquished who have either forgotten their injuries as they swear allegiance to "the grotesque mediocrity,"[2] or are reacting to the smashing of their ideals with disenchantment and pathos, finding ways of inoculating themselves against their loss by pretending that nothing was lost or by dulling the pain.

Such is the suffering at work in the "event" called the Brumaire: suffering that ventures an answer in the form of a revolution, and suffering that results from the failure of a revolution and the lost gains from previous revolutions. Even more important than the suffering that is the cause and the result of a revolution lost, is the suffering that *is* revolution. This includes the activities of bringing about revolution and the incorporations of both the suffering that is the immediate cause of the revolution as well as the suffering that is present in the memory from the actions of previous revolutions. Then there is the way of suffering a revolution, and its defeat, which is mindful of the legacy that will be lodged in the memory of those to come. This spans struggles with, and against, the meaning of suffering inherited in the stories, memories, and hardships. And when there is no possibility of changing the terms of its interpretation, inclusion and, appropriation, this involves preserving, where possible, the unappropriated suffering that can be the source of hope. So the revolution requires laboring with the suffering that must be let go, and the suffering that must be held, like silences, like unmoving gestures, like words between one's teeth, like scars only your lover must see.

What silence does, must, and can Marx's loquacious revolution keep? What relation to suffering must a communist revolution inspire, even necessitate? Where and how do we take on the imperatives to make our suffering and its memory into what the revolution can honor? Is this hope being found in the suffering missed by the language of the master, or in the labor that is an invisible extraction in the truest sense? But, maybe, the question of memory and repression can force a different reckoning of surplus value. More is at stake, and more stubbornly, in the suffering that, even as object and commodity, never truly leaves us or becomes completely other. In a commodity created with my labor, my unpaid labor (a commodity itself) is the source of someone's profit. Marx can, then, help me calculate it. And it is fair to say that the externalization and alienation of my labor is premised quite often on its physical or temporalized separation from me.

However, when I *am* my injury, where my victimhood is fetish itself, the degrees of alienation still remain stubbornly attached to my body and my being. The labor of suffering allows a context in which to understand the alienation of labor itself—to point to the alienation that, as suffering, still remains in us, in our sinews, calluses, mousetrap competitions, and memories. It is when alienation itself gets objectified and fetishized as a commodity that the possibility of revolution dwindles. But insofar as the embodied experience of the alienation—of labor and of the labor of suffering—still bears the history of this labor, it offers a space of politics not usually apprehended. What is contained in this space demands a more socialized recovery, and signifies, in its incomplete conscription or in its excess, a deferral of hope. In his account of the 1848 revolutions, Georges Duveau fills this out, "In studying 1848, Marx was struck by the fact that instead of simply taking into account their own needs and natural desires, people deliberately dug into the past and dressed up in old, cast-off revolutionary garments; they were acting out the old dramas of history once again, instead of thinking seriously about the revolution that was really called for, simply because it was easier. Human beings are held prisoner by certain catchphrases, by certain attitudes and nostalgic leanings."[3]

In his scathing criticism of memories of heroism and glory in the *Brumaire*, Marx is ill-read as a whiner scolding stupid people who do not know better or as a prematurely senile modernist endorsing a radically futurist or uncritically presentist relation to the past. Far from this, Marx asks how material conditions, actual historical locations, and the current sufferings and actions of human beings have actually (and paradoxically) insulated the actors (these historical materialists by practice) from the inscriptions of the past on their present and future (in this instance, the political, institutional legacy of the 1789 bourgeois revolution)? How have they arrived to a point where they derive sustenance from the connections and meanings conjured through commodified, alienated images?

Any adequate discussion of memory (whether individual, collective, culturally sponsored and produced, systemic, or structural) must situate it within the regimes of production and representation in capitalism and liberalism, respectively. A fetish is created, forgetful of its material basis in the tense dialectical struggle between memory and forgetting as powers, needs, and activities. This production and consumption belies an inability to suffer. It is not a relief from suffering; rather, it is its appropriation and conscription. The reference to borrowed language in the quote from the *Brumaire* also places the question of memory and sensing ontologically coeval with the need to make things sensible, understood, and present.

Perhaps, then, the biggest defeat in the *Brumaire* is not the loss of the revolution but the refuge and comprehensibility sought by revolutionaries in the fixed hegemonic order, scaffolded by ghosts of successes past. The revolution's tragedy is its inability to suffer beyond the defeat and its quickness to fill the silence of the moment with words and images from history. Whose suffering was appropriated, interpreted, translated, and alienated, and by whom? For what did the revolutionaries trade in the suffering whence their hope obtains?

Sensings and presencings are contained in the labor of suffering as representations, materializations, and materialities that an unjust liberal society necessitates. This labor spans not only the acts of creating representations but also the suffering and actions enabled by, and enabling, these representations. Evident in how various political establishments are able to render class, gender, and race farcical categories is the sad fact that the prize of inclusion often privileges forms of desperation and marginality so much so that whoever accepts the language conferred by the masters first, wins.

On top of the erasure of class as history or identity, the encouragement of deeply masculinist and misogynist discourse that sneaks into racial patronage is itself intriguing. On the one hand is the willingness of the groups to speak the language offered, and, on the other hand is the comfort this provides the aging white, male, bourgeois, privileged America. The latter is exemplified in the heraldry, in anticipation of Barack Obama's election as president, of a black family on the steps of the White House as the end of a "sour chapter" of history and as the green signal to move on to new tantrums as victims of some other guilt.[4] This exemplifies the subtle and not so subtle triumph of the discourses and self-understandings that (a) keep people speaking how they must, with thresholds of propriety and voice defined by those who had the beginning *and* have the word, and (b) deem history discrete and mechanistic, and guilt whimsical and self-serving, both used by those in power to their arbitrary ends. In the many promises Obama's election must keep, and in the story of the failed French Revolution, the moment of representation serves as an end of the past and as instrumental to a foreclosed future instead of being a material—and messy—relation to the present.

Marx suggests that perhaps the vanquished have suffered more, without being aware of it, from their will to phrase things as readily as possible for the benefit of those whose understanding they seek. Marx is no privileged or detached spectator reporting on people performing certain roles. His practice is formed within, and confronts, a society that is apt to conjure away the losses in memory in order to quickly comprehend and appropriate the story. He makes present a reality in which he is implicated as much, no less and no more, than those who don the masks and the costumes of yesteryears. He gives an account of the defeat as it is coming to be. Thus, he must not only confront this failure himself but also make sure that his representation enacts the suffering that marks their collective present. In addition, this enactment should be such that it weakens the hold of the regnant forms, and of their contents of memory and forgetfulness, in order to get a word in on what will be transmitted into the future.

Marx's comparison of the aesthetic imagination of a people faced with hardship to the mad Englishman of Bedlam recalls madness in DuBois or Nietzsche in order to unpack this seeming derogation— madness is the mode of survival, not a regret, of those who are at once invisible and incessantly exposed and those whose sight exceeds their speech. Thus, this is not about affirming the losers of the Brumaire as the oppressed destined to be duped, or as perfect authors of the revolution; neither is there a neat equation between their actions and the success of the revolution. This is about the suffering that, somewhat like the substance of madness, has not become the grist of action, yet defines it—suffering that lurks and lingers in, through, and beyond the revolution, and suffering that gets completely dismissed and ignored when the pain of a failed revolution drowns it. And, yes, this is more than suggestive of the promise of health of unregistered discourses and of voices that are as yet unheard or forcibly rendered inaudible.

Genres of Suffering, Genres of Action: From Liberal Tragedy to Tragic Art

Hegel remarks somewhere that all great world-historic facts and personages appear, so to speak, twice. He forgot to add: the first time as tragedy, the second time as farce.

—Karl Marx, *The Eighteenth Brumaire of Louis Bonaparte*

This opening statement of the *Brumaire* is a claim not only about the components of history (successive tragedy-farce dyads) but also about how this repetition can be seen as a trope of representation: making appear again of what has passed before. Following up on Chapter 4, genres of acting and action *are* genres of suffering. This is forgotten to the detriment of those who act despite their suffering and those who act on behalf of those who suffer, rendering irrelevant the issue of how action is suffered and how suffering acts beyond our presumptions.

When the flourish from the *Manifesto*—that "the history of all hitherto existing society is the history of class struggles"[5]—is read alongside the opening quote of the *Brumaire*, Marx's encounter with the loss of a historical moment he had himself wanted to make manifest can be acknowledged. The former augured the revolution, while the *Brumaire* is Marx's account of the revolution fought and lost. Together, the quotes raise some questions. If the history of society so far is the history of class struggles, are some struggles tragic and others farcical? Or are world-historic facts and personages of a different nature than the history played out in ongoing class struggles? Is history, then, a sequencing of these tragedy-farce dyads, where one dyad is a farcical representation of another? Or is the very impulse to create a macrocosmic tragedy or farce farcical? Could farce, in its unassuming and ridiculous nature, perhaps be the unwitting spur to depart from macrocosmic genres of history? Are history makings that take world-historical facts and personages to be their material more prone to farce? At the same time, Marx's exclusive reference to the species of "world-historic" events suggests that there are representational endeavors that possibly rely on different material and thus create history in modes not exhausted by tragedy or farce.

My interest here is not in reconciling the *Brumaire* and the *Manifesto* but in how history's tragedy or comedy turns on stories of grand events and personages that serve as fetishes. The 1848 French Revolution tries to reenact the first revolution, aspires to a tried genre of action, and ends up adopting chunks of it entirely detached from their context. An example of this is Robespierre gaining cult status in the nineteenth and twentieth centuries in a manner disjunct from the form of his appeal in the first French revolution. Indeed, the "technology" of cult worship also changes, as the second Bonaparte becomes a public figure through pinups and posters unlike ever before; he is literally commodified through print to forge his public appeal.[6] The material and activity of class struggles is much more varied, intricate, and subtextual than these visible representations. Seeing class struggles as tragic, comic, or farcical may miss that raw reality of suffering and action. In the *Manifesto*, Marx asks that the "present struggle" be confronted in its difference from earlier struggles. It is a struggle of a majority, waged not for privileges, rights, and recognition for an oppressed minority but for winning back the world created by this majority. This recognition may push us to bring an end to the history we know so far—the history of tragedy and farce. The genres themselves have to be transcended.

The *Brumaire* is an account of Marx's own confrontation with a struggle that finds him and other revolutionaries in the midst of a farce despite their best intentions. Any adverse judgment on farce must be withheld. This is because in the fetishes at work in the suffering and making of the farcical revolution, we can find clues to the life that the fetishes inspire. This life inheres in the modes of action available to the revolutionaries and the relations to suffering these modes imply. It is also important not to let the label "farce" say something too conclusive to us about the seriousness or import of the revolution. Genres say much about what they contain, but they also say much about what they do not—the important question is not what the discrete limits of a genre are but how its contents become what they become *by* this containment and what destiny is imposed on the remainder. The genres Marx invokes, and the remainders they suggest, aid in formulating an orientation to suffering that understands better what escapes liberalism's favored genres of human action and subjectivity.

Why Farce?

Had Marx intended a mere mood inversion from one dramatic unfolding of history to another, comedy would be the choice counterpoint
to tragedy. However, farce, not comedy, is featured in the opening
scene of the *Brumaire*. Dante named his poem *La Commedia* in keeping with the following attributes: "In the conclusion, it is prosperous,
pleasant, and desirable"; in its style, "lax and unpretending"; and it is
"written in the vulgar tongue, in which women and children speak."[7]
While their ends and pathos are antonymous, both comedy and tragedy share the features that they are conclusive, and that their ends are
not merely accidental or incidental to their status as genres but an
essential and defining feature of their composition. Additionally, both
tragedy and comedy seem to offer the illusion of actions having gone
wrong, and to rise and fall with the actions of the actors. In both cases,
the denouement that *appears* to be centered on the actions of actors in
fact occurs despite them since the narrative preexists the action.

Farce, however, is connected with laughter rather than with pleas-
antness or happiness. Something farcical is "ludicrously futile or insincere; a hollow pretense, a mockery."[8] It is clear that the juxtaposition
of farce and tragedy has little to do with the joy or sorrow of the ending. Also, the distinction between a happy ending in comedy and the
sole object of exciting laughter in farce is significant; not all happiness
inspires laughter, and, more importantly, not all laughter is joyful. In
this way, farce is liberated from the imperatives of ends and plots, and
from narratives that unfold in a certain way. The relation between
actions and consequences is very loose here, as long as the play produces laughter. Perhaps, in its mockery and ridiculousness, farce is
already a way out of the tragedy-comedy polarity domesticated as a
pain-pleasure polarity.

The etymology of farce is instructive here. "The word farce comes
from the French *farci* or *farcie*, and thence from the Latin *farsa*, or
'stuffed.' In cooking, *farcie* retains its old meaning; more or less any
food, from a pepper to a chicken, that can be hollowed out, leaving a
firm skin or shell, can be stuffed."[9] On the one hand, this shows the
roominess of this genre, devoid of a narrative form that yields a moral
linking the action and the consequences of action internal to the play.
On the other hand, however, when a farce is not willed—such as in
a revolution that does not have ridiculous laughter as its intended
end—the very relation between will, consciousness, and action seems
dysfunctional. The actors themselves incarnate the mockery.

Moreover, there may be something to note in the almost malev-
olent commodiousness of the genre that allows the playwright to

simply stuff different kinds of content into his frame. In the case of revolutionary action (such as the object of study in the *Brumaire*), farce shows that older forms of thought, action, and subjectivity, and certain memories of suffering, can be so tightly held on to that they engulf all possibilities and ruptures that would allow for new content to undo its form and define it anew. The overlaid quality and the capaciousness of old forms only symbolize their very comfortable and convenient oppressiveness. At the same time, the formlessness of whatever the farce cannot hold may presage the overcoming of existing forms.

Tempering Marx's apparent diatribe against the misguided revolutionaries in the *Brumaire* is not an apology for farce. Rather, farce has value for making us visible to ourselves. In being a contrast to old-style tragedy and a spur out of genres altogether, farce allows unsuspected insights into the real struggles and labors of revolution in a way other genres do not. A case in point is the seeming paradox of a liberalism stolidly beholden to the ascetic theater, while at the same time sticking steadfastly to its tragic self-conception. Insofar as Rawls's theatrical enterprise seems far too aware of the performances it demands, and the terms of these performances that radically reconfigure the problem of speaking *for* and *as* oneself and others, it approaches the realm of farce via a tragic structure and an ascetic substance.

This coexistence signals overcoming through the sensuousness it entails. Farce is the genre that entails fetishism and also permits of the possibility and imperative of sensing presences in different ways than the most obvious, literal, and superficial. Given the different levels at which farce "makes sensible," it forces other sensuousnesses to supplant the fetish character it sponsors on the surface. What is it, then, that fetishes force us to remember?

Bodies That Suffer to Matter: Ascetic Priests and Tragic Artists

Invoking tragedy, comedy, and, for that matter, farce, keeps the focus on assessing one's relationship to suffering in terms of emplotment, actions, and end. Even the tragic, for which Nietzsche romances the Greeks, was attached to the end and to the supposedly true meaning of the world declaimed by the pessimists to those who were not pessimists! But Nietzsche is no stock pessimist, bothered as he is by the kinds of declarations smacking of the burdensome certitude of the ascetic priest. Within his morphology of tragic art, there are certainly inklings of the tragic as a continuous sense, an ethos, or even as method. This includes privileging (a) an ordinary relation to ordinary suffering over a narrative focused on the world beyond suffering, (b) a substantial and incarnate relation *to* narrative over a preferred stock narrative, and (c) the spatiality of time over the temporality of space.

The variations and oppositions, on these terms, are not between tragedy and comedy but between tragic art and ascetic priesthood. The ascetic theater brings to light the sensuous modes taken for granted in any performance within liberalism. The ascetic's labor of suffering becomes, in effect, a denial of life—when it posits expedient ideals to put life right and constructs artifices to value, affirm, and protect degenerate forms of life that oppose and exclude "nature, world, the whole sphere of becoming and transitoriness."[10] While both the ascetic priest and the tragic artist create illusions to transform reality, the frenzied aesthetic indeterminacy of the tragic artist's labor constructs new forms not presupposed by her suffering.

The ascetic priest is emblematic of liberalism at its materialist best. In this figure, possessive individualist injury, the body's capacity to suffer, and liberalism's relation to materialism, attempt reconciliation. Seemingly disjointed logics of the possessive individualism of injury and a domesticated materialism of pain come together in the ascetic priest. These logics are disjointed because of the polarities of abstraction and concreteness underpinning each in a nondialectical materialism. The coming together of these logics is apropos of liberalism.

The ascetic priest is a personification of (or an event within) liberalism for several reasons. First, he embodies both the ultimate completion (the *vollkommenheit*) of the possessive individualism of injury, as well as what may seem the subversion of this logic by taking on the pain of others as his own. The lack of mediation between property, injury, and the self completes property, and the ascetic is completely defined by suffering he chooses to consider his own. This way, the suffering may be beholden to the property relation in general but not to property in subjectivity or property in person. The ascetic priest occupies the only subject position capable of transcending the (potential) perpetrator and (potential) victim placeholders, and of embodying suffering beyond simple individualization of harm on the basis of interests and the protection from it. Injury is internalized in a radical refiguring, but not dethroning, of the property relation conventionally understood.

Second, whatever the refiguring, the ascetic priest adheres strictly to the individual subjectivity characteristic of liberalism. He is still an exemplary sufferer, one among many victims, despite his wish to make their sufferings his own, but not without labeling them as victims (of their sins or their utopias). The sufferings of the victims are channeled into an exemplary sufferer who can bear it all, or into an imagined victim (as in the original position). This channeling happens, ironically, when the suffering has to be explained away or held in store to be encashed one day in the hereafter. This resonates, beyond religion, with the secularism of suffering discussed in Chapter 3.

Third, the ascetic priest's embodiment qua possession is complete. Fourth, the experienced pain is still in a dynamic relation to the activity of the ascetic priest. While others' suffering has been domesticated into pain, the ascetic's suffering is the potential material for his labor, completing liberalism's tryst with materialism. The ascetic priest turns out to be the only subject position to articulate the possibility of suffering the pain of, or on behalf of, others. This suffering is in the name of ideals articulated within the liberal paradigm, including the eventual abolition of the very suffering that puts the ascetic into business. The actors in the original position look like faint sketches of this priest.

The only way in which the abstraction of injury is made material and weighted down in liberalism is in this figure. It also provides the template for the very real performances—certainly ordinary versions of the grand performance by the priest—required by liberal justice as it sets up its ascetic theater, general and ubiquitous. However tentative a reconciliation may be effected between possessive individualism and materialism in this figure, accompanying notions of labor and value complicate the property relation and what counts as property. The ascetic priest's taking on of another's suffering certainly forces the concepts of property and injury to confront the complicated activity of installing injury as a fetish and representing one's own and others' suffering. The priest partakes in this process by being the incorporated representation, the personification of the fetish character. The ascetic priest cannot subvert all the conditions, surely; while his ethic of embodiment rearticulates the property relation, it does not undo it. This is because the ascetic liberal sense of justice and the possessive individualism of injury need each other.

When it comes to creating illusions and understanding suffering and memory in an aesthetic way, Nietzsche's notion of tragic art suggests an avenue for exploring what an embodied existence among, and with, fetishes might look like. Nietzsche assigns tragic art the task of creating cultural ideals and new forms in the face of the ongoing and undeniable reality of suffering. This means that the tragic artist denies the vacated comfort of alienation of, and from, memory brought about by disciplinary structures of forgetting that nourish contemporary social orders. She confronts and dialectically engages the knowledge derived from her suffering of reality.

The tragic artist, a purveyor of the faith Nietzsche baptizes as Dionysian, is one who, in her labor of suffering, stands as the life-affirming force in contrast to the life-denying ascetic priest. This character appears in a most defined and definitive form in *Twilight of the Idols*, although an understanding is enriched by borrowing from the discussion of a similar, but not identical, embodiment in *The Birth of Tragedy*.[11]

How does the tragic artist suffer? As an initial hint, let us consider Nietzsche's remark in the *Genealogy*: "Goethe claimed there were only thirty-six tragic situations: one could guess from that, if one did not know anyway, that Goethe was no ascetic priest. He [the priest] knows more."[12] This tells us, first of all, that the tragic artist's exemplary suffering does not depend on an artistic ability to invent tragic situations and painful affects. This is not what characterizes her state of being. Rather, in line with a Dionysian calling, the physiological condition that characterizes her (and is indispensable) is that of frenzy. This frenzy is to be understood more in line with Nietzsche's agonal episteme, such that we can think of it as a contest of forces, instincts, and impulses. The tragic artist is the site of the activity of creation of images, reverie, and ideals that, at the end of the day, are tropes of representation. Here, again, one is forced to revisit the art of the ascetic priest and the kinds of illusions and desire of another world. However insincere and selfish the indulgences of the ascetic priest are, they end up giving many people a reason to live, redeploying their *ressentiment*—a "good" result from incommensurate intentions. The differences between the work of the ascetic and the tragic artist lie in (a) the kind of illusions that are created, (b) the self-conscious and self-proclaimed role played by each (why, in essence, Prometheus is no tragic artist), and (c) the degree of commitment to representation understood mechanistically and primarily as an epistemic enterprise driven toward "truth" and "reality" blessed by dominant ideologies.

The tragic artist does not fetishize reality as the ascetic priest does, even in her act of escaping it. She is always ever implicated within the real world of suffering and joy, and is involved in a task not of "subtracting or discounting the inconsequential" but one driven by the aim of bringing out "the main features so that the others disappear in the process."[13] In my reading, her action is redolent of a representation that transforms—and perhaps only a semantic stone's throw away from the form of the ascetic priest's illusions, which in *his* view may also be a transformation of reality. The art of the tragic artist *is* her praxis, and perhaps what distinguishes her from the priest is that her illusions do not have instrumental value in subservience to the ideal of *merely* existing but that in the very act, in the very labor of her art, and in the very process of creating those representations and illusions, reality—suffering, life, death, the artist herself—gets transformed.

It is also interesting to note that Nietzsche uses forms of the words "sorcerer," "savior," and the like in discussing both the tragic artist and the ascetic priest. While the ascetic priest is the sorcerer in one story, art and *not* the art*ist* is the sorceress in the other. While the ascetic priest is the savior in one story, in the other story, art saves the artist and, through the artist, life. I think an important point can be gleaned from this with regard to liberalism—that it is the chimera of *willful* and *willed* salvation that sustains the ascetic priest and makes his enterprise possible; he is himself the product of his enterprise and a victim, as he is the controller and the redeemer. In a way, his enterprise infects his flock with the illusion and error of the will. On the other hand, the tragic artist does not self-consciously will what is her generosity at the end of the day. It is *art*—and I would here include a more capacious notion of the aesthetic that I have been invoking from the beginning—that acts and transforms. It is her immense fearless yes-saying ability in the face of the fearful and questionable that makes her never escape life as known by the rest of us.

The ascetic priest and the tragic artist both embody and perform their labors of suffering, but they do so in different ways. The transcendence of this dialectic is performed by the ascetic when he turns the pain against himself, even courts suffering in order to triumph over the manifest reality and power of pain, and, in doing so, places himself above himself and his suffering to inhabit a place above his misfortunes in a life of serene (not resigned) activity. In the figure of the tragic artist, however, this transcendence is of a different sort—negating and preserving at the same time in a way that renders the metaphor of being above one's pain too stratospheric for the reality of the tragic artist's art. He indulges this dialectic—engages in it—in order to traverse those stages wherein, after revealing the nausea and absurdity of human life, his will to live is still intact and allows a glimmer of convalescence—his aesthetic creation, including himself as a piece of his art, drives life forward. Both the ascetic priest and the tragic artist are involved in the dialectic between the terror of life and the enlightenment and pleasure of human transcendence and overcoming. But how is one an exemplary sufferer and the other, well, simply the ascetic priest? How does "life *against* life" become "life *for* life"? Or is the very sentence structure replaced, and with it the embedded directionality, goal, and willing *toward*, obviated, too?

Both these figures are involved in an artifice, though of markedly different kinds and substance, which does not, however, undercut the fact that the tragic artist is endowed with a Dionysian insight and wisdom that allows it a privileged knowledge of reality, whereas the ascetic priest's vision and knowledge is almost always complicit with his own lacks and search for purpose. This makes him seek the reality he wants, or better still, install a reality without ever budging on the claims to truth of his installed illusions. It is precisely because of her pact with reality that the tragic artist needs to make possible a scenario where she can submit herself to the law she herself proposes, aware of her limitations and the status of her illusions, and with the knowledge that her illusions stem from her knowledge through suffering and not by rejecting it.

While the ascetic wishes to give suffering meaning, saving it from the injury of meaninglessness and exchanging it for goods, the tragic artist confronts the confounding coexistence of profundity and mean-inglessness of suffering. The latter seeks to enable suffering to appre-hend its meaninglessness and not desire meaning when it most needs it. Nietzsche's tragic artist constructs illusions to make life livable, but those illusions are not hallucinatory, self-deceiving, or meaning to detract from reality (like the illusions of the 1848 revolutionaries were). In the work of the historical materialist, these illusions are the constructions of the form and content of history itself—of memory and of forgetting.

When tragic art is considered a practice, and a lived relation to one's own and others' suffering, tragedy's status as *the* genre for his-tory making or for seeing our own or another's suffering as an event is challenged. This happens because the relation of tragic art to suffering obviates the playing of assigned roles. Nietzsche's tragic artist is not meant to be exemplary in the artistic ability to invent tragic situations and painful affects, because that is what a tragedian does. The artifices of suffering ought not to be the domain of a master sufferer at all—they are ordinary, uneventful, and survive amid and within fetishes. Denying tragedy and accepting tragic art is to also deny the culmi-nating (dare I say affirmative) moment of the historical materialist's art form. Also, it is an overcoming of the familiar self-important and transcendent function of art, where an artist incarnates herself as the creator and is accountable only to a god complex.

For Nietzsche, the ascetic and the tragic artist are not mere antagonists—they are variations on a theme if subversion is to be understood dialectically. *Askesis* and *aisthesis* both denote modes of corporeality, relations to pain and suffering, and particular arts and labors of suffering. None is beholden to the luxury of the chorus or the pit. The priest and the artist stand to be seen less as characters in a scripted stage play than as modes of relating to suffering, of enacting stories, and of relating to them. Deindividualizing and desubjectifying the roles of the ascetic priest and the tragic artist allows them to coexist as modalities (much like what can be argued for Nietzsche's master and slave moralities), and ethical life then constitutes not simply picking and choosing what mode to adopt from one day to another, but sensing, recognizing, and suffering their coexistence itself as an aesthetic, ethical, and political labor.

Reply to Judith Shklar: The Case of Fairly Honorable Defeats

What does a tragic relation to one's and another's suffering and to stories and storytelling yield in terms of a newly figured politics of suffering? I find that Shklar's spirit must be summoned once again, and Murdoch brought in to highlight some key affinities and divergences that take us further on the path of apprehending a materialist tragic ethos.

Both Shklar and Murdoch inhabit a world of the senselessness, indeterminacy, and ordinariness of suffering where the regimes of life and politics thrive on the invisibility of countless injustice and those who suffer them. They both focus on the defeated, value liberal tolerance (in Murdoch's case, the decent, tolerant spirit of English political institutions), and take for granted the injustice of political oppression.

The sources of their philosophy and moral psychology may have something to do with these differences. Shklar owes hers to the classical liberals, while Murdoch constellates a liberal, Protestant tradition deriving from Kant and Mill with the moral psychology of Sartre and Weil. They both work with a certain separation of spheres, but Shklar's distinction between the private qua personal, and public qua political, spheres works in different ways than Murdoch's separation of the moral and the political. The latter almost allows a different and better permutation of the conservative, liberal, and antiliberal sensibilities to provide material for a materialist orientation to suffering (even though Murdoch is avowedly antimaterialist).

I am inclined to allow Murdoch's ethics and aesthetics more potency and antecedence than her politics. The contradictions between her vision of a novel as "a house fit for free characters to live in"[14] on the one hand, and the role of necessity and accident in the lives of her characters that render them unfree or differently free on the other hand are fruitful; they spotlight questions of space and time in relation to suffering and challenge freedom defined in a liberal utilitarian way. ("The character Bledyard in *The Sandcastle* defines freedom, rather like Weil does, as a 'total absence of concern about yourself.'"[15]) In other words, Murdoch is liberal in less important ways than she is not, especially when compared to Shklar, whose consistency and whose allegiance to liberalism encapsulates everything (rather like the stuffed skin of "farce" we spoke of earlier) and gravely erodes her spirit.

The way Murdoch's and Shklar's impatience with injustice manifests itself roughly parallels Murdoch's distinction between the play and the novel. Liberalism, exemplified by Shklar, relies on the high drama of suffering even when it confronts its ordinariness and invisibility, fetishizing cruelty as the worst thing we do and focusing on public injustices that ultimately bring the discussion back to the dramatic cause of the suffering. Murdoch's artistry is that of a novelist, and her focus on suffering and injustice is more suffusive, more truly in tune with the ordinariness of these experiences, which makes it the task of the artist to grant them their singularity amid their generality.

This flows into how both these thinkers—in interesting counterpoints to Bachmann—suffer their encounter with the invisibility of injustice and victims. In my view, Shklar and Murdoch differ on *what* it is they make visible, which invokes an aspect of Apollonian wisdom in Greek tragedy, their relation to tragedy working here at the level of their sensual labors. Ocular metaphors are central to the work of both.[16]

But where Shklar exposes or willfully wears blinders in her acceptance of her own liberal limits, Murdoch *attends*. The difference is in sensibility, imagination, and aesthetics. And since they both see themselves as students and practitioners of moral psychology, these are significant differences that orient them very differently to the debate about representation and the naming of victims broached in the previous chapter. The key may be entirely in their artifice and in their modes of inquiry, presentation, and representation: in the difference between liberal and postliberal aesthetics and ethos; in their relations to poetry (with a merely linguistic and analytical relation to language on the one hand and a more world-creating relation on the other); and in their embrace of tragedy as either a wish to define or an abstinence from defining. Exposure requires a naming, while attention does not—the latter has an element of reverence, a particular attunement to the *how* of language and sensing, a humility that the fiercely antiutopian vision of Shklar cannot bear to feel or is too wary of capturing.

Murdoch owes her moral psychological bent to Sartre. Liberalism and Sartre's existentialism share a focus on the subject, however contrarian in relation to each other, and end up bloating it. She also takes from him two opposing things: the ability to love anyone (derived from Sartre's self-chosen man) and to, at the same time, desire a true unselfing to be authentic. From Weil, she gets the idea that freedom has little or no relation to will or choice; suffering makes us self-absorbed in a way that the right attitude is to unself or decreate ourselves. As long as the question of suffering remains connected to will, and agency is understood in the terms of choice, then we cannot really understand the tragic as ultimately reforming our understanding of willing and of suffering.

In Murdoch's tragic embrace of contingency and necessity, and in her turn to honoring contingencies and particularities, I find ingredients of a materialist approach to suffering—a form and content of suffering and a relation to our own and others' suffering—that challenges the liberal injury enterprise and allows a different kind of representative praxis than liberal representation and postmodern critiques of the same.[17] Murdoch's worry about the self-absorbed nature of suffering ushers the imperative of unselfing—a direct response to the liberal possessive individualism of injury. However, this unselfing also has to be considered in a dialectical and materialist way. This much can be said of Murdoch in the words of David Gordon, before introducing a materialist additive: "Unselfing, after all, admits of degrees. Sometimes, it is a severe imperative, a yielding of the human to 'death,' blankness and silence. Sometimes it is a question, rather, of correcting one's own vision within and ordinary world and indeed, in good humanist fashion, of accepting responsibility for a more truthful, less egoistic understanding, even if this means a retreat from the highest good."[18]

Just as the problem of agency and the victim perspective were illustrated as being connected, the response to those also comes intertwined, and Murdoch affirms as much. I believe she needs just a dose of the materialist understanding of sensuousness and suffering that has been brewing in this project. When Murdoch brings up unselfing as an imperative, it is linked inextricably to love, to the ability to *see* the other in all its particularities. It is partially her strand of Platonism, and partially her reaction to materialism qua behaviorism and vulgar empiricism, which allows her to frame her notion of attention in a way that reifies the thought-action dichotomy. Her most elevated sense, vision, *is* sensuous activity and not pure thought—where thought itself is a material activity because it is an assemblage and effect of our sensuousness. This is another moment whereby the problem of Shklar's empiricism surfaces and runs into the dialectically opposed problem with Murdoch. Such liberal materialism cannot be opposed by a Platonic internalism. The materialism itself should be dialectically extended into the space between thought and action, between the activity and the process of representation. Hers is the Plato of the *Phaedo*, wherein we get a glimpse of a possibly dynamic protomaterialism, not unlike the tension between the body and soul in the cave in Plato's *Republic*, the soul itself as material (not unlike the very material nature of imagination in Hobbes; only matter decays, and imagination, for Hobbes, is decaying sense). If we broaden her attack on behaviorism to include those materialisms that fetishize and congeal the materiality they can grasp, and also those idealisms that consider only the materiality of certain kinds of activity to the exclusion of others, we would quickly approach the kind of materialism for which I am arguing.

Murdoch can be transported beyond the thought-action dichotomy, where attention is not an internal mental disposition but our sensual labor. That would make the notions of defeat, honor, and grace much less merely intellectual. Nietzsche and Marx both, on their own, give rather satisfying solutions to the problem: Nietzsche, by relating suffering to vision and Apollonian art to the wisdom of seeing; Marx, by making theory practical and talking about social humanity. Murdoch, if an idealist, is still able to recognize fetishes and is able to theorize, in line with Marx, the ground of, on one hand, the ability and responsibility of installing and destroying fetishes and, on the other, of temporal, historical necessity.

An overcoming of the outmoded genre of tragedy in and through human action requires an embrace of a kind of materialist ethos that is indebted to what Murdoch calls real and incomplete tragedy, *not* the eventful and commensurable tragedy of liberal justice. This ethos inheres three elements: a notion of necessity rather than the impossibility of desire and choice; a sense of hope that is not served for the comfort of the powerful and privileged; and sensuousness, individual and social, attuned to the many layers of materialities of suffering and representation. These elements of a historical materialist reframing of the subjectivity of those who suffer, are also premises of new imaginations of justice beyond the ascetic or tragic modes of guilt, redressal, or agentist redemption.[19] I address these in the next section.

ELEMENTS OF A HISTORICAL
MATERIALISM OF SUFFERING

Necessity

He never manages to conceive the sensuous world as the total living sensuous activity of the individuals composing it; and therefore when, for example, he sees instead of healthy men a crowd of scrofulous, overworked and consumptive starvelings, he is compelled to take refuge in the "higher perception" and in the ideal "compensation in the species," and thus to relapse into idealism at the very point where the communist materialist sees the necessity, and at the same time the condition, of a transformation both of industry and the social structure.

—Marx on Feuerbach in *The German Ideology*

Marx's categories of prefiguration were the categories of schism, division and alienation. The historical process, therefore, appeared to him as that "panorama of sin and suffering." His purpose was to determine the extent to which one can realistically hope for the ultimate integration of the forces and objects that occupy the historical field.

—Hayden White on Marx in *Metahistory*

Proletarian revolutions like those of the nineteenth century constantly criticize themselves, constantly interrupt themselves in their own course, return to the apparently accomplished, in order to begin anew; they deride with cruel thoroughness the half-measures, weaknesses, and paltriness of their first attempts, seem to throw down their opponents only so the latter may draw new strength from the earth and rise before them again more gigantic than ever, recoil constantly from the indefinite colossalness of their own goals—until a situation is created which makes all turning back impossible.

—Marx and Dionysus in *The Eighteenth Brumaire of Louis Bonaparte*

Necessity is not only a key element of tragedy but also a hinge for overcoming it as genre, en route to a historical materialist understanding of suffering. Liberalism frames tragic necessity as the irreconcilability of various wants, and our surrender of what we would really, really love to have. It shows, despite itself, that these necessities are not "natural" or without history. Liberalism equates necessity with tragic unfreedom, especially when it comes to taking action amid bad choices, and when it uses it to justify submission to a utilitarian calculus or to a different abstract principle of action. This concept of necessity is, however, less a mediator, a consequence, or an obstructer of free action than a self-contained material force. It emerges as the main actor that cuts through a lament over bad choices and confused wills in order to reach the suffering that is, and arises from, the absence of choice—necessity itself. And, then, when hope is understood in relation to this necessity, it becomes the lived imperative to make necessities into conditions for the possibility of transformation. In an ontic bond to suffering, hope ceases to be caught in a mutually excluding relation to memory and nostalgia.

Marx's note on Feuerbach brings up both necessity and condition, and poses necessity in terms of the activity that yields a transformation of the social structure. For Marx, the suffering is the condition as well as the necessity for this to occur. Necessity in liberalism (with or without the mediation of need) is cognate with scarcity as a precept of capitalist economics. As discussed in Chapter 1, Murdoch goes a step further and finds the scarcity more pervasive as a disposition in societies that reify individuals and their others (individuals or institutions) in conflict with each other on the basis of this scarcity. When liberalism, through its sensitivity and commitment to cruelty, pain, and fear, invokes the boundedness of our individualities through injury and harm, it remains caught within the conditions of interiorized scarcity.

Scarcity, the basic precept of popular economics, is a construct supported by the institution of private property. Recall, here, that scarcity is invoked in relation to human needs that must be met, and that economics concerns itself with the distribution of scarce resources to fulfill these needs. The form of need figured in the story of scarcity, and hence scarcity of choices, is private, positivist, abstract, and generalizable. In the regime of liberal juridical politics, the possessive individualism of injury is coeval with this scarcity, experienced by sufferers as, for one, the state's inability to do justice as it abandons mostly those in need when it is either unable to sense their suffering or does not want to.

To return to Kushner on this note, Prior Walter's demand for more life brings up necessity again in terms of the actions of suffering. Necessity conjures a sense of compulsion and has a built-in temporal, transitive element—one of a history of needs and of the hope that new needs replace old ones and that life-affirming suffering replace the superfluous suffering and injustice for which no tragic philosophy worth its name must have any tolerance. Necessity carries a more loaded temporality than need does, like the imperative for conditions to change or for certain scarcities and sufferings that pervade time one way to pervade it differently or travel elsewhere. Need (as a more spatial iteration), necessity (as a more historical, temporal one), and their definitions and temporalities must be admitted for a rethinking. One premise of my rethinking is the suspicion that while liberal tragedy keeps its declared and public focus on action, it is greatly invested in willfully and disparately valuing and revaluing the needs and necessities on which this action is based. What if the past being looked toward, whether real or fictive, is incapable of consoling? What if there are no previous gains to be lost, unlike the story that Marx tells in the *Brumaire*? This inspires consideration of the lived experience of necessity in relating to a past that allows no refuge at all and does not console.

Marx's critique of labor is not of some fixed or timeless substance, but of the form labor takes and the relations and aspects of life it infects, infests, and colonizes within capitalism. Talal Asad cautions against missing the realities of colonialism and imperialism in this scheme. He wants us to consider geopolitics in order to understand how capital's political and evolutionary needs craft, among other things, the frozen spatialized temporality called the nation. The inhabitants of the frozen space-times are dispatched their isolated narratives and national histories, and prescribed their experience of time in relation to others who labor similarly or differently. This allows the causes of suffering to be distended from the effects. Responsibility and redemption are relegated to the domain of nations whose suffering, first, may not have causes constrained by concocted national boundaries or the time of their "independent" existences, or second, would not have even taken this form if it were not for global powers and their actions. Needs, deprivations, and sufferings that are nationalized, localized, and necessitated by those in power have to be examined for this reason, their structural locations parsed out, and their neat geographical distributions questioned.[20]

Given the historicality of notions of labor and forms of sensuousness, and of necessities that sufferers confront, it is important not only to appreciate multiple modes of sensuous existence and compulsions to action but also to see the privileged ones as historical and necessarily replaceable with time and history on our side. Part of this requires seeing modes of acting out of suffering, and acting out our sufferings, as being requisite for certain moments, but not without the necessity that they give way to other modes. If tragic heroic agency is part of an era's defenses against its own realities, then one task of political practice is to help us see our sufferings and our actions, our victimhoods and our agencies, in this light. Political practice must help discover and nurture the ability to suffer. This necessity recalls the fact that tragedy had an enormous function in the life of those (such as the ancient Greeks) who knew little of the kind of suffering and strife that beset humanity in the epochs that followed or that dwelt in the periphery of the polis (this is not a question of quantity but kind), allowing us to take a close look at the kind of suffering that Marx finds almost ontological to humans. The abundant systemic injury, alienation, and exploitation that form the core experience of the majority of humanity today need to be kept from becoming an ontological condition. In this way, the claim "to be [sensuous] is to suffer" takes on an interesting normative meaning. Suffering and injury would be overcome only in terms of an implicit *telos* of recovering the human capacity to be and to suffer in ways our current injuries keep estranged from us, and of creating the conditions for this to happen.

The Swerving Atom—Hope, in Service of What and Whom?

With respect to how the wounded act, materialist necessity, understood as the condition of possibility, becomes coeval with hope and keeps it from being a mere escape from given conditions. Marx's trysts with necessity begin as he grapples with Democritus and Epicurus in his doctoral dissertation. Democritus's empiricism brings necessity to light. Epicurus's "scorn [toward] the inexorable necessity of physicists" holds on to chance, to the accidental, with not even syntactical room (in the form of the disjunctive) to acknowledge any concept of necessity.[21] For Marx, the dualities familiar to both are in need of questioning; irritated with their "polemical irritation," he writes, "The purpose of action is to be found, for Epicurus . . . in abstracting, swerving away from pain and confusion, in ataraxy. Hence the good is the flight from evil, pleasure the swerving away from suffering. Finally, where abstract individuality appears in its highest freedom and independence, in its totality, there it follows that the being which is swerved away from, is all being."[22]

The removal of time from the realm of the sensuous atoms keeps us marginal to the world of becoming that Epicurus appreciates. Becoming becomes necessity, to which we respond only by opting out, as oxymoronic as that sounds. So while Epicurus is able to grasp the philosophy of nature better than anyone before him, his atomism allows him to place our selves out of nature, where we are free only in our defiance of the motion of nature. The problem is not merely the opposition, but whether the opposition is considered to be dialectical or absolute. This potential dialectic allows Marx to call for a humanization of nature and a naturalization of human sensuousness.

Real possibility, for Marx, is comparable to intellect and thus more bounded, in contrast to abstract possibility, which, like imagination, is relatively unbounded. While real possibility "seeks to explain the necessity and reality of its object" and keeps its relation with its dialectical opposite, "abstract possibility is not interested in the object which is explained, but in the subject which does the explaining." Marx adds, "The object need only be possible, conceivable. That which is abstractly possible, which can be conceived, constitutes no obstacle to the thinking subject, no limit, no stumbling-block." The reason for, and goal of, abstract possibility is "the tranquility of the explaining subject."[23]

Given liberalism's incapacity for time, it wavers between a Democritean embrace of static realism and an Epicurean wish for deliverance through abstract possibility for a swerve from pain into ataraxy. In so doing, liberalism avoids agon, understood narrowly in a Hobbesian way, and rejects any becoming through it. In Chapter 1, liberal toleration was likened to precisely this wishful *ataraxia*, an imperturbability that, by positing happiness as lack of agon, takes to detachment and "passive" peace in the autonomous, private sphere. Marx wants necessity to reclaim precisely those aspects of Democritus and Epicurus that liberalism cordons off. The swerve must be a grounded one—unafraid and embracing of the matter that has weight and that resists, worried whether the dead will be able to bury themselves. Their insistence on burying the dead, on completing stories that do not have endings, should make us suspicious of those who want to leave the room hopeful and purged. Hope is more precious and more abundant at the same time. But it is tempting to throw it out with liberal amnesia and the assurances all our ethical and moral caretakers keep extracting from us. This especially happens when someone else's hope means a kind of tolerance for, and complacency (often thus complicity) with, injustice. If the swerve of the atom is the repository of hope, is hope not actually the negation of what feeds the liberal penchant for conclusiveness, for eventfulness, and for consoling stories with ends (consoling because they have ended)?

This incapacity for, even plunder of, time native to liberalism and other undialectical metaphysics is the hallmark of the forever new world. With so much space for the "new," history and memory matter little. However, history and memory are not left alone either. American space eats history up, without a burp. When the angel of America appears to Prior, he offers him the golden tablet and prophethood, in a riff on the story of Joseph Smith.[24] Prior ultimately rejects this offering that symbolizes how the state and religion thrive on the collusive redemptions they grant to someone's suffering. Moreover, this calls for some consideration of the spatial coordinates of revelation and prophethood in America: on the one hand, this is the new world that became home to the most persecuted religious groups that would now be free to set up their cities on the hill; on the other hand, this is the longstanding conceit, relived in different ways in war and in peace, of America as the center of the universe, only helped by Joseph Smith finding out that this is where both Eden and the promised land lay.

This is not a jab at any particular religious narrative. Even less is it a question of veracity or legitimacy. Discursive repercussions and ironies are involved in any ideological construct, truth, and, for that matter, any narrative that features hope as culmination, and these are worth absorbing. America's signature penchant for insistent proclamation, reclamation, unwriting, and rewriting of a history finds a comical vehicle in the arguments made for Prior's prophethood over the course of the said act. Prior Walters from other lands and times appear in an allegory to the prophets whose origin and location the keen, hopeful, and faithful Americanism of the Joseph Smith story supplants. All this to make it okay for Prior to take up the mantle of prophethood and to lose no sleep over America's determination of the location of revelation and prophecy. This episode is entirely at home among the antics with time and space that shape America's psychic and geopolitical dominion. It is also continuous with America's insatiable appetite for hope after making a travesty of everyone else's history, not to mention its own.

Not only is the garnering of historical narrative in the work of the angels and ghosts that appear to Prior significant and symbolic, but Prior's rejection of the messages is meaningful, too. This rejection is of the shackling narrative of the suffering god, a narrative that continues to bind the liberal state and even makes it possible despite the departure of God from the state. This narrative validates the liberal state as an underperforming savior who keeps having us claim our injuries and assure it that we are okay. Prior denies the state the comfort of his prophethood—the comfort that he is among those who have been accounted for. Septimus made a different, yet very similar, choice. Picky about what he or someone else can do with or to his suffering, Prior, like Septimus, rejects the recognition that the state provides for its own sake, with a host of presumptions about what a sufferer needs, and how best the suffering should be interpreted, logged, dissipated, and absorbed. Prior is unwilling to accept a redemption if it costs him

his life or his ability to demand for more life, retaining his preroga-
tive to not submit to the state's construals of the meaning of life and
death. The question is thrown back at those who define the "problem" of suffering and decorate themselves with its solutions, impotent
in the face of Priors who continue to ask for more life and a right to
define life and death in the first place.

Immediacies, experience, and thought all stand to change with
this recovery of time, as the case of Democritus and Epicurus shows.
There are many moments in *Angels in America* where Louis's appall-
ing linguistic confessions of vulnerability seem of a piece with his
heady abstract intellectualism, and where Prior's charm *seems* to be
not merely in his authenticity but in his unrelenting empiricism. However, these characters disallow such neat alliances: theory and thought
are redeemed as being hardly captive to Louis's idealism, and Prior
hardly cuts a figure betrothed to vulgar materialism and immediacies.
Both are able to surface from these dualities because they redeem time
and temporality, reinsinuating it within their different epistemologies.
It is through this, and only this, redemption that the play provides
hope—by its gesture of compensation for the paucities that make
America's insecure arrogance of space possible, promising the possibility of a release from its hold. Not surprisingly, those who suffer the
most, and those who are most marginal and outcast, are most capable
of making painful pacts and trusting friendships with time that all the
wimps—Louis, Joe, Roy Cohn—cannot.

Sensual Recoveries: New Orientations to Suffering and Representation

Besides enabling us to see our own and others' victimhood and subjectivities in a way that honors the imperatives—to act, in hope—that
suffering posits for those who suffer, a historical materialism of suffering must be able to encompass many relations to memory and
many relations to hope in their essential incompleteness, absurdity,
and realness. It must run counter to the paradigms that, in relying
on bounded possessive individualities, either renders the suffering
readable as injury and harm or distances the suffering by deeming it
authentically inaccessible as the sublime or too private. By considering the materiality of sense experience in a manner that departs from
these existing liberal paradigms, it may help reframe the mandates
and stakes of the aesthetic, the political, and the ethical in relation to
each other.

Dispossessing Representation

> *Wittgenstein's example of my pain inhabiting your body seems to me to suggest either the institution that the representation of shared pain exists in imagination but is not experienced, in which case one would say that language is hooked rather inadequately to the world of pain. Or, alternately, that the experience of pain cries out for this response of the possibility that my pain could reside in your body and that the philosophical grammar of pain is an answer to that call.*

> —Veena Das, "Language and Body: Transactions in the Constructions of Pain," *Social Suffering*

> *In her [Veena Das's] use of Wittgenstein's example of "feeling pain in the body of another," a passage that no one, to my knowledge, has put to more creative, nor sounder, use. I take Wittgenstein's fantasy in that passage as a working out of Descartes' sense that my soul and my body, while necessarily distinct, are not merely contingently connected. I am necessarily the owner of my pain, yet the fact that it is always located in my body is not necessary. This is what Wittgenstein wishes to show—that it is conceivable that I locate it in another's body. That this does not in fact, or literally, happen in our lives means that the fact of our separateness is something that I have to conceive, a task of imagination—that for me to know your pain, I cannot locate it as I locate mine, but I must let it happen to me. My knowledge of you marks me; it is something that I experience, yet I am not present to it, as in the experience (as Veena Das cites from Julia Kristeva) of giving birth.*

> —Stanley Cavell, "Comments on Veena Das's Essay 'Language and Body: Transactions in the Constructions of Pain,'" *Social Suffering*

Attempts to balance out the emphasis on the doer of harms in liberal theory by bringing in the perspective of the victim often either call upon the language of "perspective" in liberal diversity or ally with a compensatory antiknowledge stance familiar in, for instance, postcolonial and postmodern feminist critiques of the essential violence of knowledge.[25] These moves raise important issues of complicity. Ironically, they both affirm that we can only speak for ourselves and for our own suffering.

It may, or need, not be so. When Nietzsche addresses perspective in relation to suffering, he talks about senses that suffer to make the sufferer no longer see the world in the same way.[26] A perspectivism conceived following Nietzsche thus challenges the claim that only a possessive individualist perspective can be had on suffering. First, it encourages imagining the task of sensing the world in different ways and also understanding and performing affective and sensual labors differently. Thinking of the activity and social nature of suffering subjects us in a different way to the suffering of others and to the articulation(s) of our own suffering. Second, depending on how suffering is understood, either as the fetish of injury or as something of a broader undergoing of the senses, the sobering up, in which Nietzsche implicates the sufferer, can be posited as a shared process. This broadens the claim of Rousseauian sympathy by not restricting compassion to a translation and a mirroring, a dignified narcissism, at best, but by seeing compassion as a sensing and undergoing that brings into being *with* someone. As discussed in Chapters 2 and 5, the lack of ability to *take* the perspective of the victim already misstates the task and the stakes, and assumes the logic of possessive individualist injury.

If, to continue the discussion framed in the beginning of this chapter, the ascetic priest radically refigures the possessive individualism of injury, then tragic art can be posited as able to subvert the possessive relation altogether. What Marx means by social humanity in the tenth thesis on Feuerbach corresponds to such a common sensuousness.[27] This speaks to the work of senses that straddles the boundaries of bodies, and at least opens up questions unto what can be felt and for whom, and why a private (and) proprietary relation to pain (and joy) is so easily assumed. Sensuousness, when understood as such a species labor, recognizes itself in the fetish of injury and engages with the world in a simultaneity-oriented way.[28] In attending to the world, it is able to remember *for* the fetish and remember it *as* the fetish it is. As Murdoch points out, such an unpossessive relation necessitates a mystical element, an element of infusing the ordinary and the senseless with a certain kind of passion.[29] On that note, in opposition to the liberal mantra of scarcity, and to the abuse of scarcity as the occasion for liberalism's tragedy, the tragic artist does not interiorize scarcity like the ascetic priest must.

The question of possession, as featured in the possessive individualism of injuries, needs further examining, especially since some of the inviolable premises of property become suspect when merged too neatly with the experience of suffering. An instance is the relation to the suffering of bodies, whether our own or others', that can allow us to be a bit more wary of the autonomy, agentism, triumphalism, and confidence of owning one's own suffering either as completely alienable or completely inalienable.

The cases of unskilled labor and the reserve army of the unemployed exemplify capitalism's needed simplifications of the labor power that enters the calculus, the process being sustained by members of a class who "possess nothing but the ability to work."[30] In the case of the fetishism of injuries, liberal justice and politics requires victims and injury in order to keep itself in commission. This reserve army of the (dis)possessed comprises those who possess nothing but their injury, and are reducible to it; those who are possessed by their ability to survive; those whose sufferings do not make it into the category of injury; and those whose suffering is cheapened so much, once valued, that they will sell it for anything.

It is debatable whether this motley army survives its state of injury by dint of good calculus, thus embodying the dicta of Hobbes and Bentham, or whether its very existence fiercely refutes those dicta. The latter would be a case of clever, though blatant, disingenuity of liberalism's preoccupation with death and injury, whether in the state of nature or in the preoccupation with cruelty, or in the inescapable tragedy of juridical calculi. These limit cases provide the rationale for liberal institutions only because liberalism can count on those who will survive, just like those whose very ability to subsist makes surplus value possible.[31]

The notion of "dispossession," in the case of victims, tells of the roles, the voicings, and the performance itself. Veena Das and Arthur Kleinman write,

> Possession places emphasis on the being of the possessing agency or the person who is possessed's experience of being taken over, becoming a medium for that god, ghost, demon, or ancestor. Dispossession, in contrast, refers to an experience of splitting in cognitive and affective states so that the person becomes nearly completely absorbed in that focus. During dispossession what is inner and inexpressible can be projected outward into a culturally authorized voice. We do not wish to imply that there is a completed hidden script in the inner life that is simply waiting to be projected. Rather, the states of dispossession are able to provide the external criteria by which the person traumatized by violence can overcome the suffocation of speech. Language does not function purely as a medium of communication but is also to be viewed as experience which allows not only a message but also the subject to be projected outwards.[32]

This highlights the sophomoric quality of suspicions of representation that arise from a yearning for immediacy equated with absolute possession, and further pushes exploration of the metaphor of acting in talking about the aesthetic element of representation. The terms possession and dispossession together bring to mind "the actor's problem" in theater theory. The actor's problem is the dilemma between the impersonation necessary for all acting, on the one hand, and the fact that the success of the acting lies in how natural the impersonation is, on the other.[33]

A short detour through the paradigm of method acting provides an interesting counterpoint to the forms of acting deemed inevitable for representation. Method acting allows insight into the problems inherent to any understanding of representation or speaking *as*, and even *for*, oneself or the other, especially outside of a script and outside of the possibility of a fixed, determinate object of knowledge and understanding (in this case, the fetish character in the script).[34] Politics and real lives do not lend themselves to such luxuries. Different forms of acting as frame the ethics of representation differently. In method acting, acting as happens when the actor mines her own memory of experiences and is repossessed by them when the moment comes for her to deliver her performance. Imagination plays a crucial role, obviously, and it involves not only conjuring a set of conditions but subjecting surrounding objects to the "method" as well, where they become embodiments of their own (imagined) history.[35]

Characterized by attention to the intricacies of the character and by the effort to artifice out of the materials of one's own particular memories and experiences and the commonality of human existence, the method rests in the ability to empathize, even to raze oneself, in order to bring to presence the other. The key features are the importance of affective memory, artistry beyond the script, and the importance of action in creating emotion. Especially important is the centrality of the ensemble, where the ability to listen is more important than the wish to wait for the moment to deliver one's lines or have the other done with theirs. All are clues to what representation may involve, what it takes to act or speak *as*. The precepts of method acting suggest that liberalism even misunderstands impersonation—that is, the acting as. Then, acting for and speaking for may learn from this and, in debates on representation, cease to be simply superior to acting as and speaking as, on the one hand, or dismissable, on the other. When Rawls theorizes the acting in the original position, he sets limits for what he *considers to be* the raw material for the representation. He fundamentally does not understand the nature of this material and its relation to the sufferings to which it owes its life, and to the sufferings it is trying to channel into the original position.

A romance for authenticity and immediacy, conditioned by possessive individualism, also has implications for representation's possibilities. Such romance of immediacy has roots in the discourse of modern liberal individualism that feels requited when everyone speaks for, and as, themselves. Method acting's framing of acting as also reveals what is at stake when we criticize representation for its negation of immediacy. The removal of the space between the representer and the represented (as is the tendency of representations that represent *as*) keeps representation from being seen for the dialectical process it is, with subject and object not simply restricted to those positions.

Bertolt Brecht's understanding of acting is different, mindful of an excess and of something beyond the perfect personification. This is in opposition to conventional tragedy, as well as to the moments of immediate realism provided within a Stanislavskian paradigm. Both Brecht and Stanislavsky see the political consequences of theater—while the former employs the alienation that is an element of a fetishistic society, the latter puts into use the common sense that has kept the fetish in commission.[36]

According to Marx, communist materialism foregrounds the question of sensuousness as ontological *and* epistemological, one because of the other.[37] Treating suffering not as object requires insinuating a relation to it at the level of sensuousness. Sensuous proclivities are epistemological proclivities. Perhaps it is the character of the fetish to clog senses in a way that allows other channels of sensing to become impossible, but it is also the fetish that allows itself to be seen as such, etched within systemic oppression and a hegemonic regime of sensing and suffering our own and others' existences. To return to the questions raised in Chapter 3 by the disability-adjusted life years (DALYs) measure and the sublime events of suffering, how does beholding a statistic or a picture make distinctions that occlude something in order to make something else visible? What do we see when we see an injury? What do we hear when we hear a silence, a testimony, or someone speaking the language of law? It is at such moments that the very division of labor of senses is exposed as lodged within power structures that make dependent and independent variables of what we see and hear, and decide if and how they will be measured and in what units.

Even the recognition of injury as a fetish and an abstraction makes possible the additional step—that of finding the source of the fetish in our labors and our sufferings. The fetish may tell, once its amnesia is bore through, a lot about where we lie in the structural division of the labors of suffering. It may reveal not only who does or does not get to speak but also in what ways; whose screams, let alone silences, do not get heard; who gets heard without even an utterance; and equally important, who names the feelings that are had and decides what can and cannot be felt. More fundamentally, it may reveal how sensual labors are divided among us. When suffering is seen in this way, a materialist imperative involves not only attending to the fact of suffering created but also to how people suffer. In such an approach, the spoken is a reminder of why it is the spoken and what is unsaid, the seen a reminder of why it is the seen and what is unseen, and the spoken and the seen reminders of *who we are as the sayers and the seers*. Seeing the fetishes as active in the world allows an appreciation of the material that interacts with the fetish and bears its marks, with a history and a life not subsumed by the fetish.

Living Suffering's Labors

> *The novelist must kill the hero.*
>
> —Iris Murdoch, *Sartre, Romantic Rationalist*

Even when liberal thinkers push the envelope to register ordinary, ubiquitous, and invisible injustices, they sustain a frame of human action fashioned along an outdated and ahistorical understanding of agency and heroic tragic action. Carrying the burden of the Enlightenment that remained shackled to religion's obsession with limit cases—whereby suffering had to be glorious and eventful to strike the same nerves and to consume the space vacated by god—liberalism displays a singular and consistent partiality to the eventful, the extraordinary, and the sublime in suffering (as discussed in the Introduction). This interesting paradox in the sensuous and epistemological—thus political—propensities of liberalism occurs every time an ideology so deeply invested in suffering is so readily awestruck by it, and when liberal imaginations get easily flustered in the face of the suffering that does not fit in with their usual scales. It is now time to see how the course this inquiry has taken refigures this particular aesthetic-ethical-political moment.

The "purely" aesthetic nature of the sublime in Kant's work, and its qualitative beyondness from recordable, calculable experience, can be seen as an evacuation of its politics as well. The delimitation of injury to the sphere of harms caused by humans to other humans is in concert with the sublime as the beyond. This *beyond* may be *beyond politics*. Here, politics—reduced to what human beings control (where control and cause are coextensive with each other)—affirms a language concerned only with actions that cause suffering and with certain kinds of compensation. If our closeness to fellow beings, our ability to suffer with and for them, and the possibility for claiming redress are all conditional on representations of the sublime, then this is an instance of crisis itself—an old-fashioned tragedy, with human hubris resulting in bad stuff we never planned for. Ironically, representing the sublime is an oxymoron for Kant and hardly the condition of the possibility of hope or redress that he wants. Precisely due to the promise of its unrepresentability, the sublime has it within itself to be a prototype of a notion of species-being in the aesthetic realm. But when it is surrendered to the regime of liberal representation, the possibilities of seeing within it more than shock and awe dwindle, for it becomes tethered to the autonomous individualism that is a requisite of liberal law, politics, and morality. It becomes an excuse for favoring the abstract universal over the particular—a triumph of quantity over quality. This is the only form the sublime can take within the political economy of injury.

Kushner's *Angels* provides an excellent example of how the sublime and the extraordinary can illuminate unseen suffering and injustice. It vets the imagined locations of suffering and disease, and the division of labor, when those suffering suffer the way they do. Kushner is less interested in objectifying or ledgering the specific sufferings AIDS causes than in how it collates and coalesces those aspects of our suffering that are general and ordinary. He neither holds AIDS up as an impenetrable category, nor flaunts death itself as extraordinary. In all this, he illuminates the tragic in a responsible undertaking of Thoreau's challenge in this chapter's epigram.

Angels turns AIDS on its head, going beyond the mechanics of disease to where and how it lives and what it does to us by showing us who we are. Such a move was, in the history of philosophy, awarded to Rousseau, Hegel, Marx, and Nietzsche, for they invite us to see where what afflicts us lives within and among us. They suggest that good, evil, joy, and suffering have to be tracked down to their origins and sources that are irreducibly internal to the worlds we create and not somewhere out there. Certainly this exteriority is the start—one of the early stages of consciousness, as Hegel puts it—but it must be overcome by being understood in relation to us. This requires seeing myself as the condition of the possibility of the other and the other as the condition of my possibility. The phenomenon of experience is only a starting point and not the end of the investigation or of experience itself. For Feuerbach, and then for Marx, this process is undertaken not by an individual consciousness but by the species. This is why the alienation that both Feuerbach and Marx talk about involves alienation from the kind of immanence, and from an understanding of the other in us—the "evil"—that becomes unknown and unavailable to us.

When confronted with AIDS as an example, in this case, of an ongoing event of sublime suffering, Kushner follows Hegel and Marx to show us how this evil of suffering can reveal that it comes from within and not from outside of us, and that it could be an occasion to see where it resides and where it goes when estranged. This forces seeing suffering, evil, and suffering as evil in their instantiations within a given moment in history and within everyday lives and struggles. Ultimately, this demands a response—to the impossibility of justice— in the form of commissions of justice that hypostatize neither those who suffer nor their suffering. Kushner and Murdoch assist and affirm this move because (a) they bring heroic suffering down to earth and make us apprehend its ordinariness; (b) they do so without minimizing abject suffering—nor is the intent to ironize it away or make it more knowable, manageable, or controllable; (c) they throw the question back at those who do define the problem of suffering and decorate themselves with its solutions, effectively asking "what will you do, when I continue to ask for more life, for a right to define life and death in the first place?"; and (d) they recognize actions of suffering that are not beholden to those who make us suffer.

Murdoch carries a sense of the materiality of suffering that is not available even to any of the contemporary liberal theorists, like Shklar and Card, who emphasize the ubiquity and invisibility of injustice in their attempts to recover liberalism's originary commitment to the fact of human suffering. This is because when liberal thinkers address the ordinariness and ubiquity of suffering, they are still beholden to categories of injury and harm, and they entrust these concepts with the suffering they want liberalism to requite. However, both Murdoch and Kushner (who would self-identify as liberals) remind us that justice of the sort these other liberal thinkers imagine is ill-gotten by traversing the sensuous world already present in, and to, liberalism, and that the requital they are hoping for may require other ways of sensing and responding to suffering that are not considered. As an artist, Murdoch views her task as conveying the terribleness and shapelessness of life by giving it "a dramatic shape [and] at the same time . . . fighting against it and blurring it—even destroying it."[38] Coupled with a kind of reverence, which Murdoch and Paul Woodruff both associate with the social functions of Greek tragedy, this role of the artist overcomes both hubris and grand tragedy.[39]

Kushner's play features dream sequences that various characters share. This suggests that the fluidity and intersections of time and of our existences, and the enormity or commonality of our experiences and sufferings, does not have to translate into abstract universalism. It gestures, more importantly, to what Feuerbach and Marx mean by species existence in relation to suffering not beholden to the dichotomies of individual (qua private) and collective (qua public qua universal qua general). The attention paid to time in Kushner's work reminds us of what liberalism misses when it finds its solutions inside hegemonic time and outside of real, lived, and organic temporalities. Time brought back in allows for a sense of solidarity and nonindividualism that a spatially restricted understanding of solidarity on the basis of identity or event does not.

Thus, depending on how the activity of suffering, and hence the suffering of representation, is theorized, we can challenge the assumptions that suffering (a) is private, individual, and proprietary, and (b) either requires a certain kind of representation or can only be violated by it. By attending to the space between capacity and activity, between interiority and exteriority, and to the dialectic between materiality and representation, the processes of suffering, representation, and enactments of the same, can be kept free from the decisive dichotomies of internal-external and their convenient, yet fallacious, mapping on to individual-collective, private-public, and the like. Sensuousness, suffering, and activity can challenge, rather than assume, extant differentiations between mine and thine in order to see organic relations between our capacities and activities across the boundaries of our bodies. Articulation and speech are thus not mere privately undertaken externalizations, but are intricate social, material, embodied, and shared processes.

As discussed earlier, an individualist notion of representation is wedded to an individualist account of experience and, hence, of knowledge. Perhaps a more social understanding of this experience has to be invoked. Feuerbach writes, "What is for me or subjectively a purely immaterial, non-sensuous act is in itself, or objectively a material and sensuous one. . . . Just as for me, my body belongs to the class of imponderables or has no weight, even though in itself, or for others, it is a heavy body."[40]

If a sensuous act is an objective act, then Feuerbach thinks that the testimony of senses cannot be wrong and that sense experience is something on which all can agree. There is more going on in his claim about my body being "imponderable" to me but not to others; there is nothing private about our senses or their suffering. Feuerbach hints at the temporal nature of sensuousness itself (that Marx fully exploits) when he mentions that the immediacy of senses is a goal, not a given.

This is a statement on the social nature of suffering as a sensuous act, where "social" may cut laterally across the immediate, the personal, and the private in response to discourses on the articulation of pain in language that insist on pain's ineffable and irreducibly private nature. Feuerbach suggests that suffering can be personal without being private, that it can be social without being shared or "public," and that even to the sufferer, her suffering is not transparent. This "transparency," if at all a goal, cannot be valorized as an individual goal or effort but as a social one. Suffering includes the processes of undergoing and enduring our individual and collective sensuousness and sensibility.

Marx finds Feuerbach's "objectivity" to be in need of concreteness. He is worried that the process is too internal for Feuerbach, and for that reason, too abstract. He introduces this concreteness by bringing in his historical understanding of labor. Labor, for Marx, is a specific social form. It assumes this form "from the moment that men in any way work for one another."[41] Labor is social not just because it constructs commodities (defined as exchangeable social use values) but because it becomes the mode in which we speak to each other.

Since a nonpolitical sociality is too simplistic; since questions of power, corporeality, and language take precedence here; and since suffering's social nature is irreducible to the question of scale or numbers, the political and the aesthetic can be reintroduced into the ethical. Suffering takes a social form in tandem with the development of language and other primary social forms of association. The becoming social of suffering is not the same as mass, public, or collective suffering. Its social nature defies the accepted antinomy between the highly individualized and inarticulable nature of pain, on the one hand, and the categories of mass suffering, on the other. Of course, one can talk about the socialization and secularization of suffering in the form of representations, in the spectacle, and in the regimes of discipline and punishment. But suffering is social not because of the representations and experiences that are shared. Suffering is social because it is how we do and could speak to each other, and because it is mediated by categories that limit what can be said and heard (a problem of structures of power and of their impact on our sensuous capacities). An emphasis on the individuality of suffering is overstated: consider all the times when some form of interaction with the suffering or labor of others (in conversation, literature, art, and so on) articulates our own suffering and also makes possible the recognition of one's suffering as injustice. Liberal paternalism is this fact or privilege taken to an extreme. Suffering, even more than labor, is a social act, with our ability to make the suffering of the other our own in ways beyond what

Marx says could be possible with labor, in a way that could render irrelevant the need to own it in the first place.[42]

Marx's discussion of the suffering of labor clues us in about the social natures of labor and suffering as they cohabitate in liberal capitalism, and facilitates moving beyond this structure toward new forms of sociality, labor, and suffering. A worker is dehumanized when his senses are no longer functioning, and when machines latch on to human weakness and reduce him to a weaker and less sensuous being. However, how does the condition of alienation allow for the worker to sense his own dehumanization and his amputated senses? And what is the difference between the alienation of the capitalist and the worker? The answer may be in the alienating activity itself. Perhaps the source of the dehumanization of the worker may allow for a resensitization, available to Marx's select members of the bourgeoisie (or Jacques Ranciere's and Herbert Marcuse's margins and the excluded).[43] Marx works with a notion of a worker's sensuousness that is not merely active but also passive, also able to undergo its alienation in a way the bourgeoisie cannot. Marx's story of the evolution of the labor movement gives one instance of how this happens, consistent with his discussion of language as practical consciousness. On the one hand, workers speak through their products since they, and not the bourgeoisie, create them. In this case, the bourgeoisie does not have the privilege of such activity. On the other hand, the numerical possibilities of actual intersubjective experience are greater than those for the bourgeoisie. There are just *more* senses at work here.[44]

This notion of social sensuousness in relation to suffering does not adhere to given dichotomies of individual-collective, private-public, and communicable-ineffable, nor does it find neat overlaps between them. This formulation sees language in its materiality within other corporeal undergoings and not merely as productive of material articulations. When the sensual labors of suffering and representing are considered species activities, we are denied the luxury of working with an additive or composite principle of suffering and subjectivity. This can push us to think of the organic nature of these labors: in a naturalistic sense, they necessitate and constitute each other through relations of reciprocity as well as agon. The social, then, stands to be reconceived as entirely disconnected from attributes of transparency, commensurability of aggregates, and publicness. It can be reframed as not only a fundamental relation—via the fact that we are social beings related to suffering in a certain manner—but also a fundamental orientation, wherein the question of how we are social beings who relate to suffering would help define the condition of the social.

Perhaps it is possible to think of the work of senses—the seeing, smelling, hearing, touching, tasting, uttering—as framed within a sociality that does not rely on a discrete calculus or an additive law. Instead, it may follow a more organic and commutative nature. Commutation, literally "changing with or together," implies an *inter*change, different from the exchange relation in capitalism.[45] This is reminiscent of the dialectic itself in terms of the openness to the alteration of the factors and their relations to each other.[46] Another set of constitutive relations emerges in this materialist understanding of suffering and representation: the relations between parts of a whole that must be considered alongside the relations of an individual or group to a totality such as the state. The multiplicity of factors does not imply commensurability except in emphasizing its difficulty, especially if the variability of factors is seen as an obstacle to any neat equation. The factors themselves vary in their internal relations.

Moreover, commutation may reveal what is missed when justice is spoken of only in a distributive sense. The distributive mode necessitates abstractions that elaborate the relation of a part to a totality and that enable justice in this mode. Commutation may augment this mode by considering the relations between parts of a totality in their dynamism and incommensurability. (And it does so without romanticizing wholeness that fuses all particularities and removes all dialectical moments.) Commutation modifies any conventional account of distributive justice by seeing ethics and politics as inseparable, and the labors of suffering as detailed in this work to be intrinsic and internal to the tasks of justice, even at the cost of their instrumentality. This stands truest in the realm of suffering; as far as the division of labors of suffering remains a concern, a notion of the commutative begs the question of possession in relation to suffering. It stresses that how we relate to our own suffering is inextricable from how we relate to others, be they individuals or totalities, universals or particularities.

CODA: RETURNING SUFFERING TO THE POLITICAL AND THE POLITICAL TO SUFFERING

Modes of subjectivity, sensuousness, and enactment that evade liberalism's grasp and sensorium suggest a way of rendering the question of sensuousness in relation to suffering, one's own or others', not a merely ethical one, or a narrowly aesthetic one, or with a foregone object and archive, but a wholly and substantially political and methodological one that frees ethics and aesthetics from the finalities and autonomies they respectively feign. The labor of suffering straddles

the domains of politics, ethics, and aesthetics despite the logic of separations that I found natural to liberal thought and practice at the start
of our journey. There is probably something about the domains that
is more stable throughout and across our existences than the arbitrary
and contingent nature of the public and the private spheres in the
liberal framework.

However, I am suspicious of the move that—by affording epistemic stabilities to, and distributing ontic priorities among, politics,
ethics, and aesthetics—effectively depoliticizes the question of suffering. This happens when thinkers as disparate as Emmanuel Levinas,
Susan Sontag, and Judith Shklar consider suffering a problem but
not a question, each sacralizing suffering in a way that that renders it
untouchably unexamined, directing us to focus our worries on what
to do in response to it. An emphasis on the ethical—in the invocations
of the demand made by the other's face or of the fear of cruelty being
the worst thing we do—quite often either precludes any discussion of
subjectivity or places my subjectivity at stake in responding correctly
to another's suffering. These moves focus more on those who respond
than those who suffer, and suffering is once again rendered an object.
While these are useful mantras for going through life in some sort of
ethical and other-regarding way, it is important to remember whom
the preclusion of the question of subjectivity of the sufferer aids. Is
there any room for the sufferer herself to worry about who and what
it is whose suffering awes us into action, and who and what it is that
speaks and is spoken for—let alone to ask what this voicing is, what
sympathy is, indeed, what suffering is? The shrinking of space for
these questions, and the antipolitics of a focus on the ethical, becomes
reminiscent of the religious-moral invocation that is bound to end all
conversation. I believe the distinction between sacralization and honoring is important here, for different material relations of alienation
and intimacies are at stake in each.

In Martha Nussbaum's celebration of cosmopolitanism, the familiar move of the invocation of the worst sufferings of mankind is bound
to shut up and line everyone else in submission, not to the pain of
others (as it may appear), but more fundamentally to iterations of who
I am as one who suffers, as one who responds to suffering, and as one
troubled by each of those questions rather than having settled them.[47]
Nussbaum or Shklar, in their philosophical commitments to different metaphysics (even in explicit noncommitments to metaphysics),
do not even consider that their invocation of events of unimaginable
suffering as cautionary tales for all of humanity is beholden to the sublime in ways complicit with liberalism's political economy of suffering.

In being so, they inadvertently evacuate the political in favor of some formalistic ethical certitude that may carry its own violent obliterations, dysfunctionalizing political judgment in submission to ethical judgments already made for us. The ethicization of discourse on suffering, and the submission to the violence of violence, is a parallel to the death of the political. Similarly, as long as the aesthetic follows this logic—that representation is unethical and violent in nature and that we must somehow leave it behind—it will be limited in its vision, unable to see the deep and necessary ontological connection between suffering and representation. Beyond considering aesthetics at play in the artistry of rights and interests that privileges the Western scopic and rhetoricist regimes, the aesthetic must be seen as more closely derived from *aisthesis* (perception from the senses). The resulting essential, ontic, and experiential proximity to suffering may allow us to radically reimagine our subjection to injuries, interests, and rights.

The elements of a historical materialism of suffering introduced over the course of this chapter—necessity, hope, and a materialist sensuous ethos—reconsider woundedness and victimhood in order to illuminate the multiplicity of relations that are, and can be, had to our own and others' suffering. They expose the presumptions and certainties regarding the imperatives suffering poses for sufferers that codify a basic distance from suffering and an inability to insinuate the question of suffering in our comportments, orientations, and internal relations of simultaneity to the world.

A righteous or tolerant pluralism of sufferings, enacted wounds, and relations to our own and others' suffering is not my objective here. One only has to consider, to build to a different end, how the judgments, actions, and reactions of many among us cannot help but reject consolations that come from codified knowledges and certitudes, such as those pertaining to what suffering is, how we must despise it, and how we must fix it. Then, one only has to question the imperatives these knowledges and certitudes pose for all of us, and examine the utilitarian charm of the beguiling tragedy of "powerless" institutions and other conscriptions of sympathy, empathy, voice, and desire for a markedly different world. This may involve not giving liberal institutions or fervent recruiters of various marginalities the power to set the terms of honoring the suffering and hope of others, and not giving them the power to corner our pathos, in a moment of ethical noblesse, by emphasizing how another's suffering is impenetrable and unknowable. As much as this ethical noblesse upholds the letting be of the other, it is a preservation, first and foremost, of oneself—perversely reminiscent of the confusing touch-me-not of the Christ back from the dead, a Christ whose triumph over death ironically inspires entire cultures built on surplus fear, suffering, and death as offerings for those with terminal senses but endless lives (often the courtesy of the same historical cryogenics). It is imperative to reject both the righteous or tolerant pluralism of sufferings and the touch-me-not version of seemingly other-centered politics in favor of seeing our sufferings and our labors as coconstitutive of the world we inhabit.

What would it mean, as Louis puts it to the Rabbi, to "incorporate sickness into one's sense of how things are supposed to go," to convoke a politics that is "good with death" but asks for "more life"? Perhaps the sufferer not be incidental to the suffering when suffering is defined as a problem only in the terms we can pretend to solve, only to fail at that, too. Perhaps liberal politics should accept that statistics of diseases, mortalities, and morbidities, calculated in terms of the loss in human productivity, on the one hand, and those of prison populations and philanthropic gifts, on the other, are not graceful confessions of its mastery of suffering or death. It is not that there are no sufferings to be named, interpreted, and tended to. However, it is important to remember that this is not a random, altruistic, or unmediated process, and it benefits those with the agency and position to act on another's suffering. Perhaps politics should be able to speak to, and for, the reserve army of those with abject, yet-to-be-interpreted-and-recompensed sufferings, and those who have no ability to be injured outside of the terms native to liberal capitalist discourse. Perhaps politics can diverge from its reliance on certain frames of suffering in order to address the ubiquity and ordinariness of human tragedy and suffering. Perhaps, still, if politics is concerned with the creation and maintenance of forms of life, then the activities of this making, when they negotiate with the past, present, and future, necessitate a look at the way old and new wounds are enacted in order to yield forms that are different.

Ultimately, perhaps liberalism's colonization of suffering, and its moral dominion over it, needs to be resisted and loosened. Questioning the forms in which we suffer and are told to do so is not the same as altogether questioning the reality or centrality of suffering and our responsibility to it. The ways in which we suffer tell us what we need and do not need, what our bodies can and cannot bear. Politics must be pushed to engineer the passing of certain forms of suffering, not the passing of suffering altogether.

The claim to having nailed the problem of suffering becomes suspect when politics learns from suffering not via the question of justice but, more immediately, as it responds to the suffering that is life; when it is urgent to understand those ways of suffering that do not follow liberal logics; when attending to bodies who suffer, remember, and act out of their wounds differently is extremely necessary; when the question of the suffering of action is inseparable from the actions of the suffering; when our experience of the world and its ethical, political, and aesthetic moments is not prior to or outside of justice, but constitutive of it; and when the need to understand necessity, the lack of choice, and the ordinariness of tragedy is part of the same story as the clumsiness of our responses to grand disaster.

This is an offering toward a politics that is not modeled on the liberal, capitalist, and colonizing ideals of healthy agents who are asked to live diametrically across from the pole of victimhood. Such an approach would factor in the material experiences of destruction, tragedy, violence, defeat, wounds, memory, hope, and survival that risk obliteration even by many well-meaning victim-centered politics. The imagining of such a politics is not merely premised on suffering as something to be undone. Rather, it holds on to the ability to suffer as something to be striven for, grasped anew, and salvaged from the arbitrary dissipations imposed on it by global powers who not only refuse to take responsibility for the plight that they have every role in creating and locating but also shamelessly arbitrate how the wounded can make their suffering matter.

Modern schemes for solving the problem of human suffering succumb to their own hubris, even as they set the terms of joy and sorrow, love and death, life and hope, salvation and freedom, that those subject to these schemes *ought* to have a role in determining. Maybe these schemes have no relevance to those who suffer abjectly, or maybe the latter have lost their senses living among the dead who tyrannize us and the dead who beseech us. It is time that we confront the nauseating exploitations and self-affirming decrepitude of Western liberal capitalist arbitrations of where suffering must live and where it must die—these moralities keep themselves alive and ascendant by always invoking their choice exceptions, fixating on those marginal relations to suffering and life signified in the savage acts of, say blowing up one's own and others' bodies, often regarded as savage for no other reason than their violation of some silly rational choice maxim. There are many other exceptions that confront these dominations, not the least of which are the forms of acculturations, past and present, that see the realm of ethics as deeper and richer than the space of individual moralities acted out. Similarly, some of these exceptions to learn from hold and honor suffering as an inherently social act, as a welcome burden to carry with and for each other. If it is indeed the case that the world is so because the colonized have not stopped regurgitating, then the incipient fascisms in the metropoles today ought to make us wonder whether our problem as people of this world is not that there is not enough liberalism, but that, at best, liberalism is insufficient, and, at worst, it is complicit. Perhaps the majority of the world needs a politics that is material enough to speak to, and with, their silences, their pain, their losses, their defeats, their victories, their dispensabilities, their mutilations, their self-injuries, their fidelities, their betrayals, their memories, their justice, their humor, *and* their hope. At stake in such an imagining is nothing less than the possibility of newer forms of joy, desire, hope, and life itself.

Notes

Introduction

1. Kristin Kopp offers a really rich account of some of these issues in "The Discourse of Trauma—The Trauma of Discourse: Conquering Memory in Ingeborg Bachmann's *Malina*," in *Conquering Women: Women and War in the German Cultural Imagination*, ed. Hilary Collier Sy-Quia and Susanne Baackmann (Berkeley: University of California Press/University of California International and Area Studies Digital Collection, 2000), 104:75–90.

2. Troy Taylor, "William Hope: Secrets of the Crewe Circle of Spirit Photographers," http://www.prairieghosts.com/hope.html (2003); National Media Museum and the Science and Society Picture Library, "The Spirit Photographs of William Hope," *Flickr Commons*, http://www.flickr.com/photos/nationalmediamuseum/sets/72157606849278823/detail.

3. I am aware of, and compelled by, Jacques Ranciere's follow-up with Aristotle in Jacques Rancière, *Disagreement: Politics and Philosophy*, trans. Julie Rose (Minneapolis: University of Minnesota Press, 1998), 1–4. I am certainly informed by this distinction, but I use voice and speech in this book to refer to specific things: speech to the act and product of the speaking and voice to a superset of such expressions and representations that count as democratic assertions. Both speech and voice, then, ultimately stand in here for forms of making present in (and to) a political sense.

4. Suffering as evil and suffering as injury are two forms of objectified and alienated suffering in the enlightenment, with injury emerging as a dominant instantiation of the enlightenment in liberal modernity—and the key focus of my work.

5. Extending here Marx's statement "To be sensuous is to suffer," in Karl Marx, "Critique of Hegel's Dialectic and Philosophy as a Whole," in *Economic and Philosophic Manuscripts of 1844* (New York: International Publishers, 1964), 182. This is taken up in greater detail in Chapter 4.

6. My sincere thanks to Professor Leela Gandhi for crystallizing some crucial moments of my work in her comments and validating them with clearer and more precise formulations, from which this Introduction has greatly benefited.

Chapter 1

1. Fascinated and inspired by various interpretations of the history of liberalism around its emphasis on liberty, autonomy, and on the secular broadly understood, I find suffering to be an important facet of each of these significant elements of liberalism. In step with Jerome Schneewind's account of the "invention" of autonomy as the hallmark of liberal thought that comes about in response to the anxieties, concerns, excitement, and promises inherited from the medieval and premodern eras, I will show the "problem" of suffering to be emplotted in this invention and in other sources of liberal subjectivity. See further J. B. Schneewind, *The Invention of Autonomy: A History of Modern Moral Philosophy* (Cambridge, UK: Cambridge University Press, 1998).

2. Judith N. Shklar, "A Life of Learning," in *Liberalism Without Illusions: Essays on Liberal Theory and the Political Vision of Judith N. Shklar*, ed. Bernard Yack (Chicago: University of Chicago Press, 1996), 273, 279. The realness of memory plays a big role in Shklar's rejection of idealism. This explains her relation not only to the concept and unreality of utopia (and its horrible consequences for the present of human beings) but also to ways of analyzing problems that do not root themselves in experience. She once said that "a general deepening of self-understanding comes from confronting the remote and the alien." Perhaps this is what memory and history were to those who, in her view, sought refuge in utopian fantasies (themselves remote and alien!) that could be confronted via memory and history. Utopian fantasies could only be ill-understood without taking into account the weight of history they inhere. Shklar rejected the protection both of "sheltered despair" and "cozy optimism." This meant that a more real and more concrete liberalism had to train itself to carry more weight and see and hear more than it did.

3. The composition of this set of rights may vary across thinkers, and may derive justifications from an idea of human nature that Shklar finds too "mythical" and dogmatic to be believable, or from appeals to natural law such as in John Locke's liberalism of natural rights, where freedom is itself a right.

4. What Shklar refers to as the liberalism of self-development is credited to John Stuart Mill and holds freedom to be a good and not only a right. Freedom provides the ambience within which liberal subjects fulfill their goals. To this, the liberalism of self-development explicitly adds the enabling of the citizens that the liberalism of rights presupposes.

5. Judith N. Shklar, *Legalism* (Cambridge, MA: Harvard University Press, 1964), 5.

6. Judith N. Shklar, "The Liberalism of Fear," in *Political Thought and Political Thinkers*, ed. Stanley Hoffmann (Chicago: University of Chicago Press, 1998), 3.

7. Ibid.

8. Ibid., 10.

9. Ibid., 13.
10. Stanley Hoffmann, "Preface," in *Liberalism Without Illusions: Essays on Liberal Theory and the Political Vision of Judith N. Shklar*, ed. Bernard Yack (Chicago: University of Chicago Press, 1996), x.
11. Far from bringing liberalism into question, the failure of liberalism in Europe gets Shklar to plead for more. Only an unflinching commitment to uncorrupted(ly) liberal institutions is seen, by her, as the answer. Only a true liberalism can, in Shklar's view, furnish the tools of a political project focusing on realistic preemption and damage control. And only liberalism correctly understands the world, its people, their suffering, and the constructive and destructive relations between these.
12. Albert Hirschman tracks a gradual channeling of the mistrust of human passions and the human body into one sphere of activity where all those passions could actually take the form of reason. One of Shklar's heroes, Montesquieu, is actually one of those people who imagined commerce as being a palliative to the cruelties of human passions by being a capacious appropriator of the same. Compare Albert O. Hirschman, *The Passions and the Interests: Political Arguments for Capitalism Before its Triumph* (Princeton, NJ: Princeton University Press, 1996).
13. Shklar, "The Liberalism of Fear," 11.
14. Thomas Hobbes, *Leviathan: With Selected Variants from the Latin Edition of 1668*, ed. E. M. Curley (Indianapolis, IN: Hackett, 1994), part I, chap. 5, 22.
15. Sheldon S. Wolin, *Politics and Vision: Continuity and Innovation in Western Political Thought* (Boston: Little Brown, 1960), 328.
16. Ibid., 326, 327.
17. See also John Locke, *Second Treatise of Government*, ed. C. B. Macpherson (Indianapolis: Hackett, 1980), and John Locke, *An Essay Concerning Human Understanding* (Amherst, NY: Prometheus Books, 1995).
18. The activity of labor affirms the opposition between man and nature, where nature keeps man on a string of uncertainty and helplessness but is, at the same time, full of possible rewards for the endurance. Any conquest over nature adds to the means of life and to the value of the person who discharges himself through this labor. Private property comes into being. Life expands into liberty and property, and both are considered things to be preserved. What was merely implicit in Hobbes in terms of the possession of life and its protection and preservation is made much more explicit in Locke, where preservation and protection are predicated on the property relation and on the ownership of our lives, liberty, and our property together. Preserving the self now spans preserving what are considered the sources, as well as extensions, of the self, such as liberty and property.
19. The structure of feeling, with the increase in the sheer quantity of instantiations, on the one hand, and the replacement of intensity by suffusion, on the other, made enough room for ambient emotions. To invoke the

qualities of sound, pitch replaces loudness or frequency makes up for amplitude. I am thinking of sentiments such as anxiety and angst that have a peculiarly modern character. I see them as variations on the theme of suffering that began with Hobbes—the stimuli change from bloody religious wars to the wars of social survival, and protecting the self comes to be defined ever so broadly in the face of changes in society, economics, culture, and politics. In other words, death comes to occupy more avenues and is much slower and more ambient itself. The self knows many more threats than the purely physical since its own fiction is more material than ever before. Wolin writes, "It meant . . . that the intensity of pain suffered in the loss of wealth or status was equal to the pain of physical hurt." He adds, "The preservation of the self [became] a more formidable task for the liberal than it had been for Hobbes" (Wolin, *Politics and Vision*, 329). This is also where security as an antidote to this situation comes to be equated with an ability to count (on) things.

20. Soon, in Hume, the conception of effects and objects becomes the precursor to modern consumerism under private property. Here, the self gets extended into (rather, defined by) objects that surround it. See David Hume, *Four Dissertations. i. The Natural History of Religion. ii. Of the Passions. iii. Of Tragedy. iv. Of the Standard of Taste* (London: Printed for A. Millar, 1757). See also Páll S. Árdal, *Passion and Value in Hume's Treatise* (Edinburgh, UK: Edinburgh University Press, 1989).

21. Immanuel Kant, *The Metaphysics of Morals* (Cambridge, UK: Cambridge University Press, 1991), 71, Ak. 249.

22. Ibid., 68–69, Ak. 246–47.

23. Ibid., 43, Ak. 215.

24. Ibid., 44, Ak. 216.

25. This recalls Marx on property as the relation that unifies the four universal human rights of security, property, liberty, and equality. Karl Marx, "On the Jewish Question," in *Selected Writings*, ed. Lawrence Hugh Simon (Indianapolis, IN: Hackett, 1994), 1–26 (especially 15–18).

26. Tracy B. Strong, *Jean Jacques Rousseau: The Politics of the Ordinary* (Thousand Oaks, CA: Sage, 1994), 15.

27. John Rawls, *A Theory of Justice* (Cambridge, MA: Harvard University Press, 2005), 62, 142.

28. John Rawls, *Justice as Fairness: A Restatement*, ed. Erin Kelly (Cambridge, MA: Harvard University Press, 2001), 59.

29. Ibid., 61.

30. *Oxford English Dictionary*, 2nd ed., s.v. "tolerance, n.," http://dictionary.oed.com/cgi/entry/50253982.

31. *Oxford English Dictionary*, 2nd ed., s.v. "toleration," http://dictionary.oed.com/cgi/entry/50253991.

32. Iris Murdoch, *Sartre, Romantic Rationalist*, 1st ed. (New York: Viking Press, 1987), 31; Jean-Paul Sartre, *Critique of Dialectical Reason: Theory*

of Practical Ensembles, trans. Alan Sheridan-Smith (New York: Verso, 2004), 815.

33. Joel Feinberg, *The Moral Limits of the Criminal Law: Harm to Others,* vol. 1 (New York: Oxford University Press, 1984), 33–34.
34. Judith N. Shklar, *Ordinary Vices* (Cambridge, MA: Belknap Press of Harvard University Press, 1984), 44.
35. Shklar, "The Liberalism of Fear," 11.
36. John Kekes, "Cruelty and Liberalism," *Ethics* 106 (1996): 837.
37. See also Richard Rorty, *Contingency, Irony, and Solidarity* (New York: Cambridge University Press, 1989); Annette C. Baier, "Moralism and Cruelty: Reflections on Hume and Kant," *Ethics* 103 (1993): 436–57; Shklar, "The Liberalism of Fear"; William A. Galston, "Two Concepts of Liberalism," *Ethics* 105 (1995): 516–34; William A. Galston, "Liberal Virtues," *American Political Science Review* 82 (1988): 1277–90; and Bernard Yack, "Liberalism Without Illusions," 2.
38. Kekes, "Cruelty and Liberalism," 838.
39. Seyla Benhabib, "Judith Shklar's Dystopic Liberalism," in *Liberalism Without Illusions: Essays on Liberal Theory and the Political Vision of Judith N. Shklar,* ed. Bernard Yack (Chicago: University of Chicago Press, 1996), 57.
40. Shklar, "The Liberalism of Fear," 9.
41. In Shklar's discourse, the subject positions of victim and perpetrator, the fearful and the feared, and the tolerator and the tolerated adhere to a notion of power that is simplistic, stark, and unidirectional. She continues to focus on power that is channeled from the ruler to the ruled and sticks to very static hierarchies. This is especially surprising since Shklar dwells much on the structures of surveillance and discipline such as McCarthyism, the effects of which she describes as "less crude and immediate than subtle and latent" (Shklar, "A Life of Learning," 266). She clearly fears that complicating understandings of power and its workings may amount to a disruption that may not be worth the outcomes. Thus, her picture of political power retains rather easy subject positions. She does not understand that embracing more complex understandings of power, and our grammars of subjectivity and suffering, may itself be an ethical, even just, act, and does not automatically disavow the realities of injustice and victimization.
42. Benhabib, "Judith Shklar's Dystopic Liberalism," 57.
43. Ibid.
44. Shklar, "The Liberalism of Fear," 8.
45. Shklar wants to bring to liberalism an ethos of remembering that works both in the registers of what is seen or admitted as well as whose perspective is used (those who are beset with scars and weights of various sorts). Does memory lead to a different kind of sensitivity to pain (and hence to what is seen and heard and whose sensual testimony is admitted)? In the context of suffering and liberalism, her emphasis on memory works

in multiple registers, including liberalism's memory of its own roots and originary justifications; the memory of suffering and the suffering of it on part of her actual and potential sufferers; the relation of the memory of injustices past to those that can be assumed to recur; and the sluggishness of memory in general, as well as the human wish (and in/ability) to conquer it, recreate it, and the costs that may entail. It is also the memory that constrains and configures the hopes her liberalism can tolerate and those it cannot. The question remains, what can liberalism's memory (especially that of Shklar's liberalism) withstand? To what extent does her empiricist liberalism, out of fear, bury everything in the concrete ground of memory? To what extent does her fear command the form, content, and function of those memories and the memory of those on whose behalf she fears and sees?

46. Methodologically, Shklar's getting at fear is not a move out of the private into the public but first begins with the public. Similarly, her emphasis on the political and the public may be out of a wish to rejuvenate those spheres. How would a theory that actually did believe in reclaiming the body, and revenerating it after eons of hatred, take it back into its fold? Nietzsche was someone else who felt the same way about what philosophy and religion had, together, done to the body—it is evident from within his work that contempt does not mean exclusion, but as Foucault would tell us, an implication of the body in the systems of hatred and contempt that were created. How far is Shklar herself from this point? Her equation of neglect and contempt, naïve as it may be, then brings us full circle to her equating inclusion, benevolence, caritas, and love—a problem that besets postmodernism as much as it does liberalism, of whatever sort. *How* we bring the body back in is as important as bringing it back in, as is correcting the assumption that the body was ever out.

CHAPTER 2

1. My sense of the word aesthetic derives most centrally from Terry Eagleton's classic genealogy in *The Ideology of the Aesthetic* (Oxford, UK: Basil Blackwell, 1990) and is inspired by Herbert Marcuse's *The Aesthetic Dimension: Toward a Critique of Marxist Aesthetics* (Boston: Beacon, 1978) and *An Essay on Liberation* (Boston: Beacon, 1969), as well as Theodor Adorno's *Aesthetic Theory*, ed. Gretel Adorno and Rolf Tiedeman (Minneapolis: University of Minnesota Press, 1997) and Lambert Zuidervaart's reading of it in *Adorno's Aesthetic Theory: The Redemption of Illusion* (Cambridge, MA: MIT Press, 1991). Jacques Rancière's work is a later discovery and an encouraging and affirmative one.

2. The various deployments of the word "representation" include Hobbes's formalistic definition of representation in terms of arrangements that precede and initiate it—authorization, or the giving of authority to act. Another catches the spider by its other toe, wherein representation is

defined by accountability for the representative's actions. Hanna Pitkin, in her opus *The Concept of Representation*, situates the concept in its etymological and political history. She deems it worthy of such a detailed treatment because of its "importance and ubiquity" as well as "its complexity and consequent role in long-standing theoretical confusions and controversies" (Hanna Fenichel Pitkin, *The Concept of Representation* [Berkeley: University of California Press, 1967], 2.) Other possibilities Pitkin enumerate include representation as a "standing for" rather than an "acting for," where *inanimate* objects can be allowed to enter the scene. These kinds of representations include *descriptive representation* (the making present of something absent by resemblance or reflection, as in a mirror or in art) and *symbolic representation* (not requiring reflection or resemblance; 11–12). For helpful contextual works on the problem of representation in liberal and democratic theory, please see Claire Colebrook, "Questioning Representation," *SubStance* 92 (2000): 47–67; Jane Mansbridge, "Should Blacks Represent Blacks and Women Represent Women? A Contingent 'Yes,'" *Journal of Politics* 61 (1999): 628–57; Anne Philips, *The Politics of Presence* (Oxford, UK: Clarendon, 1995); Nadia Urbinati, "Representation as Advocacy: A Study of Democratic Deliberation," *Political Theory* 28 (2000): 758–86; and Melissa Williams, *Voice, Trust, and Memory: Marginalized Groups and the Failings of Liberal Representation* (Princeton, NJ: Princeton University Press, 1998).

For more history of the aesthetics of representation in politics, see also Frank R. Ankersmit, *Aesthetic Politics: Political Philosophy Beyond Fact and Value* (Stanford, CA: Stanford University Press, 1996) and "Representational Democracy: An Aesthetic Approach to Conflict and Compromise," *Common Knowledge* 8 (2002): 24–46.

3. Pitkin, *The Concept of Representation*, 8–9.

4. See ibid., 92–143.

5. Thomas Hobbes, *Leviathan: With Selected Variants from the Latin Edition of 1668*, ed. E. M. Curley (Indianapolis: Hackett, 1994), 101–5.

6. Ibid., 22.

7. The first two, *Vertretung* and *Darstellung*, are found juxtaposed in *The Eighteenth Brumaire of Louis Bonaparte* in the discussion of the history of bourgeois revolution and the French peasants, while the third (*Vorstellung*) appears in the "Introduction" to the *Grundrisse* in the section on the method of political economy, which is Marx's articulation of his historical method. See Karl Marx, *The Eighteenth Brumaire of Louis Bonaparte* (New York: International Publishers, 1964); Karl Marx, "The Eighteenth Brumaire of Louis Bonaparte," in *The Marx-Engels Reader*, ed. Robert C. Tucker (New York: Norton, 1978), 594–17; Karl Marx, "Introduction," in *Grundrisse: Foundations of the Critique of Political Economy*, trans. Martin Nicolaus (London; New York: Penguin Books, 1993), 100–111. See also Martha B. Helfer, *The Retreat of Representation:*

The Concept of Darstellung in German Critical Discourse (Albany: State University of New York Press, 1996).

8. In this instance, interests themselves are representations—translations, articulations, and proxies of certain needs and suffering. More importantly, they are representations that function in the world like rights, injuries, harms, and commodities do—they are alienable and exchangeable, interacting with each other, and implying that they are commensurate with the person who bears them. *Vertretung* does not necessitate or require an identity or unity of interests with the subject, and, therefore, as far as interests are alienable or transferable (like property), as happens in liberal politics, representation can take place. *Vertretung* comes up in the *Brumaire* in Marx's discussion of the French peasants who "cannot represent themselves" and "must be represented." In this case, their representative is the Bonaparte dynasty that "must at the same time appear as their master, as an authority over them, as an unlimited governmental power that protects them against the other classes and sends them the rain and the sunshine from above." Marx talks about class as position and class as consciousness, and tells us how the French peasants form a class as a descriptor of their position, but since "the identity of their interests begets no unity, no national union, no political organization, they do not form a class." Therefore they are "incapable of enforcing their class interest in their own name, whether through a parliament or through a convention" (Marx, "The Eighteenth Brumaire of Louis Bonaparte," 608). Spivak talks in this regard about the "structural principle of a dispersed and dislocated class subject" whereby "the (absent collective) consciousness of the small peasant proprietor class finds its 'bearer' in a 'representative' who appears to work in another's interest." See also Gayatri Chakravorty Spivak, "Can the Subaltern Speak?" in *Marxism and the Interpretation of Culture*, eds. Cary Nelson and Lawrence Grossberg (Urbana: University of Illinois Press, 1988), 276.

9. Gayatri Chakravorty Spivak, *The Post-Colonial Critic: Interviews, Strategies, Dialogues*, ed. Sarah Harasym (New York: Routledge, 1990), 108; Gayatri Chakravorty Spivak, *The Spivak Reader: Selected Works of Gayatri Chakravorty Spivak*, ed. Donna Landry and Gerald M. MacLean (New York: Routledge, 1996), 6.

10. Here, the relation between truth, commonness, ordinariness, and availability in Tracy Strong's work on Rousseau, is relevant. The existence of common, shared experience of joy and suffering (and the shared experience of producing a representation) forms the basis of this representation (of the people as a class). Rousseau's vision is in contrast to a society or a group which, in depending only on common and aggregated "interest," is bound to be "transitory and ineffective as human society." The analytic notion of "faithfulness" of representation is supplanted by an emphasis on how and what a representation makes available in terms of common

experience. Strong, *Jean Jacques Rousseau: The Politics of the Ordinary* (Thousand Oaks, CA: Sage, 1994), 56–57.

11. Care has to be taken not to overemphasize the seemingly oxymoronic quality of the phrases "imagined concrete," "chaotic conception," or "imagined concept." The key is not to render the "conception" or "concrete" ethereal, or something born out of reverie as commonly understood, but to appreciate the interplay of image and concept with the latter evoking the sense of "take," "seize," and "contain." This interplay allows us to posit the *(pro)active* element of this *process*. This is crucial for an understanding of representation not simply as deriving from, and invested in, the meaning of *Darstellung* but implicated in *Vorstellung* as well.

12. Marx, "Introduction," 100.

13. See Strong, *Jean Jacques Rousseau*, xxvi–xxx, 30–66.

14. John Rawls, *Justice as Fairness: A Restatement*, ed. Erin Kelly (Cambridge, MA: Harvard University Press, 2001), 7–8, 80–81.

15. John Rawls, *Political Liberalism* (New York: Columbia University Press, 1993), 15.

16. John Rawls, "Justice as Fairness: Political not Metaphysical," *Philosophy and Public Affairs* 14 (1985): 238–39.

17. Rawls, *Political Liberalism*, 27; and Bruce Ackerman, "Political Liberalisms," *Journal of Philosophy* 91 (1994): 364–86.

18. George Armstrong Kelly, "Veils: The Poetics of John Rawls," *Journal of the History of Ideas* 57, no. 2 (1996): 345–46.

19. John Rawls, *A Theory of Justice* (Cambridge, MA: Harvard University Press, 2005), 17, 19.

20. Ibid., 137.

21. Maybe it is not necessary to invoke Marx's reminder of the man-citizen dichotomy in liberal secularism. But perhaps it is important to consider whether "citizen" already connotes a circumvention (not simply of noncitizens and aliens, but of some "human" substance that is not part of the title "citizen"). This would determine whether "the represented" in this case were already in one role among many, and, hence, the original position was then in the business of representing representations; or whether the veil performed only a first-order filtering on the particular histories and sufferings of "whole" people who formed the populace of a country. Rawls said, "Since Greek times, both in philosophy and law, the concept of the person has been understood as the concept of someone who can take part in, or who can play a role in, social life, and hence exercise and respect its various rights and duties. Thus, we say that a person is someone who can be a citizen, that is, a fully cooperating member of society over a complete life" (Rawls, "Justice as Fairness," 233).

It is clear, though, that whether or not a citizen already implies a role that liberalism has been quick to accept as such (I am tempted to say it does), they are still represented in the original position as having certain attributes: free, equal, reasonable, rational. (The delegates or representatives are also included in the represented, since the former represent themselves as citizens.)

22. Rawls, *Justice as Fairness*, 23–24.
23. Ibid., 20.
24. Ibid., 18–19.
25. Michael D. Weiss, "A Jurisprudence of Blindness: Rawls's Justice and Legal Theory," *Drake Law Review* 42 (1993): 573.
26. W. E. B. DuBois, *The Souls of Black Folk* (New York: W. W. Norton, 1999), 3. On "double-consciousness," DuBois says, "After the Egyptian and Indian, the Greek and Roman, the Teuton and Mongolian, the Negro is a sort of seventh son, born with a veil, and gifted with second-sight in this American world—a world which yields him no true self-consciousness, but only lets him see himself through the revelation of the other world. It is a peculiar sensation, this double-consciousness, this sense of always looking at one's self through the eyes of others, of measuring one's soul by the tape of a world that looks on in amused contempt and pity. One ever feels his twoness, an American, a Negro; two warring souls, two thoughts, two unreconciled strivings; two warring ideals in one dark body, whose dogged strength alone keeps it from being torn asunder. . . . The history of the American Negro is the history of this strife, this longing to attain self-conscious manhood, to merge his double self into a better and truer self."
27. Rawls, *Justice as Fairness*, 81.
28. Kelly, "Veils," 359.
29. Weiss, "A Jurisprudence of Blindness," 575.
30. Sheldon S. Wolin, "The Liberal/Democratic Divide: On Rawl's Political Liberalism," *Political Theory* 24 (1996): 107. See also Roberto Alejandro, "What Is Political about Rawl's Political Liberalism?" *Journal of Politics* 58 (1996): 1–24; and Stephen L. Esquith and Richard T. Peterson, "The Original Position as Social Practice," *Political Theory* 16 (1988): 300–334.
31. John Rawls, "The Sense of Justice," in *Collected Papers*, ed. Samuel Richard Freeman (Cambridge, MA: Harvard University Press, 1999), 112.
32. Even though this onus, of being native to all moral persons and being the object of representation, is no longer functioning in *Political Liberalism*, the sense of justice still remains one of the two fundamental moral powers required to be part of justice as fairness. Even though the "person" of *Political Liberalism* has explicitly been rendered a political rather than a psychological construct, the capacities are still intact—the content now being provided by conventions and inherited ethos rather than by the definition of an ahistorical moral personality. In *A Theory of Justice*, the principles of justice are actually close descriptors of the sense of justice. Rawls writes that "one may regard a theory of justice as describing our sense of justice" and that "a useful comparison here

is with the problem of describing the sense of grammaticalness that we have for the sentences of our native language" (Rawls, *A Theory of Justice*, 46, 48). Both the sense and its articulation interact to yield a theory of justice.

33. Rawls, "The Sense of Justice," 96–97, 100, 111–12.
34. Ibid., 110–11.
35. Ibid., 111.
36. Ibid., 100.
37. Ibid., 101.
38. Ibid., 107.
39. Weiss, "A Jurisprudence of Blindness," 575.
40. David Morris, "About Suffering: Voice, Genre, and Moral Community," in *Social Suffering*, ed. Arthur Kleinman, Margaret M. Lock, and Veena Das (Berkeley: University of California Press, 1997), 29.
41. Ibid., 27.
42. Ibid.
43. Friedrich Wilhelm Nietzsche, *Daybreak: Thoughts on the Prejudices of Morality*, ed. Maudemarie Clark and Brian Leiter (Cambridge, UK: Cambridge University Press, 1997), sec. 114, 69.
44. Nietzsche, *Twilight of the Idols, or, How to Philosophize with the Hammer* (Indianapolis: Hackett, 1997), 21–22. I say "cautiously" here, since I think that, for Nietzsche, the realms of injury or suffering are one in the same (unless the cause or origin of injury is one the person locates outside of himself or within himself in the process of overcoming it). But this is more processual than dualistic. Moreover, as we learn in *On the Genealogy of Morals*, Nietzsche has an awkward relationship to Kant's notion of the intelligible. He writes, "(Incidentally, even in the Kantian concept of the 'intelligible character of things,' something remains of this lascivious ascetic discord that loves to turn reason against reason: for 'intelligible character' signifies in Kant that things are so constituted that the intellect comprehends just enough of them to know that for the intellect they are—utterly incomprehensible.)" Friedrich Nietzsche, *On the Genealogy of Morals and Ecce Homo*, trans. Walter Arnold Kaufmann and R. J. Hollingdale (New York: Vintage, 1989), 3:12, 119. Therefore, while I want intelligible injury to connote an injury which does not have to be empirical or physical in a narrow sense, but which is sensible in and through the intellect as well, it is important to clarify that I am not trying to invoke a "true" substance of suffering kept from us by "deceptive" representations that mediate our empirical experience of it.

Also, there is value in having Nietzsche and Kant converge in exposing the proclivities of Christianity and Enlightenment in crafting the prevalent sensorium. On the one hand, suffering, for Nietzsche, has to have a primarily sensible, even simply physiological, element—in *Twilight of the Idols*, he talks about how reason (Christianity, morality, etc.) has always decried the senses and made them the culprit. On the other hand, however, Nietzsche himself is not free of asserting the "reality" of suffering, and, hence, perhaps intellect has to, and must, play a role. This happens, for instance, when the sufferer is turned into a sinner, through the power of heightened affect and feeling, as it is with truth-oriented scientific methods or sensationalist surplus pathos in contemporary politics and media. Nietzsche's work thus suggests a more holistic notion of suffering in life in general that involves both the sensible, affective component as well as the perceptive component of, and on, suffering, and reconciles the abstract and the concrete elements of suffering.

45. Nietzsche, *Daybreak*, sec. 114, 69.
46. Nietzsche, *On the Genealogy of Morals*, 3:28, 162.
47. Ibid., 3:15, 127.
48. Ibid., 1:10, 36–37; 2:10, 72–73.
49. Ibid., 3:14, 122.
50. See ibid., 2:3, 60–61.
51. Ibid., 3:15, 125–28.
52. Ibid., 3:20, 140.
53. Ibid., 3:15, 126.
54. Ibid., 3:15, 126.
55. Ibid., 3:15, 127.
56. Nietzsche, *Twilight of the Idols*, 65, 91. Nietzsche's grapplings with the political and cultural role of suffering spanned his entire career, beginning with his musings on tragedy in *The Birth of Tragedy* up until his definitive incarnation of his tragic artist in *Twilight*. The move from the embodiment of the agon, understood in terms of the Apollonian and Dionysian impulses in Greek tragic theater, to the localization of this agon in the individual (artist), marks a change in concern with, or hope for, a tragic culture. There is a restriction of the domain, availability, and accessibility of Dionysian labor, which excludes it from a decidedly cultural and public communicative domain at large. (In other words, the degree of wholesome unalienated labor possible is circumscribed and limited.) Nietzsche goes on to say that efforts like those of nineteenth-century Germany to "popularize" or acculturate themselves with or to Goethian attributes are bound to fail. This is markedly different in its antipessimism, and antinegation, than Nietzsche's thoughts on culture in the *Birth*. For example, his use of collective pronouns, and of "mankind," is far more frequent in *Birth* than in *Twilight*—along with his musings in, say, sentences like "the very first philosophical problem immediately produces a painful and irresolvable contradiction between man and god and moves it before the gate of every culture, like a huge boulder. The best and highest possession mankind can acquire is obtained by sacrilege and must be paid for with consequences that involve the whole flood of sufferings and sorrows" (Friedrich Nietzsche, *The Birth of Tragedy and The Case of Wagner*, trans. Walter Arnold Kaufman [New York: Vintage Books, 1967], sec. 9, 71). Perhaps the move from tragedy as a public art

to the tragic artist as the domain of the Apollonian and Dionysian is itself a tragic, declensionist "victory" of the Apollonian over the Dionysian and not some glorious reconciliation of the two. Or, perhaps, Nietzsche is now, as *Twilight* specifically agonizes over, faced with the reality of late modernity—we are inextricably caught within a distinctly *post* and *un*tragic age, which is simply incapable of tragedy. In that sense, the tragic artist's formal likeness to the ascetic can be understood, precisely in the artist himself embodying an alternative "ascetic" ideal, since we seem to be incurable and incurably ascetic(s) beyond rescue. No wonder, then, that enough people find in Nietzsche an affirmation of the liberal individual as the embodiment of the tragic artist. See, in particular, the discussion in Morton Schoolman, *Reason and Horror: Critical Theory, Democracy, and Aesthetic Individuality* (New York: Routledge, 2001). The model, and faith, by the time of *Twilight*, is one of individuation that reiterates the fact that is perhaps the extent to which we can approximate the tragic age of the Greeks. Also see discussion in Chapter 6 of this book.

57. Nietzsche, *The Birth of Tragedy*, 65–66.
58. Reference here to Borges's Funes, who died of too much memory, of an inability to inhabit time, of an incapacity for living time, and of no choice but to die of these. Funes stands outside of time in some way, objectified by it, and able to deal with it only as object. I am certainly using "memorious" provocatively, for I have grown to see this incapacity also as a product of particular sensuous-political-economic regimes and their endemic compulsions and marginalizations. While this may be the "health" that liberalism and capitalism actually envision for their subjects, through their resident hypostatizations and Apollonian reifications that render memory only a form of jarring stone monument or *ressentiment*—never accepting their memory actually *as* memory, as is clear in Rawls—they will always take exception with those who remember (differently). See Jorge Luis Borges, "Funes, the Memorious," in *Ficciones*, ed. Anthony Kerrigan, trans. Anthony Bonner (New York: Grove, 1994), 107–16.
59. Nietzsche, *On the Genealogy of Morals*, 3:11, 117.
60. Ibid., 3:11, 117.
61. Ibid., 3:13, 120.
62. Ibid.

CHAPTER 3

1. Look for a parallel discussion of need, hope, and sensuousness in the final chapter of this book.
2. Tony Kushner, *Angels in America: A Gay Fantasia on National Themes* (New York: Theater Communications Group, 1995), 266–67.
3. Ibid., 28, end of scene 4 into scene 5.

4. Ibid., 31.
5. I have in mind Gunter Grass's *The Tin Drum*, where the "child" Oskar is an allegory to Nazi Germany, and Milan Kundera's *The Book of Laughter and Forgetting*, *which* ends with a nightmare of an island of children and repeatedly regards "infantocracy" as horror. Gunter Grass, *The Tin Drum* (New York: Vintage, 1990); Milan Kundera, *The Book of Laughter and Forgetting* (New York: Harper Perennial Modern Classics, 1999), 231–60.
6. Kushner, *Angels in America*, 259; in scene 5 of *Millennium Approaches* (part II of *Angels in America*), excerpted in the Introduction of this book.
7. Ibid., 41.
8. Rousseau resents the indulgences of the likes of Voltaire who digest the Lisbon earthquake by launching wholesale attacks on the goodness and rationality of Providence and the universe in general. Rousseau's *Discourse on the Origin of Inequality* separates natural from moral inequality and foreshadows the separation of the domains of God and man in relation to suffering. Designed to bring the discussion back to earth and to those who were suffering, Rousseau's move meets its fate in Kant, who takes it upon himself to write the script for the injured and their suffering. See, thus, the *Doctrine of Right*, part I of Kant, *The Metaphysics of Morals (New York: Cambridge University Press, 1991)*, for Kant's discussion of injury in relation to right and property that is the fountainhead for the approach to suffering in liberal law and politics. By securing a place for humans and their suffering, this serves as a counterpoint to Voltaire, who feels comfortable speaking for the sufferers and tells them in rather comedic, eighteenth-century nihilism that he *knows* that the world is worthless.
9. Arthur Kleinman, Veena Das, and Margaret M. Lock, eds., *Social Suffering* (Berkeley: University of California Press, 1997).
10. Christopher J. L. Murray and Alan Lopez, eds., *The Global Burden of Disease: A Comprehensive Assessment of Mortality and Disability from Diseases, Injuries, and Risk Factors in 1990 and projected to 2020* (Cambridge, MA: Harvard School of Public Health, 1996).
11. Arthur Kleinman and Joan Kleinman, "The Appeal of Experience, The Dismay of Images: Cultural Appropriations of Suffering in Our Times," in *Social Suffering*, ed. Arthur Kleinman, Margaret M. Lock, and Veena Das (Berkeley: University of California Press, 1997), 11–15.
12. George Thomas Kurian, *The Illustrated Book of World Rankings*, 5th ed. (Armonk, NY: Sharpe Reference, 2001).
13. Clive Staples Lewis, *The Problem of Pain* (New York: HarperCollins, 2001), 91.
14. Susan Sontag, "Regarding the Torture of Others," *New York Times Magazine*, May 23, 2004, http://www.nytimes.com/2004/05/23/magazine/23PRISONS.html?pagewanted=2.

15. Friedrich Nietzsche, *On the Genealogy of Morals and Ecce Homo*, trans. Walter Arnold Kaufmann and R. J. Hollingdale (New York: Vintage, 1989), 2:1, 58.

16. Susan Neiman, *Evil in Modern Thought: An Alternative History of Philosophy* (Princeton, NJ: Princeton University Press, 2004).

17. Ibid., 1–4.

18. See also Claudia Card, *The Atrocity Paradigm: A Theory of Evil* (New York: Oxford, 2005).

19. Marx gestures to this—either vitriolically (in his tirade against the debasement of man through religion) or ironically (at least in comparison to Hegel, in seeing evil historically and as a historicizable form and not as a force *an sich* in history)—in his critique of, and departure from, Hegel, for whom evil is still a substantial and denotative concept ("a motive force in historical development"). Marx further distances himself in his critique of Feuerbach's tendency to hold on to Hegel's dichotomies between good and evil but more superficially than the latter—a stance also explicated in Friedrich Engels, *Ludwig Feuerbach and the End of Classical German Philosophy* (Honolulu: University Press of the Pacific, 2005). Shlomo Avineri's "The Instrumentality of Passion in the World of Reason: Hegel and Marx," *Political Theory* 1 (1973): 388–404, provides a link between the issues of evil and labor in history, challenged in my treatment in Chapter 4 of the emphasis on a form of productive activity in many readings of Marx.

20. The enlightenment is the superset of assumptions and (very material) positings within which liberalism as an ideology becomes possible. My use of the phrase "liberal modernity" is meant to separate enlightenment and modernity and to suggest that alternate modernities are possible.

21. See Ludwig Feuerbach, *The Fiery Brook: Selected Writings of Ludwig Feuerbach*, ed. Zawar Hanfi (Garden City, NY: Anchor Books, 1972); Ludwig Feuerbach, *The Essence of Christianity* (Amherst, NY: Prometheus Books, 1989).

22. A helpful volume for plumbing the question of the sublime is Jean-François Courtine, ed., *Of the Sublime: Presence in Question* (Albany: State University of New York Press, 1993).

23. Thomas Hobbes, *Leviathan: With Selected Variants from the Latin Edition of 1668*, ed. E. M. Curley (Indianapolis: Hackett, 1994), 38. When Hobbes invokes "the natural" as opposite to "the acquired" in terms of intellectual virtue, and so on, we get an interesting look at what "natural" means. For the materialist that Hobbes is, the notion of the natural did not grasp anything that was innate: not even our senses could bespeak of knowledge, as there is no factual knowledge that came naturally to human beings. Rather, the way that he talks about the natural is to talk about education and constitution. The notion of natural and acquired distinguished between what the object of the virtue was and what its origin is. Passions remained natural virtues, cultivated over time, and then,

among the acquired, came wit and reason, where the passions were to be supportive of them.

24. Refer to discussion in Chapter 2 of this book. See also Annette C. Baier, "Moralism and Cruelty: Reflections on Hume and Kant," *Ethics* 103 (1993): 436–57; John Kekes, "Cruelty and Liberalism," *Ethics* 106 (1996): 834–44; Richard Rorty, *Contingency, Irony, and Solidarity (New York: Cambridge University Press, 1989)*; Judith N. Shklar, *Ordinary Vices* (Cambridge, MA: Belknap Press of Harvard University Press, 1984); and Judith N. Shklar, "The Liberalism of Fear," in *Political Thought and Political Thinkers*, ed. Stanley Hoffmann (Chicago: University of Chicago Press, 1998).

CHAPTER 4

1. The liminal potentiality that this exposure may open up will be dealt with in the discussion of farce in Chapter 5.

2. Karl Marx, *Grundrisse: Foundations of the Critique of Political Economy (Rough Draft)*, trans. Martin Nicolaus (London: Penguin Books, 1993), 106.

3. Moishe Postone, *Time, Labor, and Social Domination: A Reinterpretation of Marx's Critical Theory* (New York: Cambridge University Press, 1993), 18.

4. Karl Marx, *Capital: A Critique of Political Economy*, ed. Friedrich Engels, trans. Samuel Moore and Edward Aveling (New York: International Publishers, 1967), 176. *Capital* thus resonates with "On the Jewish Question" but with the nuance desired by the conversion of the question of private property into that of labor.

5. Ibid., *176*.

6. Robert L. Heilbroner, *Teachings from the Worldly Philosophy* (New York: W. W. Norton, 1996), 200.

7. Marx, *Capital*, 176.

8. For a more detailed discussion, see R. N. Berki, "On the Nature and Origins of Marx's Concept of Labor," *Political Theory* 7 (1979): 42, 44; David McLellan, *The Thought of Karl Marx: An Introduction* (London: Macmillan, 1971), 139; and C. J. Arthur, *Dialectics of Labour: Marx and his Relation to Hegel* (Oxford: Blackwell, 1986).

9. Marx, *Capital*, 168. Marx writes, "Labour-power can appear upon the market as a commodity, only if, and so far as, its possessor, the individual whose labour-power it is, offers it for sale, or sells it, as a commodity. In order that he may be able to do this, he must have it at his disposal, must be the untrammelled owner of his capacity for labour, i.e., of his person. He and the owner of money meet in the market, and deal with each other as on the basis of equal rights, with this difference alone, that one is buyer, the other seller; both, therefore, equal in the eyes of the law."

10. Karl Marx, "Wage Labour and Capital," Marx/Engels Internet Archive (1993), chap. 5, http://www.marxists.org/archive/marx/works/1847/wage-labour/index.htm.

11. See Postone, *Time, Labor, and Social Domination*, 82, 158–66.

12. Diane Elson, "The Value Theory of Labour," in *Value: The Representation of Labour in Capitalism*, ed. Diane Elson (London: CSE Books, 1980), 115–80.

13. Marx, *Capital*, 92.

14. Ibid., 645.

15. See Ludwig Feuerbach, *The Fiery Brook: Selected Writings of Ludwig Feuerbach*, ed. Zawar Hanfi (Garden City, NY: Anchor Books, 1972).

16. Karl Marx, *The Poverty of Philosophy* (New York: International Publishers, 1963), 13–14. Engels writes in the preface to the first German edition of *The Poverty of Philosophy*, "And the determination of value of commodities by labour and the free exchange of the products of labour, taking place according to this measure of value between commodity owners with equal rights, these are, as Marx has already proved, the real foundations on which the whole political, juridical and philosophical ideology of the modern bourgeoisie has been built. Once it is recognized that labour is the measure of value of a commodity, the better feelings of the honest bourgeois cannot but be deeply wounded by the wickedness of a world which, while recognizing the basic law of justice in name, still in fact appears at every moment to set it aside without compunction. And the petty bourgeois especially, whose honest labour—even if it is only that of his workmen and apprentices—is daily more and more depreciated in value by the competition of large-scale production and machinery, this small-scale producer especially must long for a society in which the exchange of products according to their labour value is at last a complete and invariable truth. In other words, he must long for a society in which a single law of commodity production prevails exclusively and in full, but in which the conditions are abolished in which it can prevail at all, viz., the other laws of commodity production and, later, of capitalist production." Marx, *The Poverty of Philosophy*, 13–14.

17. A detailed discussion of the fetishism of injuries awaits in Chapter 5. See Lucio Colletti, "Bernstein & the Marxism of the Second International," in *From Rousseau to Lenin: Studies in Ideology and Society* (London: New Left Review Books, 1972), 77–78; and Postone, *Time, Labor, and Social Domination*, 147.

18. My critique of liberal suffering and theorization of a materialist alternative to the liberal approach is in methodological (i.e., epistemological, ontological, and practical) debt to materialist dialectics. Dialectics entails a way of viewing things and offers a language that considers things as moments in their own development in, with, and through, other things. Bertell Ollman identifies that the words "relation," "moment," "movement," "contradiction," "mediation," and "determination," which

dominate much of Marx's writing, are part of the dialectical vocabulary. Therefore, not only is dialectics a way of seeing things, but it is also an approach to studying problems that privileges a search for relationships. These relationships are not only between different (posited) entities but also between the same one in times past, present, and future. (Bertell Ollman, *Alienation: Marx's Conception of Man in Capitalist Society* [New York: Cambridge University Press, 1976], chap. 1–6.)

Dialectics is important to my task not merely as a methodological tool but as a substantive component of the labor of suffering. Abiding dualities, dichotomies, oppositions, and separations in liberalism must be responded to not by granting independence to each, neatly reconciling them, or simply fusing the separates or subsuming one under the other but by employing dialectics. Let us take, for instance, the abstract and the concrete. These are terms that often occur in critiques of liberal universalism, tolerance, autonomy, and modes of (dis)embodiment. Materialist dialectics assures that the abstract and the concrete are not independent of, or indifferent to, each other. Stressing that both the abstract and the concrete are material and real, and that the abstract feeds off the edifications it necessitates and is necessitated by, the materialist dialectical method finds abstract foundations interesting precisely because of how they are realized, materialized, and embodied in the edifices they support. Dialectics emphasizes not only the fact of internal relations but also the dynamic interaction and reconstitution of categories in and through these relations. Independent realms in the clouds, to allude to Feuerbach and Marx, would be of less interest if it were not for why and how they were installed, who installed them, and how they affect the installers in turn. Those installers are not static parties in exchange or subject to unilateral determination but are suspended within the multilateral processes of justification, realization, and materialization involved.

19. Daniel Brudney, *Marx's Attempt to Leave Philosophy* (Cambridge, MA: Harvard University Press, 1998), 230.

20. Ibid., 228–36.

21. Ibid., 233.

22. Karl Marx, "Critique of Hegel's Dialectic and Philosophy as a Whole," in *Economic and Philosophic Manuscripts of 1844*, ed. Dirk J. Struik, trans. Martin Milligan *(New York: International Publishers, 1964)*, 182. Marx continues, "Man as an objective, sensuous being is therefore a suffering being—and because he feels what he suffers, a passionate being. Passion is the essential force of man energetically bent on its object."

23. *Oxford English Dictionary*, 2nd ed., s.v. "suffer, v.," http://dictionary .oed.com/cgi/entry/50241626.

24. Marx W. Wartofsky, *Feuerbach* (New York: Cambridge University Press, 1977), 416.

25. Ibid., 371–77.

26. Ibid., 385.

27. Wartofsky explains further: "If the species nature consists in the relations among individuals, then however concrete the individuals are asserted to be, they can, in the logic of interdependence of individuals on each other for their individuality itself be no more concrete than the relations in which they stand to each other; a point Marx was to drive home." Ibid., 426.

28. Bertell Ollman, *Dance of the Dialectic: Steps in Marx's Method* (Urbana: University of Illinois Press, 2003), chap. 2–4.

29. Karl Marx, "Private Property and Communism," in *Economic and Philosophic Manuscripts of 1844*, ed. Dirk J. Struik, trans. Martin Milligan *(New York: International Publishers, 1964)*, 141.

30. Ollman, *Alienation*, 74, 87.

31. Ibid., 83.

32. In this discussion, however, man's essential powers are the "stated or implied" subject. Ollman's commentary on appropriation will be useful in thinking about the complexity of this externalization: "For Marx, the individual appropriates the nature he perceives and has become oriented to by making it in some way a part of himself with whatever effect this has on his senses and future orientation. To 'capture' a sunset, it is not necessary to paint, write or sing about it. *It becomes ours in the experiencing of it.* The forms and colors we see, the sense of awakening to beauty that we feel and the growth in sensitivity that accompanies such an event are all indications of our new appropriation. To paint the sunset, or to write and sing about it, if joined by genuine emotions, would achieve an even higher degree of appropriation, would make this event even more a part of us" (Ollman, *Alienation*, 89. Emphasis mine).

The language of experiencing something in order to make it a part of us may be benign if we broaden our current meanings of possession. But, how does this play out in the context of suffering? As subjects of experience, we are subject to it and undergo it. Feuerbach uses the word "incorporation," which Marx replaces with "appropriation." Ollman continues, "Appropriation means to utilize constructively, to build by incorporating." However, the implication is that the goal of existence or any action is such an incorporation or building I wonder if there is a way of talking about incorporation that allows the other to be recognized in all its live corporeality but not merely as object or project. Perhaps Ollman is not grasping the tension between *energeia* and *kinesis* that Marx wants to reform and reside in. (For more detail on these as Marx inherits them from Aristotle, please see Eugene Garver, "Aristotle's Genealogy of Morals," *Philosophy and Phenomenological Research* 44 [1984]: 471–92). Ollman's favored language of making something ours, and self-actualization, sneaks in an anthropocentric and self-absorbed valorization. There is a lightness in his account of everything contributing to human growth—as if all experiences have value in this abstractly equalizing and strongly subject-centered way, no matter how (in)coherent the sets of human powers that confront them. It suggests, almost haughtily, that even our passivity is okay as long as it *gives us* something! (See also Clement Dore's discussion of suffering as activity or end in "Does Suffering Serve Valuable Ends?" *Philosophy and Phenomenological Research* 45 [1984]: 103–10).

In contrast, want to endorse a sense of embrace and suffusion, and an ambient reverence, does not necessitate appropriation in Ollman's way—and might suggest that an orientation in a materialist sense already implies a live interaction with living things, with the other, with the world, with the living and with the dead. This orientation may be slower and more still than Ollman imagines, without being static. Perhaps this allows a way out of insistent externalization and incorporation that only sees life as one hell of a productive and frenetic motion!

33. Karl Marx, "Private Property and Communism," 138–39.

34. The question of translation between individual and collective has to contend with the body as property. Marx's discussion of social humanity in the *Theses of Feuerbach* suggests that the individual as we know it today is possible only as part of a particular social form, and that other individualities accompany other social formations. Marx does not find it essential that individuality be owned in merely one way—he does, after all, find appropriation (as a dialectical moment within productive activity) not to be reducible to private property.

35. Marx reformulates the question of essence and separates himself from Aristotle in this way. See also Joseph Margolis, "Praxis and Meaning: Marx's Species Being and Aristotle's Political Animal," in *Marx and Aristotle: Nineteenth-Century German Social Theory and Classical Antiquity*, ed. George E. McCarthy (Savage, MD: Rowman & Littlefield, 1992), 329–55.

36. Marx, "Private Property and Communism," 141.

37. Brudney, *Marx's Attempt to Leave Philosophy*, 236–37.

38. Brudney explains, "The injunction is against (a) the view that, for human beings, the fundamental relation to the world is that of an agent disengaged from the world and mentally grasping something external to and (as yet) unchanged by her, and against (b) the view that a correct understanding *of* the fundamental relation to the world is to be attained from the agent as described in (a). In contrast to the feedback model, [the simultaneity model] involves no three-step sequence of analysis, practical action, and reassessment in light of practical action. Rather, understanding inheres in one's actions. . . . In the phrase from 1844, 'the senses have . . . become theorists directly in their practice.' Changing the world is the correct way to interpret it." Ibid., 237.

39. See also ibid., 240–42.

40. Karl Marx, "Theses on Feuerbach," in *Selected Writings*, ed. Lawrence Hugh Simon (Indianapolis: Hackett, 1994), 101.

41. One of the abiding perplexities in my relation to Nietzsche on the question of suffering is his ambiguous relation to the man of action and his rather modern fervor for frenzy and activity. It is despite this that I find a consistent importance given to the art of suffering, whether as passivity or as activity, from *The Birth of Tragedy* to *On the Genealogy of Morals*. Nietzsche's story in the *Genealogy* that ends with the ascetic priest requires an update for contemporary times: the problem is no longer the internalization of humans as ascetic moderns; instead, it is the ways we externalize. The first essay begins the story of the triumph of slave morality, with the actively discharging and all-powerful noble warriors who succumb to the mutiny of the priests, who have too much time to think, reflect, and resent, and to whose damning "creative" passivity both the warriors and the slaves (both active, working people) fall prey. The end of the story was the ascendance of conscience and the sovereign individual, with almost more biological space than the nobles had—the entire genealogy lodged right inside the human body. This almost indiscriminate celebration of "activity" is disconcerting in a consumer society where the differential ability of bodies to hold and to bear on one hand, and to act and frantically externalize on the other, bespeaks of a social structural order. The present-day sovereign consumer is defined precisely by how quickly he does externalize, how minimal the capacity of the body is to endure and hold—where, to allude to Kundera's image in *The Book of Laughter and Forgetting*, all orgasms are logged. (We bear too much by bearing too little—real suffering gets occluded by the consolation of activity!) I feel that such a relation to activity is actually very reminiscent of the nobles who acted for the sake of action, since the activity of consumption is an end in itself, thus a perfect action. (I am also thinking of the affliction in the film *28 Days Later*, where the diseased do not actually eat people but "consume" only through infection). The actively discharging individual is very much at home in contemporary culture. Perhaps what lay beyond Nietzsche's sovereign individual was a certain Dionysian selflessness, but Dionysus in the terrain of value creation is very similar to the noble warrior from the first essay of the *Genealogy*. This forces us to think that the tragic artist, with his thirty-six or more ways to suffer, cannot be a weird look-alike of this noble warrior. So when the regime of value creation and productivity provides a mold for all our activities, Marx and Nietzsche can be read as raising the question of activity and passivity in a crucial critique of liberal capitalism. Both Marx and Nietzsche can be approached in this way, precisely because neither is hope merely as an escape from given conditions, nor suffering merely productive. I do not see the actions of the wounded as valuable only if they affirm an instrumental relation to actions and suffering. The notions of materialist necessity and hope can be broadened—as the necessity of making necessities into conditions for the possibility of a new form, and for the possibility of going beyond form itself. (See *28*

Days Later, DVD, directed by Danny Boyle [Gloucestershire, UK: DNA Films, 2002].)

42. Postone, *Time, Labor, and Social Domination*, 30.

CHAPTER 5

1. For instance, in trying to grasp the logic at work in the depiction of the suffering of Jesus (*The Passion of the Christ*, directed by Mel Gibson, [Basilicata, Italy: Icon Productions, 2004]), I am baffled by the way "God" (given that Jesus was pointedly *not* all too human) abides by such a calculus and how redemption stands refigured in a rather capitalist way (he suffered, nay died, for you, it is time to redeem him, so pay back). The film is troubling because it shows the suffering of Christ in completely anachronistic and narcissistic ways (the narcissism is also extremely unironic); it transfers onto Jesus the relation we currently have to our acknowledged injuries and harms as insiders to a liberal hegemonic apparatus. It exhibits a superficial and possessive individualistic relation to our own and others' suffering, faithful to the precepts of utilitarian notions of justice, the demands of juridical politics, and the subsequent terms of inclusion, exclusion, punishment, reward, speech, and silence. Christ and angels take the form of clearing agents, keeping a ledger of his suffering and those of others on his behalf, with an ethos of quantification and measurability that ought to keep us captive until we have finally paid him back for his suffering. There have been, and are, other ways of understanding the suffering of Christ that do not employ, still less, impute, a possessive individualist and economistic mentality. But it is testament to our times and capacities that the suffering of anyone, even Jesus, could be reduced to our inane, senile, and depleted liberal capitalist sensorium. My issue here is not with an accurate interpretation or representation of Jesus or his suffering. I instead want to highlight two things: (1) that there is something to be taken from Feuerbach's understanding of religion as the projection of the collective capacities of the species at a given moment; thus, Jesus can only be understood in the way we understand suffering at this moment, regardless of the origins of the latter; and (2) that this explicitly shows the limits of our understanding of why people suffer and how one must respond to suffering, and it may also show the interest of institutions of power (whether in religion, economics, politics, or law) in reinforcing those understandings. If the first observation is not entirely true in the sense that some of us *do* have capacities that are differently human or that resist the discourse of utilitarian suffering, then Feuerbach's celebration of the species needs an update for contemporary times: some discourses are powerful enough to preempt the possibility of a truly democratic installation of our "gods." Thus, when liberal approaches to suffering predominate, by universalizing pain and fear and our modes of and relations to our own and others'

pain and fear, the result is similar. Rousseau tells a comparable story in the *Discourse on the Origin of Inequality* about the installation of private property and civil society. See Jean-Jacques Rousseau, *The Discourses and Other Early Political Writings*, ed. Victor Gourevitch (New York: Cambridge University Press, 1997).

2. This comes as no surprise, since representation of labor by the value of its product is only part of this problem for Marx. The other part of the problem is that of the representation of labor-*time* by the magnitude of the same value. In other words, value represents both the labor as well as the labor-power in terms of time, as discussed earlier. Thus, the fetish character of the commodity derives from both aspects of this representation and its ability to convince us that they are the same.

3. For instance, the need to prove explicit harmful intent or individual harm in disparate treatment cases in the late 1980s, or the loud assertion of the *purely* "political" nature of liberalism in Shklar's work that, with its bleeding heart for the invisibility of injustice and victims, can only find a way of *making* them more visible, with no input of theirs nor an ethos of expecting them to pitch in the labor of suffering that they continue to keep alive.

4. Karl Marx, *Capital: A Critique of Political Economy*, ed. Friedrich Engels, trans. Samuel Moore and Edward Aveling (New York: International Publishers, 1967), 75.

5. Jean-Luc Nancy, "The Two Secrets of the Fetish," *Diacritics* 31 (2001): 3. Nancy makes the case that we ought not to take the fetish's revelation as a demystification—a question Marx also clearly raises where he sees the limitations of Feuerbach's account as resolving the problem of fetishes and its closet idealism. Nancy asks, "Does the living humanity inscribed in a work become visible as something other than the idea of an incommensurable measure? By definition, he who topples idols promises the truth of a god that is neither ensured nor saturated by any presentation. It is always a negative theology that which unmasks idolatries: and the divine superessence, at the same time that it confirms the transcendence and authority of the true god, does not itself appear" (5). Nancy talks about how the uncovering of the secret still leaves behind an undisclosed secret: "The very presence of the thing, whether it is named commodity or product, paid for in cash or by credit card, worshipped or utilized, the thing itself, the pro-duced thing: the thing driven to the foreground, brought forward in the strange element of presence in and for itself" (6). The secret is of the immeasurability of alienation and hence of fetish. The secret is called "revealed secret" and "demystified fetish"—but these expressions do not yet show the truth of production, or rather the truth of the producer in person or in subject, the truth of his singular and communal existence, whose future portrait Marx, at times, sketches out. But let us recognize that if he came upon us in the person, the living (natural, not artificial—the nonfabricated fabricator) producer would offer his

face, his true presence. He would present himself, and he would be pre-sented to us. Still, what theology or philosophy finds reprehensible in the idol is presence as the presentation of truth.

6. *Oxford English Dictionary*, 2nd ed., s.v. "character, n.," http://dictionary.oed.com/cgi/entry/50036832.

7. Marx, *Capital*, 72.

8. Ibid., 84–85.

9. Ibid., 86.

10. Ibid., 72.

11. In a crass analogy to the stock market, for instance, this is the move from M-C-M` to M-M` in Marx's analysis of the stages of capital. Thus, just like the gaping, inviting absence of labor and its production in M-M` can-not be construed as absence per se, I persist in the claim that Rawls does show us the production process of bodies and their suffering in liberal society so closely because he is so obviously trying to hardest to localize, segregate, and, one may say, noumenalize it in the original position.

12. Marx, *Capital*, 131–32.

13. Friedrich Nietzsche, *On the Genealogy of Morals and Ecce Homo*, trans. Walter Arnold Kaufmann and R. J. Hollingdale (New York: Vintage, 1989), 3:13, 120.

14. Ibid., 3:28, 118.

15. Ibid., 3:1, 58.

16. Karl Marx, "The Meaning of Human Requirements," in *Economic and Philosophic Manuscripts of 1844*, ed. Dirk J. Struik, trans. Martin Milligan (New York: International Publishers, 1964), 153–54.

17. Chandra Talpade Mohanty, "Under Western Eyes," in *Third World Women and the Politics of Feminism*, ed. Chandra Talpade Mohanty, Ann Russo, and Lourdes Torres (Bloomington: Indiana University Press, 1991), 62.

18. Marnia Lazreg, "Feminism and Difference: The Perils of Writing as a Woman on Woman in Algeria," *Feminist Issues* 14, no. 1 (Spring 1988): 81–107. Quoted by Mohanty in "Under Western Eyes," 62. See also Nayereh Tohidi, "Gender and Islamic Fundamentalism: Feminist Politics in Iran," in *Third World Women and the Politics of Feminism*, 252.

19. See Marx's discussion of political and human emancipation in Karl Marx, "On the Jewish Question," in *Selected Writings*, ed. Lawrence Simon (Indianapolis: Hackett, 1994), 1–26.

20. However, as far as slave morality is concerned, the very need of the first world to fetishize the "East" or "orientalize" it allows them to "name" themselves—hence, the myth of Narcissus is even more applicable: slave morality *rebounds*.

21. They cease to become "impositions" from the outside because they become culturally embedded, dominant symbols and signs. The "objects" (think of any Mira Nair film) themselves become part of the machine of reproducing these images.

22. Mohanty, "Under Western Eyes," 65. Mohanty is referring to Maria Mies's work on lacemakers in Narsapur, India. See also Maria Mies, *Lace Makers of Narsapur: Indian Housewives in the World Market* (London: Zed Books, 1982).

23. See also Martha C. Nussbaum, "Victims and Agents: What Greek Tragedy Can Teach Us About Sympathy and Responsibility," *Boston Review* 23 (February/March 1998); Jean Bethke Elshtain and J. Timothy Cloyd, *Politics and the Human Body: Assault on Dignity* (Nashville, TN: Vanderbilt University Press, 1995).

24. Gayatri Chakravorty Spivak, "Can the Subaltern Speak?" in *Marxism and the Interpretation of Culture*, ed. Cary Nelson and Lawrence Grossberg (Urbana: University of Illinois Press, 1988), 271–313.

25. Nietzsche, *On the Genealogy of Morals*, 2:10, 36–37.

26. Catharine A. MacKinnon, *Toward a Feminist Theory of the State* (Cambridge, MA: Harvard University Press, 1989), 180.

27. Richard H. Bell, *Simone Weil: The Way of Justice as Compassion* (Lanham, MD: Rowman & Littlefield, 1998), 52–53. Bell is quoting MacKinnon from "Rape: On Coercion and Consent," in *Writing on the Body: Female Embodiment and Feminist Theory*, ed. Katie Conboy, Nadia Medina, and Sarah Stanbury (New York: Columbia University Press, 1997), 44.

28. Wendy Brown, *States of Injury: Power and Freedom in Late Modernity* (Princeton, NJ: Princeton University Press, 1995), 26–27, 66–70.

29. Ibid., 74–76.

30. Part of Shklar's wish was framed in the way MacKinnon's rhetoric is—in terms of the visibility of injustice—but the degree to which each of them is invested in the problematic of injustice is vastly different. Shklar's wish to see the invisible injustices is circumscribed by the political, while for MacKinnon, the idea is to overload the structure of law with meaning, in a way that will eventually, in a Marxist sense, undo it; that is, to render the law illegal, as it were. The contrast to Rimbaud's move is Mallarme's sundering of language and meaning altogether. The critical analog to the latter would be entirely detaching something from the logic of liberalism and its institutions. Brown wants a way in-between, but she thinks she can allow the terrain to remain unreframed. I do not think so. How the relations between materiality and representation are theorized is where the answer lies. Overloading the language, or dethroning it, comes with its set of material processes. Please see Iris Murdoch, *Sartre, Romantic Rationalist* (New York: Viking, 1987), 64–68.

31. Brown, *States of Injury*, 55.

32. See Judith Butler, "Burning Acts: Injurious Speech," *University of Chicago Law School Roundtable* 3 (1996): 199.

33. Brown, *States of Injury*, 75.

34. Ibid., 137. Brown's awareness is evidenced in her claim that Carole Pateman only "criticiz[es] the fetish."

35. Spivak, "Can the Subaltern Speak?" 308.

36. See also Wendy Brown, *Politics Out of History* (Princeton, NJ: Princeton University Press, 2001), 119.

CHAPTER 6

1. Virginia Woolf, *Mrs. Dalloway* (Orlando, FL: Harcourt, 1990), 49–109.
2. Karl Marx, "Preface to the Second Edition (1869) of *The Eighteenth Brumaire of Louis Bonaparte*," http://www.marxists.org/archive/marx/works/1852/18th-brumaire/preface.htm.
3. Georges Duveau, *1848: The Making of a Revolution* (New York: Vintage Books, 1967), 207–8.
4. *Democratic Underground*, "Garrison Keillor Endorses Obama," February 3, 2008, http://www.democraticunderground.com/discuss/duboard.php?az=view_all&address=132x4368598.
5. Karl Marx, "Manifesto of the Communist Party" in *Selected Writings*, ed. Lawrence Simon (Indianapolis: Hackett, 1994), 158.
6. R. R. Palmer and Joel G. Colton, *A History of the Modern World* (New York: McGraw-Hill, 1992), xxxi, 506.
7. *Oxford English Dictionary*, 2nd ed., s.v. "comedy, n.," http://dictionary.oed.com/cgi/entry/50044658.
8. *Oxford English Dictionary*, 2nd ed., s.v. "farce, n.2," http://dictionary.oed.com/cgi/entry/50082266.
9. Albert Bermel, *Farce: A History from Aristophanes to Woody Allen* (New York: Simon and Schuster, 1982), 61; *Oxford English Dictionary*, s.v. "farce, n.1," http://dictionary.oed.com/cgi/entry/50082265.
10. Friedrich Nietzsche, *On the Genealogy of Morals and Ecce Homo*, trans. Walter Arnold Kaufmann and R. J. Hollingdale (New York: Vintage, 1989), 3:11, 117.
11. The Dionysian's lack of affiliation to any individuation principle renders it the creative principle of ecstasy and mystical rapture that brings wisdom, insight, and energy and that pushes and tests the Apollonian limits and guidelines to human activity. In its manifestation of artistic and creative expression in intoxication, sexuality, community, the Dionysian works to break moral and conceptual limits. In Dionysian frenzy, the artist experiences the excitement and enhancement of his entire affective system. Interestingly enough, within the ambit of the Dionysian, Nietzsche includes all its means of expression at once and the simultaneously driving forth of the "power of representing, imitating, transfiguring, transforming, and every kind of mimicking and acting" (Friedrich Nietzsche, *Twilight of the Idols, or, How to Philosophize with the Hammer* [Indianapolis: Hackett, 1997], 56). The Apollonian, with its introduction of limits and boundaries, is responsible for demarcating the cultural and social world—the world of symbolic metaphors, cognitive frames, moral order, dreaming, visual arts, is Apollonian.

While the Apollonian gives us the norms, institutions, and interpretive frames, the Dionysian is the generous giver of the creative power that constantly renews our dynamic energies and drives toward a higher form of wisdom. This wisdom is the tragic vision. The Dionysian stands for the creative deployment of the passions and the affirmation of life in spite of suffering—as it were, it represents a synthesis of the Dionysian, as originally conceived in *Birth*, with the Apollonian. In other words, when the tragic artist is termed Dionysian in *Twilight*, he is an embodiment of this very synthesis of the Dionysian and Apollonian.

The fact that this synthesis even occurs is owed to the oceanic desire for oneness and wholeness on part of the Dionysian, but it is the Apollonian that affords a form, a representation, a demarcation, an "embodiment" to this wholeness. (In other words, not unlike Socrates' characterization of pain and pleasure being joined at their heads at birth, I feel the Apollonian and Dionysian coexist in the same way, as necessary conditions for the validation of the other.)

On another level, it seems appropriately historical and dialectical that through Nietzsche's meditation on these instincts, and as they continued to play out while Nietzsche meditated, they each became more like the other. Nietzsche writes in *Birth*, "Where the Dionysian powers rise up impetuously as we experience them now, Apollo, too, must already have descended among us, wrapped in a cloud; and the next generation will probably behold his most ample beautiful effects" (Friedrich Nietzsche, *The Birth of Tragedy and The Case of Wagner*, trans. Walter Arnold Kaufman [New York: Vintage Books, 1967], 143–44). If this teleology is too repulsive, the transition from *Birth* to *Twilight* is one from tragedy of the chorus to the "drama" or from the Dionysian and Apollonian to the Apollonian-Dionysian (as discussed in Chapter 2).

12. Nietzsche, *On the Genealogy of Morals*, 3:20, 141.

13. Art also makes apparent much that is ugly, hard, and questionable in life. For example, if one were to talk about the art form of tragedy, the utility of tragedy was found, according to Schopenhauer, in its ability to "evoke resignation." In his preface to the *Birth*, Nietzsche disavows this resignation, and hence his use of tragedy purported to do actually the opposite: negate Schopenhauer's use of tragedy as the negation of will and of life.

14. Iris Murdoch, "The Sublime and the Beautiful Revisited," in *Existentialists and Mystics: Writings on Philosophy and Literature*, ed. Peter J. Conradi (New York: Allen Lane/Penguin, 1998), 286.

15. David J. Gordon, *Iris Murdoch's Fables of Unselfing* (Columbia: University of Missouri Press, 1995), 20.

16. For a contextual discussion of the status of these metaphors, see David Michael Kleinberg-Levin, *Sites of Vision: The Discursive Construction of Sight in the History of Philosophy* (Cambridge, MA: MIT Press, 1997).

17. Murdoch's avowed Platonism and antimaterialism do not help here, but I do not find that to be a huge hurdle since her major critiques of

materialism are critiques of mechanistic philosophy, which carry over also into her relation to language itself (and, in my view, to representation).

18. Gordon, *Iris Murdoch's Fables of Unselfing*, 108.

19. The redemptive gaze of Walter Benjamin's Angelus Novus (his use of Paul Klee's painting in "Theses on the Philosophy of History") is helpful in visualizing this overcoming when applied to the task of creating forms that are not subservient to tragedy, farce, or any preexistent or predetermined form whatsoever, and of responding to injustice, fetishistic injury, and enforced forgetting. The generously redemptive, yet uncomfortably tentative, gaze backward suggests that such an outdoing is consistent with a recovery or return that amounts to a transformative confrontation. This confrontation may release the possibilities of alternative presents without glancing away from the reality of the present at the same time. An essential part of that reality is the fact that our identities have been rendered inextricable from our memory of suffering, not to mention the all-too-human propensity to look to the past for comfort and shelter, even if it requires the extra work of reconstructing the past in this new consoling mode. The passage of outmoded forms of history is not achieved in replacing old fetishes and institutions with new ones in language only, but in allowing them to pass because our own sufferings cannot be borne by them—that they cannot hold. See Walter Benjamin, "Theses on the Philosophy of History," in *Illuminations: Essays and Reflections* (New York: Schocken Books, 1988), sec. 9, 257.

20. See Talal Asad, *Formations of the Secular* (Stanford, CA: Stanford University Press, 2003).

21. Karl Marx, "The Difference Between the Democritean and the Epicurean Philosophy of Nature," in *Activity in Marx's Philosophy*, ed. Norman D. Livergood (The Hague, Netherlands: Martinus Nijhoff, 1967), 42–43.

22. Ibid., 51.

23. Ibid., 43–44.

24. The connection to the stone inscriptions in Ingeborg Bachmann's *Malina* is unmistakable, whether or not intended by Kushner. It is worth thinking what these dream sequences and their attendant injunctions tell us about the relations and redemptions of suffering posited, idealized, and imagined in the liminalities invoked and harnessed by Bachmann and Kushner.

25. For example, Dawn Rae Davis, "(Love Is) the Ability of Not Knowing: Feminist Experience of the Impossible in Ethical Singularity," *Hypatia* 17, no. 2 (2002): 145–61.

26. As discussed earlier, Nietzsche often brings up the eye of the sufferer and the suffering that sobers up and reorients the senses to the world. See Friedrich Nietzsche, *Daybreak: Thoughts on the Prejudices of Morality*, ed. Maudemarie Clark and Brian Leiter (New York: Cambridge University Press, 1997), 114.

27. Marx, "Theses on Feuerbach" in *Selected Writings*, ed. Lawrence Simon, 101.
28. Please refer back to my discussion of Brudney in Chapter 4.
29. Iris Murdoch, *Sartre, Romantic Rationalist* (New York: Viking Press, 1987), 31.
30. Marx, "Wage Labour and Capital," Marx/Engels Internet Archive (1993), http://www.marxists.org/archive/marx/works/1847/wage-labour/index.htm.20.
31. Those who survive carry the weight of the surplus value equation: reproducing labor-power costs less than the exchange value of the products produced. On a different but related note, I find the following excerpt from the Harry Cleaver's introduction to Antonio Negri's *Marx Beyond Marx* to be rather provocative and powerful: "Although he paints a true horror story of living labor being dominated by capitalist-controlled dead labor, Marx also makes clear that living labor cannot be killed off totally or capital itself would die. The irony of capitalist reproduction is that it must assure the continued reproduction of the living subject. The antagonism is recreated on higher and higher levels as capital develops. What begins as the horror of zombie-like dead labor being summoned against living labor, becomes, over time, an increasingly desperate attempt by capital to protect its own existence against an ever-more-powerful-and-hostile working class. Capital can never win, totally, once and for ever. It must tolerate the continued existence of an alien subjectivity which constantly threatens to destroy it. What a vision: capital, living in everlasting fear of losing control over the hostile class it has brought into existence! This is the peacefully placid capitalist hegemony of traditional Marxism turned inside out, become a nightmare for the ruling class." Harry Cleaver, Introduction to in Antonio Negri, *Marx Beyond Marx: Lessons on the Grundrisse*, ed. Jim Fleming, trans. Harry Cleaver, Michael Ryan, and Maurizio Viano (New York: Autonomedia/Pluto, 1996), xxiii.
32. Veena Das and others, eds., *Remaking a World: Violence, Social Suffering, and Recovery* (Berkeley, CA: University of California Press, 2001), 21.
33. Aldo Tassi, in his work on the metaphysics of performance, writes, "To be sure, impersonation as it takes place outside the theater is a matter of pretending to be what one is not: that is to say, of using one's body in such a way as to refer the spectator to someone else. In the theater, however, impersonation is a matter of becoming what one is not. The actor's body is used as the site of a metamorphosis. In order to accomplish this, the actor engages in a number of preparatory exercises directed at breaking down the body's tendency to become a referential site during the acting situation. In other words, the goal to be achieved in the theatrical performance is one where the character in the play appears onstage not as someone the actor refers us to, but rather as someone who has come to full-blooded presence in the actor's body. The primordial function of the theater performance, then, is to bring this character to presence, using

the actor's body as a threshold." Aldo Tassi. "The Metaphysics of Performance: The 'Theater of the World'" (paper presented at the Twentieth
World Congress of Philosophy, Boston, Massachusetts, August 10–15,
1998), *The Paideia Project Online: Proceedings of the 20th World Congress
of Philosophy.* http://www.bu.edu/wcp/Papers/Aest/AestTass.htm.

34. See Konstantin Stanislavsky, *An Actor's Handbook: An Alphabetical
Arrangement of Concise Statements on Aspects of Acting* (New York: Theater Arts Books, 1963) and also David Krasner, *Method Acting Reconsidered: Theory, Practice, Future* (New York: St. Martin's Press, 2000).

35. See also Harold Rosenberg, *Act and the Actor: Making the Self* (New
York: World Publishing, 1970) and Tracy Strong, *The Idea of Political
Theory: Reflections on the Self in Political Time and Place* (Notre Dame,
IN: University of Notre Dame Press, 1990) for two very thoughtful and
different approaches to the theater and artistry of the self as actor.

36. See Walter Benjamin, *Understanding Brecht* (London: Verso, 2003) and
Krasner, *Method Acting Reconsidered.*

37. See, in particular, Marx's discussion of Feuerbach in Karl Marx and others, *The German Ideology* (London: Lawrence & Wishart, 1970), 62–64.

38. Jack I. Biles, "An Interview with Iris Murdoch," *Studies in the Literary
Imagination* 11 (1978): 117.

39. See Paul Woodruff, *Reverence: Renewing a Forgotten Virtue* (Oxford:
Oxford University Press, 2001).

40. Marx W. Wartofsky, *Feuerbach* (New York: Cambridge University Press,
1977), 407. Wartofsky quotes Feuerbach from Feuerbach's *Collected
Works* (1st ed.) 10:125 and note. This edition was published sometime
between 1903 and 1910 (see "Author's Note," xvi).

41. In Marx's view, the development of society—the evolution of language,
labor, and primary social forms—is marked by the making distinct of
the processes of production and consumption. The immediacy of production and consumption is riven in this historical process—the space
between consumption and production is precisely where society comes
into existence. This allows for the objectification of a social universe and
of human history. In capitalist society, the labor takes a specific form
because of what and how it produces within the strictures of the production process within which it performs.

42. The question of translation between individual and collective has to contend with the body as property. Marx's discussion of social humanity
in his theses on Feuerbach forces us to think of the individual as being
possible only within a particular social form. Marx does not find it essential that individuality be owned in merely one way; he does, after all,
find appropriation (as a dialectical moment within productive activity)
to be not reducible to private property. Wartofsky explains: "The species
being does not exist in itself, but only in the relation, the interaction, of
I and thou; that is, it is constituted only among individuals. The community, the commonality, is not an entity, therefore not a hypostatized,

independent being, but a relation, or as Marx was to say, an ensemble of relations. The bond, existential relation itself, remains vague, abstract. It is love, or sensibility, or dependence." Marx W. Wartofsky, *Feuerbach* (New York: Cambridge University Press, 1977), 426.

43. See also Herbert Marcuse, *An Essay on Liberation* (Boston: Beacon, 1969), and Jacques Rancière, *Disagreement: Politics and Philosophy* (Minneapolis: University of Minnesota Press, 1998).

44. The question, however, that is raised is of the quality, not quantity. I have argued that the very interaction is shaped by liberalism, even if the interactions are multiplied. But, the difference is that the intersubjectivity and excess are not recognized. Is it Marx's claim that the worker is capable of a different experience by virtue of his social existence that would lead to the creation of his consciousness as the only emancipatory one?

45. *Oxford English Dictionary*, 2nd ed., s.v. "commutative, a.," http://dictionary.oed.com/cgi/entry/50045249. Defined as "relating to or involving substitution or interchange; as the commutative principle in arithmetic and algebra, i.e., the principle by which the order of terms or factors may be altered."

46. Both Aristotle and Aquinas speak of commutative versus distributive justice, but in different ways, and I am not importing their language since I am not talking about forms of justice here. But I do want to suggest that a particular relation of exchange begets a corresponding relation among parts of the whole. In the present division of labor (and of the labor of suffering), where the emphasis on the distribution of suffering sees the welfare state as the broker, the notion of distributive justice in Aquinas is brought to mind, where the focus is on the relation of one to the whole.

47. See Martha Nussbaum, "Patriotism and Cosmopolitanism" and "Reply," in *For Love of Country*, ed. Joshua Cohen (Boston: Beacon, 2002), 3–20, 131–44.

BIBLIOGRAPHY

28 Days Later. Directed by Danny Boyle. Gloucestershire, UK: DNA Films, 2002. DVD.

Ackerman, Bruce. "Political Liberalisms." *Journal of Philosophy* 91 (1994): 364–86.

Adorno, Theodor W. *Aesthetic Theory.* Edited by Gretel Adorno and Rolf Tiedeman. Minneapolis: University of Minnesota Press, 1997.

Aldridge, A. O. "The Pleasures of Pity." *ELH* 16 (1949): 76–87.

Alejandro, Roberto. "What Is Political About Rawl's Political Liberalism?" *Journal of Politics* 58 (1996): 1–24.

Ankersmit, Frank R. *Aesthetic Politics: Political Philosophy Beyond Fact and Value.* Stanford, CA: Stanford University Press, 1996.

———. "Representational Democracy: An Aesthetic Approach to Conflict and Compromise." *Common Knowledge* 8 (2002): 24–46.

Arthur, C. J. *Dialectics of Labour: Marx and his Relation to Hegel.* Oxford: Blackwell, 1986.

Asad, Talal. *Formations of the Secular.* Stanford, CA: Stanford University Press, 2003.

Aslam, Nadeem. *Maps for Lost Lovers.* London: Knopf, 2005.

Avineri, Shlomo. "The Instrumentality of Passion in the World of Reason: Hegel and Marx." *Political Theory* 1 (1973): 388–404.

Árdal, Páll S. *Passion and Value in Hume's Treatise.* Edinburgh, Scotland: Edinburgh University Press, 1989.

Bachmann, Ingeborg. *The Book of Franza & Requiem for Fanny Goldmann.* 1st English language ed. Evanston, IL: Northwestern University Press, 1999.

———. *Malina: A Novel.* New York: Holmes & Meier, 1990.

Baier, Annette C. "Moralism and Cruelty: Reflections on Hume and Kant." *Ethics* 103 (1993): 436–57.

Bandes, Susan A. *The Passions of Law.* New York: New York University Press, 1999.

Baudrillard, Jean. *The Mirror of Production.* St. Louis, MI: Telos, 1975.

Baynes, Kenneth. "Rights as Critique and the Critique of Rights: Karl Marx, Wendy Brown, and the Social Function of Rights." *Political Theory* 28 (2000): 451–68.

Beiser, Frederick C. *Early Political Writings of the German Romantics.* Cambridge, UK: Cambridge University Press, 1996.

Bell, Richard H. *Simone Weil: The Way of Justice as Compassion.* Lanham, MD: Rowman & Littlefield, 1998.

Bellamy, Richard, and Martin Hollis. "Liberal Justice: Political and Metaphysical." *The Philosophical Quarterly* 45 (1995): 1–19.

Benhabib, Seyla. "Judith Shklar's Dystopic Liberalism." In *Liberalism Without Illusions: Essays on Liberal Theory and the Political Vision of Judith N. Shklar,* edited by Bernard Yack, 55–63. Chicago: University of Chicago Press, 1996.

Benjamin, Walter. *Illuminations: Essays and Reflections.* Edited by Hannah Arendt. New York: Schocken Books, 1988.

———. "Theses on the Philosophy of History." In *Illuminations,* edited by Hannah Arendt, 253–64. New York: Schocken Books, 1988

———. *The Origin of German Tragic Drama.* London: Verso, 2003.

———. *Understanding Brecht.* London: Verso, 1998.

Berki, R. N. "On the Nature and Origins of Marx's Concept of Labor." *Political Theory* 7 (1979): 35–56.

Berkowitz, Peter. "John Rawls and the Liberal Faith." *The Wilson Quarterly* (2002).

Berlin, Isaiah. *Four Essays on Liberty.* Oxford: Oxford University Press, 1969.

Berman, Marshall. *All That Is Solid Melts into Air: The Experience of Modernity.* New York: Viking Penguin, 1988.

Bermel, Albert. *Farce: A History from Aristophanes to Woody Allen.* New York: Simon and Schuster, 1982.

Biles, Jack I. "An Interview with Iris Murdoch." *Studies in the Literary Imagination* 11 (1978): 115–25.

Birch, Charles. *Feelings.* Sydney: University of New South Wales Press, 1995.

Borges, Jorge Luis. "Funes, the Memorious." In *Ficciones,* edited by Anthony Kerrigan, translated by Anthony Bonner, 107–16. New York: Grove, 1994.

Bove, Cheryl Browning. *Understanding Iris Murdoch.* Columbia: University of South Carolina Press, 1993.

Bowie, Andrew. *Aesthetics and Subjectivity from Kant to Nietzsche.* Manchester, UK: Manchester University Press, 1990.

Broad, C. D. "Emotion and Sentiment." *Journal of Aesthetics and Art Criticism* 13 (1954): 203–14.

Brown, Wendy. *Politics Out of History.* Princeton, NJ: Princeton University Press, 2001.

———. *States of Injury: Power and Freedom in Late Modernity.* Princeton, NJ: Princeton University Press, 1995.

Brudney, Daniel. *Marx's Attempt to Leave Philosophy.* Cambridge, MA: Harvard University Press, 1998.

Butler, Judith. "Burning Acts: Injurious Speech." *University of Chicago Law School Roundtable* 3 (1996): 199.

———. *Excitable Speech: A Politics of the Performative*. New York: Routledge, 1997.

Card, Claudia. *The Atrocity Paradigm: A Theory of Evil*. New York: Oxford University Press, 2005.

———. "Review of Elizabeth Spelman's *Fruits of Sorrow: Framing Our Attention to Suffering*." *Ethics* 109 (1998): 181–84.

Carse, Alisa L. "The Liberal Individual: A Metaphysical or Moral Embarrassment?" *Noûs* 28 (1994): 184–209.

Cazeaux, Clive. *The Continental Aesthetics Reader*. London: Routledge, 2000.

Chambliss, J. J. *Imagination and Reason in Plato, Aristotle, Vico, Rousseau, and Keats: An Essay on the Philosophy of Experience*. The Hague, Netherlands: Martinus Nijhoff, 1974.

Chopp, Rebecca S. *The Praxis of Suffering: An Interpretation of Liberation and Political Theologies*. Maryknoll, NY: Orbis Books, 1986.

Cleaver, Harry. Introduction to *Marx Beyond Marx: Lessons on the Grundrisse*, by Antonio Negri. Edited by Jim Fleming. Translated by Harry Cleaver, Michael Ryan, and Maurizio Viano. New York: Autonomedia/Pluto, 1996.

Cohen, Joshua, ed. *For Love of Country?* Boston: Beacon, 2002.

Colebrook, Claire. "Questioning Representation." *SubStance* 92 (2000): 47–67.

Colletti, Lucio. *From Rousseau to Lenin: Studies in Ideology and Society*. London: New Left Review Books, 1972.

Conniff, James. "Burke, Bristol, and the Concept of Representation." *The Western Political Quarterly* 30 (1977): 329–41.

Courtine, Jean-François, ed. *Of the Sublime: Presence in Question*. Albany: State University of New York Press, 1993.

Das, Veena, Arthur Kleinman, Margaret Lock, Mamphela Ramphele, and Pamela Reynolds, eds. *Remaking a World: Violence, Social Suffering, and Recovery*. Berkeley: University of California Press, 2001.

Davis, Dawn Rae. "(Love is) the Ability of Not Knowing: Feminist Experience of the Impossible in Ethical Singularity." *Hypatia* 17, no. 2 (2002): 145–61.

Dieke, Ikenna. "Tragic Faith and the Dionysian Unconscious: An Interfacing of Novelist Baraka and Friedrich Nietzsche." *Black American Literature Forum* 24 (1990): 99–116.

Democratic Underground. "Garrison Keillor Endorses Obama," February 3, 2008. http://www.democraticunderground.com/discuss/duboard .php?az=view_all&address=132x4368598.

Dore, Clement. "Does Suffering Serve Valuable Ends?" *Philosophy and Phenomenological Research* 45 (1984): 103–10.

DuBois, William Edward Burghardt. *The Souls of Black Folk*. New York: W. W. Norton, 1999.

Duveau, Georges. *1848: The Making of a Revolution*. New York: Vintage Books, 1967.

Eagleton, Terry. *The Ideology of the Aesthetic*. Oxford, UK: Basil Blackwell, 1990.

———. *Sweet Violence: The Idea of the Tragic*. Malden, MA: Blackwell, 2003.

Eldridge, Richard. "How Can Tragedy Matter for Us?" *Journal of Aesthetics and Art Criticism* 52 (1994): 287–98.

Elshtain, Jean Bethke, and J. Timothy Cloyd. *Politics and the Human Body: Assault on Dignity*. Nashville, TN: Vanderbilt University Press, 1995.

Elson, Diane, ed. *Value: The Representation of Labour in Capitalism*. London: CSE Books, 1980.

———."The Value Theory of Labour." In *Value: The Representation of Labour in Capitalism*. edited by Diane Elson, 115–80. London: CSE Books, 1980.

Engels, Friedrich. *Ludwig Feuerbach and the End of Classical German Philosophy*. Honolulu, HI: University Press of the Pacific, 2005.

Esquith, Stephen L., and Richard T. Peterson. "The Original Position as Social Practice." *Political Theory* 16 (1988): 300–34.

Faiz, Faiz Ahmad. *Poems by Faiz*. Translated by V. G. Kiernan. London: Allen and Unwin, 1971.

Feinberg, Joel. *The Moral Limits of the Criminal Law: Harm to Others*. Vol. 1. New York: Oxford University Press, 1984.

Feuerbach, Ludwig. *The Essence of Christianity*. Amherst, NY: Prometheus Books, 1989.

———. *The Fiery Brook: Selected Writings of Ludwig Feuerbach*. Edited by Zawar Hanfi. Garden City, NY: Anchor Books, 1972.

Finch, Henry Le Roy, and Martin Andic. *Simone Weil and the Intellect of Grace*. New York: Continuum Books, 1999.

Foucault, Michel. *Language, Counter-Memory, Practice*. Ithaca, NY: Cornell University Press, 1980.

Franklin, Benjamin. "A Dissertation on Liberty and Necessity, Pleasure and Pain." New York: Facsimile Text Society, 1930.

Fraser, Nancy. *Justice Interruptus: Critical Reflections on the "Postsocialist" Condition*. New York: Routledge, 1997.

Fraser, Nancy, and Axel Honneth. *Redistribution or Recognition? A Political-Philosophical Exchange*. New York: Verso, 2003.

Freud, Sigmund. *Civilization and its Discontents*. New York: Dover, 1994.

Galloway, A. D. "The Meaning of Feuerbach: The Hobhouse Memorial Lecture, 1974." *The British Journal of Sociology* 25 (1974): 135–49.

Galston, William A. *Liberal Pluralism: The Implications of Value Pluralism for Political Theory and Practice*. New York: Cambridge University Press, 2002.

———. "Liberal Virtues." *American Political Science Review* 82 (1988): 1277–90.

———. "Two Concepts of Liberalism." *Ethics* 105 (1995): 516–34.

Garver, Eugene. "Aristotle's Genealogy of Morals." *Philosophy and Phenomenological Research* 44 (1984): 471–92.

Gordon, David J. *Iris Murdoch's Fables of Unselfing*. Columbia: University of Missouri Press, 1995.

Grass, Gunter. *The Tin Drum*. New York: Vintage, 1990.

Gray, John. *Post-liberalism: Studies in Political Thought*. New York: Routledge, 1993.

Gutmann, Amy. "Communitarian Critics of Liberalism." *Philosophy and Public Affairs* 14 (1985): 308–22.

Habermas, Jurgen. "Reconciliation Through the Public Use of Reason: Remarks on John Rawls's Political Liberalism." *Journal of Philosophy* 92 (1995): 109–31.

Halpern, Cynthia. *Suffering, Politics, Power: A Genealogy in Modern Political Theory*. Albany: State University of New York Press, 2002.

Harris, John. "The Marxist Conception of Violence." *Philosophy and Public Affairs* 3 (1974): 192–220.

Heilbroner, Robert L. *Teachings from the Worldly Philosophy*. New York: W. W. Norton, 1996.

Helfer, Martha B. *The Retreat of Representation: The Concept of Darstellung in German Critical Discourse*. Albany: State University of New York Press, 1996.

Hinden, Michael. "Ritual and Tragic Action: A Synthesis of Current Theory." *Journal of Aesthetics and Art Criticism* 32 (1974): 357–73.

Hirschman, Albert O. *The Passions and the Interests: Political Arguments for Capitalism Before its Triumph*. Princeton, NJ: Princeton University Press, 1996.

Hobbes, Thomas. *Leviathan: With Selected Variants from the Latin Edition of 1668*. Edited by E. M. Curley. Indianapolis: Hackett, 1994.

Hoffmann, Stanley. "Preface." In *Liberalism Without Illusions: Essays on Liberal Theory and the Political Vision of Judith N. Shklar*, edited by Bernard Yack, ix–xii. Chicago: University of Chicago Press, 1996.

Irwin, Alexander. *Saints of the Impossible: Bataille, Weil, and the Politics of the Sacred*. Minneapolis: University of Minnesota Press, 2002.

Jackson, Ned. "Reading Kemple Reading Marx Writing." *History and Theory* 37 (1998): 124–38.

Jaffe, Raymond. "Conservatism and the Praise of Suffering." *Ethics* 77 (1967): 254–67.

James, Susan. "The Duty to Relieve Suffering." *Ethics* 93 (1982): 4–21.

Jameson, Fredric. *Marxism and Form: Twentieth-Century Dialectical Theories of Literature.* Princeton, NJ: Princeton University Press, 1972.

Jay, Martin. *The Dialectical Imagination: A History of the Frankfurt School and the Institute for Social Research, 1923–1950.* Berkeley: University of California Press, 1996.

———. *Marxism and Totality: The Adventures of a Concept from Lukács to Habermas.* Berkeley: University of California Press, 1984.

Jenson, Deborah. *Trauma and Its Representations: The Social Life of Mimesis in Post-Revolutionary France.* Baltimore: Johns Hopkins University Press, 2001.

Jones, Peter. "Two Conceptions of Liberalism, Two Conceptions of Justice." *British Journal of Political Science* 25 (1995): 515–50.

Kant, Immanuel. *The Metaphysics of Morals.* Cambridge, UK: Cambridge University Press, 1991.

———. *Critique of Judgment.* Translated by Werner S. Pluhar. Indianapolis, IN: Hackett, 1987.

Kariel, Henry. "Review of The Idea of Political Theory: Reflections on the Self in Political Time and Space by Tracy Strong." *Political Theory* 20 (1992): 345–48.

Kekes, John. "Cruelty and Liberalism." *Ethics* 106 (1996): 834–44.

Kelly, George Armstrong. "Veils: The Poetics of John Rawls." *Journal of the History of Ideas* 57, no. 2 (1996): 343–64.

Kleinberg-Levin, David Michael. *Sites of Vision: The Discursive Construction of Sight in the History of Philosophy.* Cambridge, MA: MIT Press, 1997.

Kleinman, Arthur, Veena Das, and Margaret M. Lock, eds. *Social Suffering.* Berkeley: University of California Press, 1997.

Kleinman, Arthur, and Joan Kleinman, "The Appeal of Experience, The Dismay of Images: Cultural Appropriations of Suffering in Our Times." In *Social Suffering,* edited by Arthur Kleinman, Margaret M. Lock, and Veena Das, 11–15. Berkeley: University of California Press, 1997.

Kopp, Kristin. "The Discourse of Trauma—The Trauma of Discourse: Conquering Memory in Ingeborg Bachmann's Malina." In *Conquering Women: Women and War in the German Cultural Imagination,* edited by Hilary Collier Sy-Quia and Susanne Baackmann, 104:75–90. University of California Press/University of California International and Area Studies Digital Collection, 2000.

Krasner, David. *Method Acting Reconsidered: Theory, Practice, Future.* New York: St. Martin's Press, 2000.

Kundera, Milan. *The Book of Laughter and Forgetting.* New York: Harper Perennial Modern Classics, 1999.

Kurian, George Thomas. *The Illustrated Book of World Rankings.* 5th ed. Armonk, NY: Sharpe Reference, 2001.

Kushner, Tony. *Angels in America: A Gay Fantasia on National Themes.* New York: Theater Communications Group, 1995.

Lazreg, Marnia. "Feminism and Difference: The Perils of Writing as a Woman on Woman in Algeria." *Feminist Issues* 14, no. 1 (Spring 1988): 81–107.

Lewis, Clive Staples. *The Problem of Pain.* New York: Harper Collins, 2001.

Livergood, Norman D., and Karl Marx. *Activity in Marx's Philosophy.* The Hague, Netherlands: Martinus Nijhoff, 1967.

Locke, John. *An Essay Concerning Human Understanding.* Amherst, NY: Prometheus Books, 1995.

———. *A Letter Concerning Toleration.* Edited by James Tully. Indianapolis: Hackett, 1983.

———. *Second Treatise of Government.* Edited by C. B. Macpherson. Indianapolis: Hackett, 1980.

MacKinnon, Catharine A. *Toward a Feminist Theory of the State.* Cambridge, MA: Harvard University Press, 1989.

———. "Rape: On Coercion and Consent." In *Writing on the Body: Female Embodiment and Feminist Theory,* edited by Katie Conboy, Nadia Medina, and Sarah Stanbury, 42–58. New York: Columbia University Press, 1997.

Manent, Pierre. *An Intellectual History of Liberalism.* Princeton, NJ: Princeton University Press, 1994.

Mansbridge, Jane. "Should Blacks Represent Blacks and Women Represent Women? A Contingent 'Yes.'" *Journal of Politics* 61 (1999): 628–57.

Marcuse, Herbert. *The Aesthetic Dimension: Toward a Critique of Marxist Aesthetics.* Boston: Beacon, 1978.

———. *Eros and Civilization.* Boston: Beacon, 1966.

———. *An Essay on Liberation.* Boston: Beacon, 1969.

Margolis, Joseph. "Praxis and Meaning: Marx's Species Being and Aristotle's Political Animal." In *Marx and Aristotle: Nineteenth-Century German Social Theory and Classical Antiquity,* edited by George E. McCarthy, 329–55. Savage, MD: Rowman & Littlefield, 1992.

Marx, Karl. *Capital: A Critique of Political Economy.* Edited by Friedrich Engels. Translated by Samuel Moore and Edward Aveling. New York: International Publishers, 1967.

———. *A Contribution to the Critique of Political Economy.* New York: International Publishers, 1970.

———. "The Difference Between the Democritean and the Epicurean Philosophy of Nature." In *Activity in Marx's Philosophy*, edited by Norman D. Livergood. The Hague, Netherlands: Martinus Nijhoff, 1967.

———. *Economic and Philosophic Manuscripts of 1844*. Edited by Dirk J. Struik. Translated by Martin Milligan. New York: International Publishers, 1964.

———. "Private Property and Communism." In *Economic and Philosophic Manuscripts of 1844*. 132–46.

———. "The Meaning of Human Requirements." In *Economic and Philosophic Manuscripts of 1844*. 147–64.

———, "Critique of Hegel's Dialectic and Philosophy as a Whole." In *Economic and Philosophic Manuscripts of 1844*. 170–96.

———. "The Eighteenth Brumaire of Louis Bonaparte." In *The Marx-Engels Reader*, edited by Robert C. Tucker, 594–617. New York: Norton, 1978.

———. *The German Ideology*. London: Lawrence & Wishart, 1970.

———. *Grundrisse: Foundations of the Critique of Political Economy (Rough Draft)*. Translated by Martin Nicolaus. London: Penguin Books, 1993.

———. "Introduction." In Karl Marx, *Grundrisse: Foundations of the Critique of Political Economy*. Translated by Martin Nicolaus, 100–111. London: Penguin Books, 1993.

———. *Marx: Later Political Writings*. Edited by Terrell Carver. New York: Cambridge University Press, 1996.

———. *Political Writings Volume I: The Revolutions of 1848*. Edited by David Fernbach. New York: Vintage Books, 1974.

———. "Preface to the Second Edition (1869) of The Eighteenth Brumaire of Louis Bonaparte." http://www.marxists.org/archive/marx/works/1852/18th-brumaire/preface.htm.

———. *The Poverty of Philosophy*. New York: International Publishers, 1963.

———. *Selected Writings*. Edited by Lawrence Hugh Simon. Indianapolis: Hackett, 1994.

———. "On the Jewish Question." In *Selected Writings*, 1–26.

———. "Theses on Feuerbach." In *Selected Writings*, 97–101.

———. "Wage Labour and Capital." Marx/Engels Internet Archive, 1993. http://www.marxists.org/archive/marx/works/1847/wage-labour/index.htm.

Marx, Karl, and Mark Cowling. *The Communist Manifesto: New Interpretations*. Washington Square, NY: New York University Press, 1998.

Marx, Karl, and Friedrich Engels. *Karl Marx, Frederick Engels: Collected Works*. London: Lawrence & Wishart, 1975.

———. *The Marx-Engels Reader*. Edited by Robert C. Tucker. New York: Norton, 1978.

McCarthy, George E. *Dialectics and Decadence: Echoes of Antiquity in Marx and Nietzsche*. Lanham, MD: Rowman & Littlefield, 1994.

———. *Marx and the Ancients: Classical Ethics, Social Justice, and Nineteenth-Century Political Economy*. Savage, MD: Rowman & Littlefield, 1990.

McLellan, David. *The Thought of Karl Marx: An Introduction*. London: Macmillan, 1971.

Mendus, Susan, ed. *Justifying Toleration: Conceptual and Historical Perspectives*. New York: Cambridge University Press, 1988.

Mies, Maria. *Lace Makers of Narsapur: Indian Housewives in the World Market*. London: Zed Books, 1982.

Miller, James. "Carnivals of Atrocity: Foucault, Nietzsche, Cruelty." *Political Theory* 18 (1990): 470–91.

Mohanty, Chandra Talpade, Ann Russo, and Lourdes Torres, eds. *Third World Women and the Politics of Feminism*. Bloomington: Indiana University Press, 1991.

Mohanty, Chandra Talpade. "Under Western Eyes." In *Third World Women and the Politics of Feminism*, edited by Chandra Talpade Mohanty, Ann Russo, and Lourdes Torres, 51–80. Bloomington: Indiana University Press, 1991.

Morris, David. "About Suffering: Voice, Genre and Moral Community." In *Social Suffering*, edited by Arthur Kleinman, Margaret M. Lock, and Veena Das, 25–46. Berkeley: University of California Press, 1997.

Murdoch, Iris. *A Fairly Honourable Defeat*. New York: Viking, 1970.

———. *Metaphysics as a Guide to Morals*. New York: Allen Lane, Penguin, 1993.

———. *Sartre, Romantic Rationalist*. New York: Viking, 1987.

———. "The Sublime and the Beautiful Revisited." In *Existentialists and Mystics: Writings on Philosophy and Literature*, edited by Peter J. Conradi, 261–86. New York: Allen Lane/ Penguin, 1998.

Murray, Christopher J. L., Alan D. Lopez, Harvard School of Public Health, World Health Organization, and World Bank. *The Global Burden of Disease: A Comprehensive Assessment of Mortality and Disability from Diseases, Injuries, and Risk Factors in 1990 and projected to 2020*. Cambridge, MA: Published by the Harvard School of Public Health on behalf of the World Health Organization and the World Bank; distributed by Harvard University Press, 1996.

Nancy, Jean-Luc. "The Two Secrets of the Fetish." *Diacritics* 31 (2001): 3–8.

National Media Museum and the Science and Society Picture Library. "The Spirit Photographs of William Hope." *Flickr Commons*. http://www.flickr.com/photos/nationalmediamuseum/sets/72157606849278823/detail.

Neal, Patrick. "Justice as Fairness: Political or Metaphysical?" *Political Theory* 18 (1990): 24–50.

———. "Vulgar Liberalism." *Political Theory* 21 (1993): 623–42.

Negri, Antonio. *Marx Beyond Marx: Lessons on the Grundrisse.* Edited by Jim Fleming. Translated and Introduced by Harry Cleaver, Michael Ryan, and Maurizio Viano. New York: Autonomedia, 1996.

Neiman, Susan. *Evil in Modern Thought: An Alternative History of Philosophy.* Princeton, NJ: Princeton University Press, 2004.

Newman, Peter K., Murray Milgate, and John Eatwell. *Marxian Economics.* New York: Norton, 1990.

Nietzsche, Friedrich. *On the Genealogy of Morals and Ecce Homo.* Translated by Walter Arnold Kaufmann and R. J. Hollingdale. New York: Vintage Books, 1989.

Nietzsche, Friedrich Wilhelm. *Basic Writings of Nietzsche.* Translated by Walter Arnold Kaufmann. New York: Modern Library, 2000.

———. *The Birth of Tragedy and the Case of Wagner.* Translated by Walter Arnold Kaufmann. New York: Vintage Books, 1967.

———. *Daybreak: Thoughts on the Prejudices of Morality.* Edited by Maudemarie Clark and Brian Leiter. Cambridge, UK: Cambridge University Press, 1997.

———. *Twilight of the Idols, or, How to Philosophize with the Hammer.* Indianapolis: Hackett, 1997.

———. *Untimely Meditations.* Edited by R. J. Hollingdale. Cambridge, UK: Cambridge University Press, 1997.

Nussbaum, Martha C. "Exactly and Responsibly: A Defense of Ethical Criticism." *Philosophy and Literature* 22 (1998): 343–65.

———. "Patriotism and Cosmopolitanism." In *For Love of Country*, edited by Joshua Cohen, 3–20. Boston: Beacon, 2002.

———. "Reply." In *For Love of Country*, 131–44.

———. "Tragedy and Justice: Bernard Williams Remembered." *Boston Review* (October/November 2003).

———. "Victims and Agents: What Greek Tragedy Can Teach Us About Sympathy and Responsibility." *Boston Review* 23 (February/March 1998).

Ollman, Bertell. *Alienation: Marx's Conception of Man in Capitalist Society.* New York: Cambridge University Press, 1976.

———. *Dance of the Dialectic: Steps in Marx's Method.* Urbana: University of Illinois Press, 2003.

Oxford English Dictionary, 2nd ed. http://dictionary.oed.com.

Palmer, R. R., and Joel G. Colton. *A History of the Modern World.* New York: McGraw-Hill, 1992.

The Passion of the Christ. Directed by Mel Gibson. Basilicata, Italy: Icon Productions, 2004. DVD.

Philips, Anne. *The Politics of Presence*. Oxford, UK: Clarendon, 1995.

Pinch, Adela. *Strange Fits of Passion: Epistemologies of Emotion, Hume to Austen*. Stanford, CA: Stanford University Press, 1996.

Pitkin, Hanna Fenichel. *The Concept of Representation*. Berkeley: University of California Press, 1967.

Plato. *Phaedo*. Boston: Focus Books, 1998.

Postone, Moishe. *Time, Labor, and Social Domination: A Reinterpretation of Marx's Critical Theory*. New York: Cambridge University Press, 1993.

Prato, Bettina. "Victims, Martyrs, and Survivors: The 'New Wars' and the Politics of Pain." *Art & Thought*. http://www.qantara.de/uploads/496/fwf77_12prato.pdf.

Punter, David. *Writing the Passions*. Harlow, UK: Longman, 2001.

Rancière, Jacques. *Disagreement: Politics and Philosophy*. Translated by Julie Rose. Minneapolis: University of Minnesota Press, 1998.

Rawls, John. *Collected Papers*. Edited by Samuel Richard Freeman. Cambridge, MA: Harvard University Press, 1999.

———. *A Theory of Justice: Original Edition*. Cambridge, MA: Harvard University Press, 2005.

———. *Justice as Fairness: A Restatement*. Edited by Erin Kelly. Cambridge, MA: Harvard University Press, 2001.

———. "Justice as Fairness: Political not Metaphysical." *Philosophy and Public Affairs* 14 (1985): 223–51.

———. *Political Liberalism*. New York: Columbia University Press, 1993.

———. "The Sense of Justice." In *Collected Papers*, edited by Samuel Richard Freeman, 96–116. Cambridge, MA: Harvard University Press, 1999.

Rorty, Richard. *Contingency, Irony, and Solidarity*. New York: Cambridge University Press, 1989.

Rose, Gillian. *Mourning Becomes the Law: Philosophy and Representation*. Cambridge, UK: Cambridge University Press, 1996.

Rosenberg, Harold. *Act and the Actor: Making the Self*. New York: World Publishing, 1970.

Rousseau, Jean-Jacques. *The Discourses and Other Early Political Writings*. Edited by Victor Gourevitch. Cambridge, UK: Cambridge University Press, 1997.

Sartre, Jean-Paul. *Critique of Dialectical Reason: Theory of Practical Ensembles*. Translated by Alan Sheridan-Smith. New York: Verso, 2004.

Scarry, Elaine. *The Body in Pain: The Making and Unmaking of the World*. New York: Oxford University Press, 1985.

———. "Consent and the Body: Injury, Departure, and Desire." *New Literary History* 21 (1990): 867–96.

Schneewind, Jerome B. *The Invention of Autonomy*. New York: Cambridge University Press, 1998.

Schoolman, Morton. *Reason and Horror: Critical Theory, Democracy, and Aesthetic Individuality.* New York: Routledge, 2001.

Sellars, R. W. "Reformed Materialism and Intrinsic Endurance." *Philosophical Review* 53 (1944): 359–82.

Sen, Amartya Kumar, Martha Craven Nussbaum, and World Institute for Development Economics Research. *The Quality of Life.* New York: Oxford University Press, 1993.

Shapiro, Ian. *The Evolution of Rights in Liberal Theory.* New York: Cambridge University Press, 1986.

Shell, Susan Meld. *The Rights of Reason: A Study of Kant's Philosophy and Politics.* Toronto: University of Toronto Press, 1980.

Shklar, Judith N. *Ordinary Vices.* Cambridge, MA: Belknap Press of Harvard University Press, 1984.

———. "The Liberalism of Fear." In *Political Thought and Political Thinkers*, edited by Stanley Hoffmann, 3–20. Chicago: University of Chicago Press, 1998.

———. "A Life of Learning." in *Liberalism Without Illusions: Essays on Liberal Theory and the Political Vision of Judith N. Shklar*, edited by Bernard Yack, 263–80. Chicago: University of Chicago Press, 1996.

———. *Legalism.* Cambridge, MA: Harvard University Press, 1964.

Silk, M. S., ed. *Tragedy and the Tragic: Greek Theatre and Beyond.* New York: Oxford University Press, 1996.

Skinner, Quentin. "Meaning and Understanding in the History of Ideas." *History and Theory* (1969): 1–53.

Sontag, Susan. *Regarding the Pain of Others.* New York: Farrar, Straus and Giroux, 2003.

———. "Regarding the Torture of Others." *New York Times Magazine.* http://www.nytimes.com/2004/05/23/magazine/23PRISONS.html?pagewanted=2.

Spelman, Elizabeth V. *Fruits of Sorrow: Framing Our Attention to Suffering.* Boston: Beacon, 1997.

Spivak, Gayatri Chakravorty. "Can the Subaltern Speak?" In *Marxism and the Interpretation of Culture*, edited by Cary Nelson and Lawrence Grossberg, 271–313. Urbana: University of Illinois Press, 1988.

———. *A Critique of Postcolonial Reason: Toward a History of the Vanishing Present.* Cambridge, MA: Harvard University Press, 1999.

———. *The Post-Colonial Critic: Interviews, Strategies, Dialogues.* Edited by Sarah Harasym. New York: Routledge, 1990.

———. "Scattered Speculations on the Question of Value." *Diacritics* 15 (1985): 73–93.

———. *The Spivak Reader: Selected Works of Gayatri Chakravorty Spivak.* Edited by Donna Landry and Gerald M. MacLean. New York: Routledge, 1996.

Sprinker, Michael. *Imaginary Relations: Aesthetics and Ideology in the Theory of Historical Materialism.* New York: Verso, 1987.

Stanislavsky, Konstantin. *An Actor's Handbook: An Alphabetical Arrangement of Concise Statements on Aspects of Acting.* New York: Theater Arts Books, 1963.

Stone, Alan. "Reflections on the Causes of Human Misery and Upon Certain Proposals to Eliminate Them." *The American Political Science Review* 70 (1976): 1286–88.

Strong, Tracy B. *The Idea of Political Theory: Reflections on the Self in Political Time and Space.* Notre Dame, IN: University of Notre Dame Press, 1990.

———. "Identity/Difference: Democratic Negotiations of Political Paradox." *Ethics* 102 (1992): 863–65.

———. *Jean Jacques Rousseau: The Politics of the Ordinary.* Thousand Oaks, CA: Sage, 1994.

———. *The Self and the Political Order.* New York: New York University Press, 1992.

Tassi, Aldo. "The Metaphysics of Performance: The 'Theater of the World.'" Paper presented at the Twentieth World Congress of Philosophy, Boston, Massachusetts, August 10–15, 1998. *The Paideia Project Online: Proceedings of the 20th World Congress of Philosophy.* www.bu.edu/wcp/Papers/Aest/AestTass.htm.

Taylor, Troy. "William Hope: Secrets of the Crewe Circle of Spirit Photographers," 2003. http://www.prairieghosts.com/hope.html.

Terkel, Studs. *Working: People Talk About What They Do All Day and How They Feel About What They Do.* New York: Pantheon Books, 1974.

Thoreau, Henry David. "Wednesday." In *A Week on the Concord and Merrimack Rivers,* edited by Carl Hovde, 278. Princeton, NJ: Princeton University Press, 1980.

Troyer, John, ed. *The Classical Utilitarians: Bentham and Mill.* Indianapolis, IN: Hackett, 2003.

Turner, Bryan S. *The Body and Society: Explorations in Social Theory.* Thousand Oaks, CA: Sage, 1996.

Urbinati, Nadia. "Representation as Advocacy: A Study of Democratic Deliberation." *Political Theory* 28 (2000): 758–86.

Vaggalis, Ted. "John Rawls' Political Liberalism." *Academic Dialogue on Applied Ethics.* http://caae.phil.cmu.edu/Cavalier/Forum/meta/background/Rawls_pl.html.

Vertosick, Frank T. *Why We Hurt: The Natural History of Pain.* New York: Harcourt Brace Jovanovich, 2000.

Waldron, Jeremy. "Theoretical Foundations of Liberalism." *The Philosophical Quarterly* 37 (1987): 127–50.

Wall, Patrick D. *Pain: The Science of Suffering*. New York: Columbia University Press, 2000.

Wartofsky, Marx W. *Feuerbach*. New York: Cambridge University Press, 1977.

Weiss, Michael D. "A Jurisprudence of Blindness: Rawls' Justice and Legal Theory." *Drake Law Review* 42 (1993): 565–91.

Welton, Donn. *The Body: Classic and Contemporary Readings*. Malden, MA: Blackwell, 1999.

White, Hayden V. *Metahistory: The Historical Imagination in Nineteenth-Century Europe*. Baltimore: Johns Hopkins University Press, 1973.

Williams, Melissa S. "Justice toward Groups: Political Not Juridical." *Political Theory* 23 (1995): 67–91.

———. *Voice, Trust, and Memory: Marginalized Groups and the Failings of Liberal Representation*. Princeton, NJ: Princeton University Press, 1998.

Wolff, Robert Paul. *Understanding Rawls: A Reconstruction and Critique of A Theory of Justice*. Princeton, NJ: Princeton University Press, 1977.

Wolin, Sheldon S. *Politics and Vision: Continuity and Innovation in Western Political Thought*. Boston: Little Brown, 1960.

———. "The Liberal/Democratic Divide. On Rawl's Political Liberalism." *Political Theory* 24 (1996): 97–119.

Wood, Allen W. "The Marxian Critique of Justice." *Philosophy and Public Affairs* 1 (1972): 244–82.

Woodruff, Paul. *Reverence: Renewing a Forgotten Virtue*. New York: Oxford University Press, 2001.

Woolf, Virginia. *Mrs. Dalloway*. Orlando, FL: Harcourt, 1990.

Yack, Bernard. *The Fetishism of Modernities: Epochal Self-Consciousness in Contemporary Social and Political Thought*. Notre Dame, IN: University of Notre Dame Press, 1997.

———., ed. *Liberalism Without Illusions: Essays on Liberal Theory and the Political Vision of Judith N. Shklar*. Chicago: University of Chicago Press, 1996.

———. "Liberalism Without Illusions: An Introduction to Judith Shklar's Political Thought." In *Liberalism Without Illusions: Essays on Liberal Theory and the Political Vision of Judith N. Shklar*, edited by Bernard Yack, 1–16. Chicago: University of Chicago Press, 1996.

———. "Liberalism Without Illusions: An Introduction to Judith Shklar's Political Thought." In

Young, Shaun P. *Beyond Rawls: An Analysis of the Concept of Political Liberalism*. Lanham, MD: University Press of America, 2002.

———. *Political Liberalism: Variations on a Theme*. Albany: State University of New York Press, 2004.

Yovel, Yirmiahu. *Kant and the Philosophy of History*. Princeton, NJ: Princeton University Press, 1980.

————., ed. *Kant's Practical Philosophy Reconsidered: Papers Presented at the Seventh Jerusalem Philosophical Encounter, December 1986*. Boston: Kluwer Academic, 1989.

Zuidervaart, Lambert. *Adorno's Aesthetic Theory: The Redemption of Illusion*. Cambridge, MA: MIT Press, 1991.

INDEX

abstraction, 50, 130; in liberalism, 19, 42, 156; in materialism, 146, 175

abstract labor v. concrete labor, 103, 105–6, 141

abstract v. concrete, 168, 199–200n44, 205–6n18

acting, 53–54, 116, 123–24, 148, 151; acting as, 51, 53, 58, 127, 174–75; acting for, 51, 58, 174. *See also* method acting

action, 5, 37, 113–14, 118–20, 162, 163, 164–66, 176

activity, 107–8, 110, 114, 115–18, 209n41

actor, 28, 47, 124–25, 217–18n33; in ascetic theater, 53, 127–28; citizen as, 57–63, 67; in original position, 57–65. *See also* acting

aesthetic(al), the, 3–6, 12, 33, 47–49, 55, 68–70, 74, 89, 92, 158, 160, 176–77, 184, 194n1

aesthetics, 5, 64, 70, 81, 88, 130, 160–61

agency, 33, 37, 133–35, 137, 139, 162

agent, 13, 22, 32–33, 34–38, 112–13, 133, 135; v. victim, 6, 13, 22, 31, 33, 35–38, 41, 61, 113, 122, 130, 133–42, 162, 166, 186

alienation, 22, 80, 105–7, 110–11, 123, 129, 148, 177–78, 181

America, United States of: hope and, 150; religion and, 169; space and, 169, 170; speech and, 76–77, 169; stories and, 169; time, memory, and, 129, 150

amnesia, 33, 42, 55, 123, 128, 131, 132, 168, 175

Apollonian, 5, 161, 163; v. Dionysian, 69–70, 200–201n56, 214–15n11

Aquinas, 219n46

Aristotle, 207–8n32, 219n46

Asad, Talal, 166

ascetic ideals, 66, 71, 74, 88, 128, 200–201n56

ascetic priest, 66–69, 71, 155–56; v. tragic artist, 68, 155–60, 200–201n56, 209n41

ascetic theatre, main features of, 47, 53–55, 64, 127–28, 132, 145, 154

autonomy, 19, 20, 21, 35, 37, 80, 112, 122, 172, 177, 190n1

Bachmann, Ingeborg, 1–3, 5, 161, 216n24

Baier, Annette, 37

Baumgarten, Alexander, 5

Bentham, Jeremy, 57, 103, 108, 173

Bermel, Albert, 153–54

body, 5, 21, 23, 25–26, 29, 33, 42, 43, 48, 112, 127, 140, 141, 144–45, 148, 155, 194n46, 217–18n33; in materialism, 118–19, 129–30, 163, 172, 179; of the worker, 106, 110, 129–30

Borges, Jorge Luis, 7, 201n58

Brown, Wendy, 136–42

Brudney, Daniel, 113–14, 118, 208n38

capital, 3–4, 14–15, 92, 102, 106, 109, 111, 130, 166; as dead labor, 14, 111, 4, 105–6, 110, 123, 217n31

capitalism and liberalism, 29, 30, 35, 55, 100–103, 104, 107, 109, 111–13,

120, 123–24, 133, 138, 158, 172–73, 201n58, 209n41

cartography of suffering, 13, 99, 166. *See also* space: of suffering

character, 47, 70, 75–76, 107, 124, 154, 160–61, 170, 174, 217–18n33; ascetic, 55, 56, 60, 65, 68, 97, 128–29, 156; fetish, 122, 194–99, 133, 175, 211–12n5

citizen, 28, 30, 40, 53, 67, 98, 197–98n21; as actor, 53–61

class, 30, 49, 61, 85, 92, 129, 151, 152, 173, 196n8, 196–97n10, 217n31

Colletti, Lucio, 111

comedy, 54, 152–55. *See also* farce; tragedy

commodification, 105, 107–10, 133, 148, 180, 211–12n5

commodities, 30, 60, 102, 103, 130; fetishism of, 119, 123–28

commutation, 182, 219n46

compassion, 6, 15, 65, 98, 172

compensation, 30, 31, 45, 46, 98, 100, 170, 176–77

concrete, the, 20, 23, 29, 103, 105, 115, 118, 144, 146, 155, 180, 197n11, 205–6n18; v. the abstract, 168, 199–200n44, 205–6n18

conflict, 43, 58, 99, 120; in liberalism, 20, 21, 27, 30, 35, 38, 79, 165, 168; in materialism, 120, 157, 181, 200–201n56

content v. form, 11, 21, 26, 28, 29, 41, 46, 55–56, 59, 62–63, 65, 68, 73, 86, 97, 110, 140, 152, 154, 159

cruelty, 19–21, 32, 36–40, 51, 90, 161, 165

Das, Veena, 84, 171

death, 1–11 passim, 24, 69, 71, 76, 78, 83–86, 89–90, 99, 106, 128, 162, 170, 177–78, 184–86; closure, 2, 3, 7–8; dead labor, capital as, 4, 14, 105–6, 110, 111, 123, 217n31; dead suffering, injury as, 2, 13, 15, 91, 103, 121, 131, 144, 173; ends, 2, 8, 56, 150, 152; finitude, 7, 54, 84, 90; ways of dying, 2, 15

Democritus, 119, 167–68, 170

dialectics, 38, 42, 43, 50, 73, 112, 123, 139, 141, 146, 149, 155, 158, 162–63, 168, 175, 179, 182, 205–6n18

dichotomies, 8, 33, 41, 75, 116, 162, 179, 205–6n18. *See also* secularization and separation

Dionysian, 69–70, 137, 159, 200–201n56, 209n41, 214–15n11; v. Apollonian, 69–70, 200–201n56, 214–15n11

disability, 66; v. handicap, 84–85

disability-adjusted life year (DALY), 85–87, 175

disaster, 13, 80, 81, 87–89, 186

discourse, 10, 11–13, 22, 32, 33, 35, 47, 65, 87, 90, 108, 116, 141, 150, 180, 184–85

dispossessed, reserve army of the, 172–73, 185

dispossession, 3, 60, 171–73

distribution, 30, 80, 123, 165; distributive justice, 86; of suffering, 13, 14, 15, 31, 32, 39, 92, 98–100, 104, 131, 182, 219n46. *See also* cartography of suffering; political economy of injury

double-consciousness, 59, 198n26

economics, 13, 20, 22, 29–30, 33, 35, 75, 91, 98, 101, 102, 104, 108, 120, 122, 165

Elson, Diane, 109

empiricism, 26, 62, 88, 105, 113, 162, 170; the ancients and, 167–68; idealism and, 14, 22, 41–42, 91, 199–200n44; liberals and, 20, 26–28, 37, 41–43, 51, 60, 91, 163, 194n46; utilitarianism and, 37–38. *See also* materiality

Enlightenment, the, 88–89, 176, 189, 203n20

Epicurus, 167–70

essentialism, 131, 132, 139

ethical, the, 6, 11, 55, 75, 90, 101, 104, 132, 160, 182–86

ethics, 84, 85, 156, 182, 186

ethnography, critical, 101–3

eventful, the, 1, 37, 52, 75, 87–89, 131, 147, 152, 159, 163, 168, 175–79, 183

evil, 21, 32, 35, 38, 88–90, 101, 167, 177–78, 189, 203; v. injury, 189n4

exchange, 29, 31, 68, 97, 99–100, 102–9, 124, 130–31, 180, 182, 196, 219n46; exchange value, 105–9, 205n16, 217n31

exclusion, 15, 32–33, 41, 43, 46, 53, 71, 73, 81–82, 124, 132, 181, 194n46. *See also* marginality

experience, 5, 6, 7, 12, 14, 15, 23, 24, 27–28, 39–43, 46, 51, 61, 67, 74, 77, 80, 88, 106, 111–13, 121, 125, 133–34, 137, 144, 166, 170, 174, 177, 179

exploitation, 82, 101; v. alienation and fetishism, 107–8, 110, 122, 138

exteriority, principle of, 14, 21, 79, 138, 144, 177, 179

externalization, 14, 25, 63, 65, 74, 82, 107, 108, 110, 114, 116–17, 121, 140, 144, 148, 179, 207–8n32, 208n28, 209n41, 218–19n42

failed state, 92

farce, 90, 151–54, 161. *See also* comedy; tragedy

fear, 24; cruelty and, 37; interaction, models of, 118–19, 125, 180, 218–19nn41–42, 219n44; labor and, 25; liberalism of, 19–25, 32, 36–37, 39–40, 136, 193–94nn45–46; pain and, 25, 31; universalism of, 37, 210–11. *See also* Brudney, Daniel

fetish, 55, 88, 119, 121–32, 141–42, 148, 163, 175–76, 211–12n5

fetishism of injuries, 100, 109, 111–12, 121, 133

Feuerbach, Ludwig, 88, 111, 115, 117–19, 146, 165, 172, 177–78, 179–80, 203n19

form, 5, 11, 29, 41, 58, 75, 127, 153, 209n41; history of, 13–15, 30, 49, 54, 83, 92, 100–106, 116, 120, 121, 124, 133, 144, 150–56, 166, 137, 180, 185, 218n41; v. content,

11, 21, 26, 28, 29, 41, 46, 55–56, 59, 62–63, 65, 68, 73, 86, 97, 110, 140, 152, 154, 159

formalism, 42, 46, 48, 51

Foucault, Michel, 69, 134, 194n46

genre, 23, 47, 54–55, 146, 151–54, 159, 163, 164. *See also* narrative; story

good, 29–31, 56, 58, 63, 98, 159

guilt, 2, 12, 62–68, 79, 82, 135, 150, 163

handicap, 85; v. disability, 84–85

harm, 11–12, 20, 22, 26, 33, 35–36, 41, 96, 100, 120, 155, 176

health, 15, 34, 41, 57–61, 66, 67–69, 84–85, 112–13, 133–34, 186

Hegel, Georg Wilhelm Friedrich, 76, 90, 146, 177, 178, 203n19

history, 14, 42, 50, 61, 62, 63, 75, 88, 90, 92, 102, 122, 146–52, 164–70, 174, 178, 190n2. *See also* memory

Hobbes, Thomas, 24–25, 40, 48–49, 163, 168, 191–92n19, 203–4n23

hope, 15, 71, 79, 118, 147–50, 163, 167–70

humanitarianism, 6, 65, 75, 79, 89, 90

humanity, standpoint of social, 119, 163, 172, 211–12n5, 218–19n42

human rights, 3

Hume, David, 37–38, 192n20

idealism, 7, 8, 38, 79, 127, 132–33, 135, 170; empiricism and, 14, 22, 41–42, 91, 199–200n44; in justice, 22, 41; v. materialism, 14, 102–3, 112, 163, 211n2, 211–12n5

identity, 11, 13, 26, 29, 37, 40–41, 58–59, 62, 97, 104, 129–30, 135, 139–41, 150, 196n8, 216n19

imagination, 50, 58–59, 125, 150, 163, 168, 174, 197n11

impartiality, 22, 59, 127. *See also* tolerance

inclusion, 11, 22, 39, 41, 43, 53, 55, 59–60, 73, 97–99, 144–45, 194n46 injury, 10, 26, 202n8; as dead suffering, 2, 13, 15, 42, 65, 91, 103, 121, 131, 144, 173; defined, 21–28, 41, 87; intelligible v. sensible, 26–28, 66, 199–200n44; political economy of, 15, 22–23, 45, 64, 70, 88, 92, 100, 116, 119, 132, 133, 177, 183; v. evil, 189n4. *See also* injury play; political economy of injury

injury play, 47, 52, 53–56, 68, 75–81, 128, 132, 140, 153, 157, 159, 160–61, 184, 197–98n21. *See also* ascetic theater, main features of

instrumentalism, 11, 79, 84, 90, 119, 144, 150, 158, 182, 209n41

interest, 29, 31, 35, 48–49, 55–56, 104, 196n8, 196–97n10

intimacy v. sympathy, 12, 39, 45, 90

justice, 10, 13, 21, 22, 28

justice, sense of, 12, 30, 58, 61–65, 67, 198–99n32

justice, types of: commutative, 182, 219n46; distributive, 31, 45, 86, 98, 108, 182, 219n46; idealist, 27, 32, 78–79, 138, 144, 161, 165; liberal, 28, 31, 36, 38, 45, 46, 84, 103, 108, 125–37, 130, 135–36, 145, 156, 173, 180, 210–11n1; materialist, 75, 78, 144, 146, 161, 185–86, 213n30, 216n19

justice as admission, 23, 39–43, 60, 97–98

justice as fairness, 30, 52–54, 56, 61, 132

Kant, Immanuel, 20, 25–28, 33, 37–38, 41, 42, 66, 87, 89, 160, 202n8; Hume and, 37–38; Nietzsche and, 199–200n44; on property and injury, 25–28; Rousseau and, 202n8; on the sensible v. the intelligible, 26–28, 66, 199–200n44; on the sublime, 176–77

Kekes, John, 36–37

Kelly, George, 54

knowing, 22, 29, 35, 55–57, 85, 116, 125, 128, 178

knowledge, 12, 26–43, 49, 56–57, 61, 63, 65–66, 88, 98, 118, 127, 137, 139, 171, 174, 179, 184, 203–4n23

Kushner, Tony, 5, 8–10, 75–81, 83, 90, 146, 165, 169, 170, 177–79, 216n24

labor, 4, 14, 25, 101–5, 138, 180, 211n2, 218n41; abstract and concrete, 103, 105–6, 141; as commodity, 102, 103, 107, 125; division of, 120, 137, 145, 166, 172, 175; labor-power and, 103, 211n2; living and dead, 4, 97, 106, 107, 110–11, 122, 123, 139, 144, 217n31; movement, 141, 172, 181; suffering and, 29, 37, 81, 100, 109, 111, 112, 130, 137, 140, 144, 180, 181, 191n18

labor of suffering, 10, 11, 12, 82, 92, 99–100, 102, 108, 119, 131–32, 148–49, 181, 182; defined, 100; labor distinguished from, 129–30

language, 2, 13, 31, 41, 46–48, 63–65, 77, 86, 107, 133, 138, 149, 175, 180, 181; composite view of, 41, 64, 119, 181

Levinas, Emmanuel, 183

liberalism: capitalism and, 29, 30, 35, 55, 100–103, 104, 107, 109, 111–13, 120, 123–24, 133, 138, 158, 172–73, 201n58, 209n41; critiques of, 38–39, 134, 137–42, 179; defined, 10; democracy and, 12, 69, 92–93; genre and, 23, 53–55; as method, 8, 11, 13, 21, 22, 28, 39, 33–34, 37–43, 45, 65, 74–75, 87–89, 91, 113–14, 155–56, 176; modernity and, 34; origins of, 20–21, 136, 178, 190nn1–4, 193–94n45; political, 32–35, 56, 191n11, 211n3; representation in, 46–47, 51–57, 64, 120; secularism and, 33, 36, 80–83, 108; separations in, 36, 81, 183

linguistic materialism, 13, 47, 73

linguistic turn, 13, 101, 133, 135, 140, 141, 161

living labor, 105, 106, 110, 112, 217n31
living suffering, 2, 4, 12, 91, 100, 103, 106, 107, 131
Locke, John, 25, 27, 37, 104, 190n3, 191n18
love, 2, 62, 69, 75–80, 83, 92, 116, 162, 194n46, 218–19n42

MacKinnon, Catherine, 136–43, 213n30
marginality, 15, 23, 30, 39–40, 92, 112, 149, 170, 181, 184, 186. *See also* exclusion
Marx, Karl: on alienation, 110–11; on class, 49, 181, 196n8, 217n31; on exploitation v. fetishism v. alienation, 101, 110–11, 122–23, 148, 211n5; on fetishism, 127; hope in, 106, 111, 138; on labor, 14, 100, 101–2, 104–5, 107, 141, 166, 180–81; materialism and, 108, 114–19, 123, 163–68 passim, 175, 180, 203n19, 218–19n42; materialist method of, 5, 14, 50, 101–3, 114, 123, 141, 146, 149, 150, 152, 177, 178, 195n7, 205–6n18, 209n41, 213n30; on religion and secularism, 88, 133, 197n21; representation in, 47–50, 196n8, 211n2; revolution and, 148, 151–52, 154; on value, 109, 141, 211n2; senses and, 115–17, 123, 135, 131, 168, 172, 175, 179, 181, 189n5, 207n32; suffering and, 107, 115, 119, 150, 165, 167, 178, 179, 181, 189n5, 206n19; theater and artifice in, 124–25, 137, 152, 153–54; time and, 131
materialist method, 5, 7, 13–15, 50, 88, 90, 101–3, 109, 112–20, 123, 135, 141, 146, 149, 150, 152, 159, 160–67, 176–79, 182, 184, 195n7, 205–6n18, 208n32, 213n30
materiality, 6, 7, 11, 14, 15, 41, 42, 55, 106, 111, 112, 118, 120, 141, 163, 170, 178, 179, 181, 213n30
memory, 2, 4, 7, 42, 47, 49, 62–67, 123, 127–29, 131, 147–50, 156, 159, 165, 168, 174, 190n2, 193n45, 216n19; as representation,
47, 63; voice and, 112, 122, 127, 132, 144, 145–46
method, 14, 15, 23, 27, 39, 50, 60, 73–74, 91, 100–102, 129–30, 146, 154, 194n46, 195n7, 200n44, 205–6n18
method acting, 173–75
modernity, 3, 5, 10, 13, 14, 20, 22, 34, 35, 77, 82, 88–89, 116, 149, 162, 174–75, 186, 189, 190n1, 192nn19–20, 201n56, 203n20, 209n41
Mohanty, Chandra Talpade, 132, 134, 138
Morris, David, 63–64
mourning in capitalism, 7
Murdoch, Iris, 5, 6, 34–35, 79, 146, 160–63, 172, 176, 178, 213n30, 215–16n17

naming, 3, 40, 41, 87, 90, 134, 145, 147, 161, 175, 185, 212n20
Nancy, Jean-Luc, 124, 211–12n5
narrative, 2, 7, 15, 41, 45, 46, 79, 80, 86, 139, 153–55, 166, 169. *See also* genre; story
nation, 7, 20, 92, 166, 196n8
necessity, 8, 59, 68, 105, 114, 130, 135, 147, 160–68, 184, 186, 219n41; v. need, 165–66, 186
need, 22, 35, 41, 49, 75–83, 107, 115–16, 149, 165–66, 185, 196n8; v. necessity, 165–66, 186
Neiman, Susan, 88–89
Nietzsche, Friedrich: Apollonian and Dionysian in, 69–70, 157, 158, 200n56, 214–15n11; on ascetic ideals, 128; the genealogist, 14, 86; on guilt, 68, 82; Kant and, 199–200n44; materialist method of, 14, 114, 135, 139, 157, 160, 163, 177, 194n46, 209n41; Rawls and, 64, 65; on ressentiment, 66, 69, 129, 139; senses and, 66, 171–72, 216n26; suffering and, 66, 67–68, 70, 135, 163, 171–72, 200n44, 209n41; on tragedy, 154, 201n56, 215n13; tragic artist and

ascetic priest in, 66–71 passim, 128, 156, 159, 201n56
Nussbaum, Martha, 134, 183

object, 11, 14, 25, 26–27, 33–35, 57, 63, 68, 102, 104, 108, 110, 115, 124, 134, 168, 174–75, 182, 192n20, 206n22; suffering as, 6, 14, 15, 22, 51, 74, 82, 91, 97, 98, 100–101, 122, 144, 148, 175, 183, 189n4
objectification, 3, 5–7, 26–27, 29, 70, 73–74, 91, 105, 110, 116–18, 129, 133, 144, 148, 177, 180, 201, 218n41. See also externalization
Ollman, Bertell, 116, 205–6n18, 207–8n32
orientation v. relation, 110–19, 172, 181
ownership, 25–27, 29, 36, 41–42, 87, 102–4, 126, 171–72, 204n9, 205n16, 218–19n42. See also possession; property

pain, 11, 14, 22, 24–25, 27, 29, 31, 32, 35–37, 38, 41, 45, 57, 59, 63–64, 67–69, 85, 105, 128, 136, 153, 155–60, 167–68, 171, 180, 183
passion, 21, 61, 65, 89, 146, 172, 191n12, 203–4n23, 206n22
passivity, 7, 13, 21, 28, 35, 39, 42, 74, 110, 115–17, 145, 168, 181, 208n32, 209n41
performance: of liberal justice, 99, 126–27, 132, 145, 154–55; of suffering, 10, 46, 52–57, 64–67, 70, 74–77, 81–82, 108, 125, 129, 130, 144–45, 154, 156, 158, 173–74, 217–18n33. See also acting; presence; theater; voice
Pitkin, Hanna Fenichel, 47–50, 195n2
pity, 67, 198
Plato, 162–63, 215–16n17
political, the, 1, 4, 6, 7, 11, 14, 21, 25, 74, 80, 81, 92, 112, 148, 160, 180, 184
political economy, 15, 22, 45, 88, 92, 119, 132, 183; of injury, 15, 22–23, 45, 64, 70, 88, 92, 100, 116, 119, 132, 133, 177, 183

political liberalism, 32–35, 56, 191n11, 211n3
politics: democratic, 7, 12, 73, 81, 75, 92; identity, 11, 130, 136, 140; liberal, 3, 6, 8, 10–13, 19, 24, 28, 38–40, 43, 46, 49, 53, 73–76, 80–81, 101, 107, 133, 160, 165; materialist, 7, 8, 10–11, 14–15, 75, 86, 91–93, 101, 110, 113, 129–30, 135, 144, 147–48, 165–66, 176, 182–87
possession, 33, 126, 156, 172–74, 182, 191n18, 207–8n32. See also ownership; property
possessive individualism, 22, 26–30, 60, 97, 103–4, 131, 155, 156, 162, 165, 170, 172
Postone, Moishe, 102
presence, 4, 7, 10–11, 13, 15, 47–48, 50, 51, 74–75, 112, 125, 154, 174, 217–18n33. See also representation
production, 7, 21, 80, 87, 110, 115, 119, 121–22, 127, 131, 141, 149; consumption and, 104–7; of suffering, 13–14, 28, 30–32, 67, 86, 92, 99–100, 104, 108, 120, 124
productivity, 7, 37, 67, 87, 98–100, 108–10, 116, 140
property, 24–29, 33, 36, 60, 103–4, 117, 122, 155–56, 165, 172, 191n18, 202n8, 218–19n42. See also ownership; possession
public sphere, 11, 34, 39, 40, 59
public v. private, 20, 21, 24, 33, 40, 57, 59, 75, 76, 81, 97, 136, 152, 160, 161, 179–80, 183, 194n46

Rancière, Jacques, 181, 189n3
rationalism, 21, 24, 40, 56–58, 89–90, 112, 186, 202n8
Rawls, John: asceticism in, 64, 65; ascetic theater in, 52–57, 127, 145, 154, 197–8n21; history and, 59, 62, 63, 122, 132, 201n58; on original position, 31, 47, 52–64, 67, 91, 97–98, 127–28, 145, 156, 174; original position as injury play in, 53–54, 60, 145, 174, 212n11; on

overlapping consensus, 52, 53, 60; political liberalism and, 81; primary goods as index of suffering in, 30–31; on primary goods, 30, 31, 53, 58, 98; representation and, 46–47, 51–53, 57, 60, 62, 98, 125, 154, 174; on sense of justice, 30, 58, 61–65, 67, 156, 198n32; suffering and, 30; on veil of ignorance, 47, 50, 52–57, 59, 61, 63, 128, 132; victims and, 127–28, 201n58

reason, 5, 27–28, 38, 53–54, 56–58, 61, 71, 191n12, 199–200n44

relation: external, 13, 14, 26, 46, 74, 122, 132; fundamental, 113–14, 118, 181; internal, 14, 41, 42, 51, 80, 119–20, 123, 144, 177, 182, 205–6n18; v. orientation, 110–19, 172, 181

religion, 5, 20, 32–33, 75, 79–83, 108, 111, 156, 169, 179, 194n46, 203n19, 210n1

representation, 5, 6, 10, 29, 45–46, 100, 109, 125, 130, 134, 139, 151–52, 157, 182, 196n10; acting and, 48, 53–54, 57–61, 126–27, 174; as action within liberalism, 30, 39, 41, 46, 51, 98, 100, 121; critiques of, 13–14, 39; different senses of, 14, 47–48, 194–95n2, 196n8; fetish as, 123–25, 131; Hobbes and, 48–49; Marx and, 49–50; sense experience and, 51, 61–65, 73–74, 122, 129, 131, 150, 161, 172–75, 177; stages of, in Rawls, 52–57; subjects of, 45–46, 55–57, 86, 111–12, 121–23, 125; of suffering, 22, 29, 30, 41, 45–46, 51, 111, 120, 135, 138, 179; voice and, 134, 137

resentment, 62

ressentiment, 63, 66–70, 128, 131–39, 157, 201n58

revolution, 80, 146–54

right, 3, 6, 19, 27–30, 41, 45, 92, 98, 101, 103, 104, 152, 178, 184, 190nn3–4; as fetish, 138, 140; human, 3

Rorty, Richard, 37, 177

Rousseau, Jean-Jacques, 172, 177, 196–97n10, 202n8, 210–11n1

Sartre, Jean-Paul, 160, 162

scarcity, 22, 35, 54, 79, 86, 98, 165, 172

secularism, 5, 14, 79, 83, 103, 133, 190n1; liberal, 33, 56, 74, 80, 108, 112, 197–98n21; of suffering, 80–82, 87, 110, 156, 180. See also secularization and separation

secularization and separation, 3, 6, 27, 35, 41, 43, 59, 76–77, 80–82, 88, 112, 118, 160, 202n8, 205–6n18

self, 19, 24–26, 29, 39, 41, 45, 47, 54, 56, 57, 59, 69, 71, 73, 113–14, 144–46, 155, 157, 162, 174, 177, 191–92nn18–20, 198n26, 207–8n32, 209n41

sense of justice, 12, 30, 58, 61–65, 67, 198–99n32

sensuousness, 12–14, 47, 51, 55, 63, 65, 70, 73, 75, 87–88, 92, 101, 107, 115–17, 119–21, 123, 131, 133, 143, 154, 162–64, 166–68, 172, 175, 178, 182, 206n22; social, 179–82

Shklar, Judith, 19–24, 32, 36–43, 51, 81, 160–63, 178, 183, 190nn2–4, 191n18, 193n41, 193–94nn45–46, 211n3, 213n30

silence, 6, 10, 63–65, 73, 77, 79, 83–86, 89–90, 135, 143, 148–49, 162, 175

social, the, 111, 172, 179–81

social humanity, 119, 172

sociality, 102, 117, 119, 121–27, 133

social sensuousness, 179–82

Sontag, Susan, 85, 183

space, 3, 4, 10, 34, 60, 76–77, 81, 87, 88, 110, 120, 130–33, 141, 148, 155, 161, 166, 168–70, 175, 179, 209n41, 218n41; species-being, 88, 111, 141, 164, 177, 179, 207n7, 210n41, 218–19n42; of suffering, 10, 12, 34, 77, 81, 87, 120, 133, 145, 202n8

species powers, 116, 172, 181

speech, 2, 10–12, 46–47, 51, 63–65, 73–74, 83, 86, 88–92, 98, 124,

135, 139, 146, 150, 173, 179, 189n3; in the original position, 63–65; v. voice, 74, 91–92, 135, 179, 189n3

speechlessness, 73, 135

Spivak, Gayatri Chakravorty, 49, 134, 140, 196n8

state, 20–23, 35, 36, 46, 74–83, 85, 92, 103, 145, 165, 169–70, 182

statistics, 85–87

story, 2–4, 6–8, 22, 41, 80, 86, 88, 112, 152, 160, 168. *See also* genre; narrative

Strong, Tracy, 196n10

sublime, 88–89, 170, 175–78

sympathy, 6, 15, 39, 172, 183–84

theater, 51, 69, 70, 124–25, 148, 153, 174, 175, 178, 217–18n33; ascetic, main features of, 47, 53–55, 64, 127–28, 132, 145, 154; liberalism's affinity for, 47, 51, 53, 55, 83, 145, 161. *See also* injury play

Thoreau, Henry David, 143

time, 3, 14, 41, 50, 60, 61, 83, 88, 102, 110, 113, 117–18, 122, 130–33, 141, 155, 165–70, 178–79, 201n58

tolerance, 20, 22, 32–35, 40, 58, 60, 90, 91, 99, 113, 160, 165, 168, 184–85, 193n41

tragedy, 12, 54, 151–54, 161, 163, 167, 178, 185–86, 200–201n56,

214–15n11, 215n13; as genre of action and suffering, 153–55, 159; liberalism and, 35, 53–55, 145, 166, 172, 184; of the revolution, 149

tragic art, 68, 70, 154–60, 172

tragic artist v. ascetic priest, 68, 155, 157–60, 201n, 209n41

universalism, 22, 24, 26, 29, 37, 85, 97, 98, 126, 131–32, 139, 177

unselfing, 1, 57, 163

utilitarianism, 5, 22, 30, 35, 38, 104, 108–9, 113, 119, 141, 161, 164, 184, 210–11n1

victim v. agent, 6, 13, 22, 31, 33, 35–38, 41, 61, 113, 122, 130, 133–42, 162, 166, 186

voice, 11, 12, 39–41, 46, 59, 63–64, 86–87, 91–92, 98, 113, 129, 133–35, 150, 173; memory and, 112, 122, 127, 132, 144, 145–46; v. speech, 74, 91–92, 135, 179, 189n3

Weil, Simone, 160, 161, 162

Weiss, Peter, 59

Wittgenstein, Ludwig, 171

Wolin, Sheldon, 24, 61, 191–92n19

Woolf, Virginia, 5, 145

worker, 101–8, 122, 125, 129–30, 181, 219n44